THE LAST STAND
OF FOX COMPANY

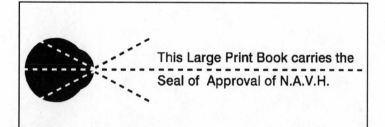

This Large Print Book carries the
Seal of Approval of N.A.V.H.

THE LAST STAND
OF FOX COMPANY

A TRUE STORY OF
U.S. MARINES IN COMBAT

BOB DRURY AND TOM CLAVIN

THORNDIKE PRESS
A part of Gale, Cengage Learning

GALE
CENGAGE Learning·

Detroit • New York • San Francisco • New Haven, Conn • Waterville, Maine • London

GALE
CENGAGE Learning™

LIBRARY OF CONGRESS CATALOGING-IN-PUBLICATION DATA

Drury, Bob.
    The last stand of Fox Company : a true story of U.S. Marines
in combat / by Bob Drury and Tom Clavin. — Large print ed.
      p. cm. — (Thorndike Press large print nonfiction)
    Originally published: New York : Atlantic Monthly Press,
c2009.
    "Published ... in arrangement with Grove/Atlantic"—T.p.
verso.
    Includes bibliographical references.
    ISBN-13: 978-1-4104-1413-7 (hardcover : alk. paper)
    ISBN-10: 1-4104-1413-2 (hardcover : alk. paper)
    1. Korean War, 1950–1953—Campaigns—Korea
(North)—Changjin Reservoir Region. 2. Korean War,
1950–1953—Regimental histories—United States. 3. United
States. Marine Corps. Marines, 1st—History—20th century. 4.
United States. Marine Corps—Officers—Biography. 5.
Marines—United States—Biography. 6. Changjin Reservoir
Region (Korea)—History, Military—20th century. 7. Large type
books. I. Clavin, Thomas. II. Title.
DS918.2.C35D78 2009
951.904'242—dc22   2008049610

Published in 2009 by arrangement with Grove/Atlantic, Inc.

To the United States Marines
who fought and died on Fox Hill

CONTENTS

"If we are marked to die, we are enough."

— *Henry V*

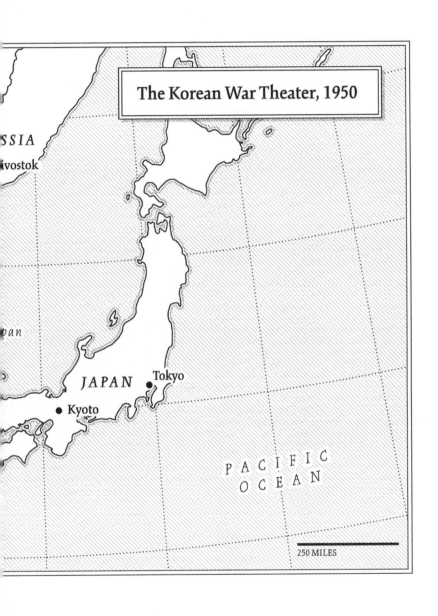

The Korean War Theater, 1950

RUSSIA

vostok

JAPAN
Tokyo

Kyoto

PACIFIC
OCEAN

250 MILES

PROLOGUE

NOVEMBER 2 TO 4, 1950

Only the officers knew that the dark railway tunnel a few hundred yards up the road marked the official entrance to the Sudong Gorge. The enlisted men didn't carry maps, but they sensed it. Over the past several miles the broad rice paddies and vineyards, the neat rows of persimmon trees, and the tiny farmhouses with their empty oxcarts had disappeared and had been replaced by the stark granite hills of upper North Korea. "Injun Territory," one of the Marines said. A few others forced a grim laugh. To most of the Marines, hostile terrain had begun as soon as they'd crossed the 38th Parallel and started the long slog north. Still, that dark tunnel looked ominous.

They were Fox Company, and just before they rounded the sharp bend in the road and humped into the tunnel they spotted Dog Company engaged in a firefight, maybe half a mile to the west, along the slopes of

13

one of the broken-tooth mountains. They found this strange. By this point in the war — more than four months since Kim Il Sung's invasion of South Korea, and six weeks after the United States' successful counterattack at Inchon — the North Koreans could be counted on to cut and run at the first sign of Americans. But Dog Company seemed to be meeting serious opposition, and some of the Marines in Fox Company began to wonder if the regimental commander's warning hadn't been the usual shinola; perhaps the Chinese had indeed crossed the Yalu River and entered the war.

In any event, that was Dog's problem, at least for the time being, and as Fox emerged from the north end of the tunnel and into the dusk, the sheer hills on either side of the company loomed high and tight.

It was a good place to call a halt, and the outfit's enigmatic commander, Captain Elmer Zorn, decided to bed down the column for the night. One of the actions that had Zorn's men often glancing at him warily was calling in an air strike uncomfortably close to their own position. On another occasion he mistakenly radioed for artillery support on Fox Company's own coordinates. The sun was dipping over the stout,

14

charcoal-colored western hills, and an eerie gray mist shrouded the forbidding taller mountains to the north. Fox was still four miles south of its objective, the tiny crossroads hamlet of Sudong, but Zorn's men had slept hardly at all for two days. The CO considered the odds: with the First Battalion out in front, and the Third Battalion following close behind, he expected no trouble. Before assigning night watches, however, Zorn did take one precaution. He ordered the leaders of his three rifle platoons to have each of their men take a good long look at four Marines from the First Battalion who had been bayoneted in their sleeping bags twenty-four hours earlier. Their cold bodies, laid in a small depression between a creek bed and the dirt road, were still wrapped in their bloody mummy bags. Sergeant Earl Peach of the Second Platoon spat. He'd seen worse, on Tarawa and Iwo. Still, he never got used to the sight.

As darkness fell and the temperature dropped, Fox was strung out perhaps four hundred yards along the road, with sentries snaking up the overhanging ridgelines. All the scuttlebutt about the Red Chinese spooked the company, and scattered small arms fire and an occasional howitzer report punctuating the cold air from up ahead didn't help. At midnight a rumor started that a North Korean tank was prowling the area, and this put everyone's nerves on edge. But there were no incidents.

Not long after sunrise, a few Marines spotted the column of soldiers exiting the tunnel, seventy-five yards south of their bivouac. These were definitely troopers, maybe 200 all told, marching in twos with a brisk, jaunty step — far too crisp for them to be the weary Marines of the Third Battalion's rear guard. And they were wearing unfamiliar uniforms. But Fox Company had been relieving numerous South Korean infantrymen all along the road north, and these were most likely more of the same. The Americans had taken to calling their allies ROKs, after South Korea's official name, the Republic of Korea.

Corporal Alex "Bob" Mixon, a forward artillery observer attached to Fox from the Second Battalion's 81-mm mortar unit, was the first to see them — and the first to sense that something was not right. They were no more than forty or fifty yards away when he hollered, "Halt. Who goes there?"

The answer was a fusillade of automatic weapons fire. Mixon dived behind a rock. When he emptied the clip of his carbine into the two columns, they broke to both sides of the road and assumed firing positions. Mixon was impressed by their discipline — a trait heretofore lacking among most of the Reds he'd encountered. Now Mixon could hear Captain Zorn running toward him, yelling, "Hold your fire! Friends! Friends!"

But the bullets snapping over Bob Mixon's head were far from friendly, and as he shouldered his carbine and squeezed off another clip he watched Fox Company's civilian interpreter tackle the captain and pull him down into a ditch on the side of the road.

By now the Chinese — as Mixon had concluded they were — had set up two heavy machine guns on either side of the tunnel entrance and were pouring fire into the company's mortar squad strung out along the creek bed. Half a dozen Marines fell instantly. Mixon was debating what to do when a helmet popped up beside him. It was Sergeant Peach, who had crawled through a culvert under the road.

"Gotta keep 'em off those mortar men," Peach said. He began picking off enemy soldiers with his M1. Mixon reloaded and joined in with his carbine, aiming especially for the machine gunners. When they had both run out of ammunition they fell back to Captain Zorn's ditch. The captain was on the field phone, ordering several fire teams to take the high ground and secure the main ridgeline on the east side of the gorge. Simultaneously, a large unit of Chinese broke off from the gunfight in the valley and began scrabbling up the steep hills.

A BAR man from the Second Platoon watched them: maybe a hundred or so soldiers no more than three hundred yards away, climbing a parallel peak. They were hopping along the ridgeline like jackrabbits, and he was so impressed with their agility and the sharp cut of their uniforms — hell, even their backpacks looked impossibly squared away — that he initially thought they might be some hotshot Marine outfit he didn't recognize.

But when his squad reached the top of the ridge they were stopped in their tracks by the disconcerting sight of a lone Chinese officer standing atop a giant boulder and dragging casually on a cigarette. At the Americans' approach he flicked his butt in their direction, jumped from the rock, and disappeared over the reverse slope. The Marines had been too stunned by his presence to shoot him. When they reached the boulder they found field telephone wires running down the cleft in the ridgeline. A couple of men unsheathed K-bar knives to cut the wires, and someone said, "The bastard's been watching us the whole time."

From the top of the hill the Marines of Fox Company could again see Dog Company, fighting for its life far to the west. Not a few men wondered what the hell was happening.

Meanwhile, down in the creek bed, one of the wounded Marines cried for help. A Navy corpsman squatting next to Captain Zorn made a move to rise from the ditch, but the company's gunnery sergeant shouldered him back to the ground. Because of the Chinese machine-gun fire, any attempt at rescue seemed futile. But Sergeant Peach decided to chance it. He scooped up the corpsman's medical kit and took off. Zorn and the few Marines behind him opened up with covering fire. Peach made the creek bed. The Americans near Zorn whooped with admiration. Peach was unlashing the med kit from his shoulder when he was stitched across the face by machine-gun fire. The top of his skull seemed to lift off his head, as if pulled by invisible wires.

Captain Zorn ordered a counterattack, and the remaining Chinese fled up the hill, leaving perhaps fifty of their dead strewn across the road. The rest of the day became a long, tense standoff as the Marines and

Chinese regulars attempted to outflank each other on the ridgelines. Sniper fire and the occasional *pop* of small mortar rounds echoed off the hills. Zorn radioed Division and then ordered Fox Company to dig in for the night as he and his staff laid plans for a dawn attack.

But by sunrise the Chinese had vanished, and the Marines of Fox were left to wonder if this disappearance was permanent, or if they had just taken part in the opening salvo of World War III.

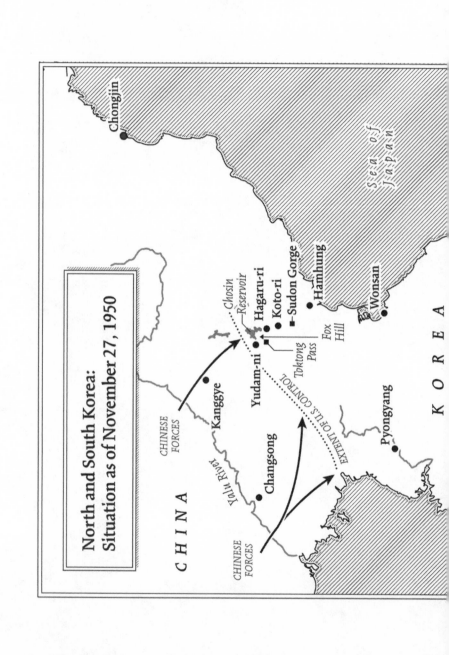

North and South Korea:
Situation as of November 27, 1950

Chongjin

Sea of Japan

Hamhung

Wonsan

Chosin Reservoir

Hagaru-ri

Koto-ri

Sudon Gorge

Fox Hill

Toktong Pass

Yudam-ni

Kanggye

EXTENT OF U.S. CONTROL

Changsong

CHINESE FORCES

Yalu River

CHINESE FORCES

CHINA

KOREA

Pyongyang

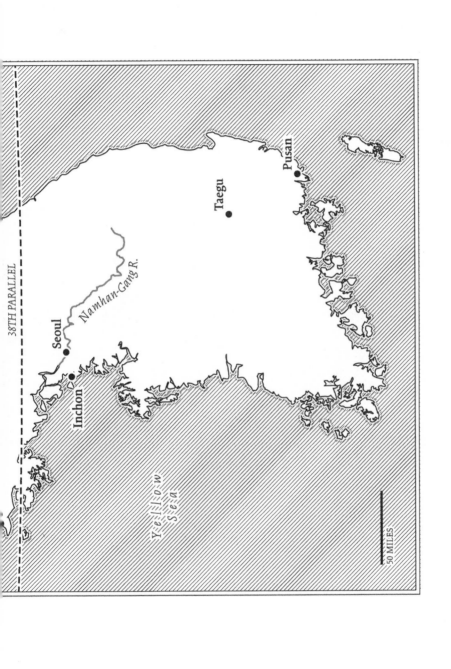

38TH PARALLEL

Seoul

Inchon

Namhan-Gang R.

Taegu

Pusan

Yellow Sea

50 MILES

■ ■ ■ ■

THE HILL

■ ■ ■ ■

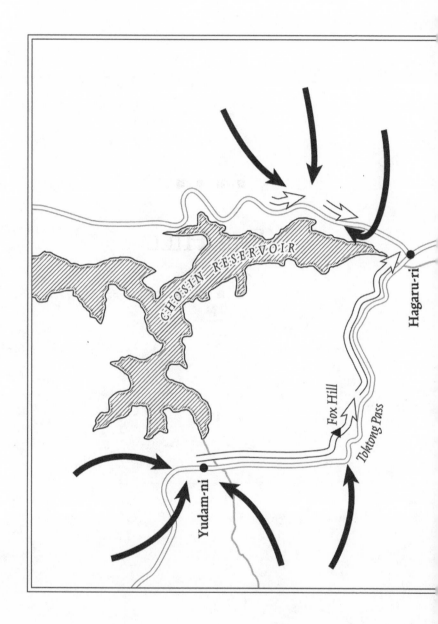

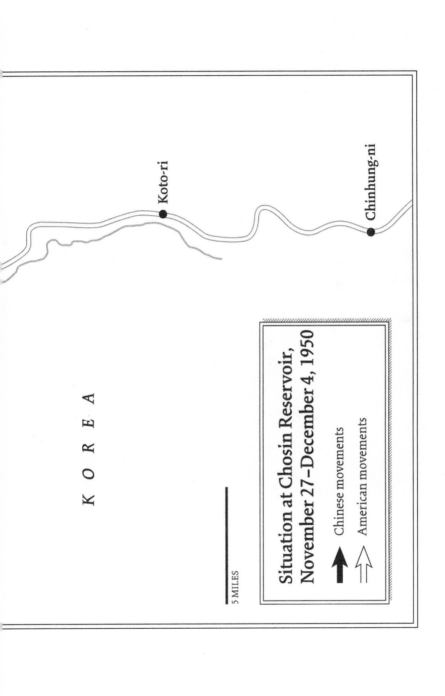

KOREA

5 MILES

Koto-ri

Chinhung-ni

Situation at Chosin Reservoir,
November 27–December 4, 1950

Chinese movements

American movements

DAY ONE
NOVEMBER 27, 1950

1

The Americans moved in slow motion, as if their boots were sticking to the frozen sludge of snow, ice, and mud. They had been dug in on this godforsaken North Korean hillside for less than forty-eight hours, yet when the 192 officers and enlisted men of Fox Company, Second Battalion, Seventh Regiment were ordered to fall in, gear up, and move out, their mood became almost wistful — or what passed for wistful in the United States Marines.

Just past sunrise, Dick Bonelli, a nineteen-year-old private first class, crawled from his foxhole, stomped some warmth into his swollen feet, and took a look at the new line replacements. Most of these men — boys, really — were reservists who had joined the company within the past couple of weeks. He knew few of their names. "Greenhorns," he spat. "Don't know how good they had it

29

sitting up here fat and happy."

The words came out in a voice so gravelly you could walk on it, all the more menacing because of Bonelli's tough New York City accent. The sky began to spit snow as he packed his kit and continued to gripe. Corporal Howard Koone, Bonelli's twenty-year-old fire team leader from the Second Squad, Third Platoon, shot him a sideways glance. *Fat and happy?* Two men from the outfit had been wounded on a recon patrol the previous night. But Koone, a taciturn Muskogee Indian from southern Michigan, let it slide. Bonelli had been in a foul mood since Thanksgiving, when his bowels were roiled by the frozen turkey he had wolfed down outside the battalion mess.

At first the holiday feast served three days earlier had seemed a welcome respite from the greasy canned bacon, lumpy powdered milk, and gristly beef turdlets that the mess cooks seemed to specialize in. But at least a third of the outfit had picked up the trots from eating the ice-cold candied sweet potatoes, sausage stuffing, and young toms smothered in gravy — served hot, of course, but flash-frozen to their tin trays by the time the Marines took the meals back to foxholes that felt more like meat lockers. Elongated strips of frozen diarrhea now littered the trench latrine.

Bonelli threw his pack over his shoulders. "Off to kill more shambos in some other shithole for God, country, and Dugout Doug," he said. A couple of guys choked out a laugh at his scornful reference to the Supreme Allied Commander, General Douglas MacArthur.

With his jet-black pompadour, high cheek-bones, and (often broken) Roman nose, Bonelli could have been cast as one of the quick-draw artists stalking Gregory Peck in *The Gunfighter,* the hit movie being shown on a continuous loop in the holds of Navy troopships steaming from California to northeast Asia. This was apt. Cowboys versus outlaws was an overriding American theme in 1950, almost as fashionable as cowboys versus communists. It was the year when Alger Hiss was convicted and Klaus Fuchs was arrested for spying for the Soviet Union, and an obscure senator from Wisconsin named Joseph McCarthy propelled himself into the headlines by charging that the State Department employed more than two hundred communist agents. It was the year President Harry S. Truman authorized the construction of the first hydrogen bomb, and Germany had settled into separate countries. It was the year when Winston

Churchill warned in the House of Commons of a "looming World War III," and across the Atlantic more than 100,000 U.S. National Guardsmen and reservists were recalled to active duty. Half a decade after the hottest war in history, the world in 1950 was on the cusp of George Orwell's "cold war." Though Orwell had died ten months earlier, his phrase was destined to live on, not least in the craggy mountains of North Korea.

But Dick Bonelli and the enlisted men of Fox Company were not much given to geopolitical strategy. Theirs was a tactical clash, not even dignified (as they noticed) by an official declaration of war; it had been designated, instead, a United Nations "police action." It was a dirty little conflict in a faraway Asian country the size of Florida, a "Hermit Kingdom" that most Americans couldn't even find on a map. The fighting was on foot and deadly: hilltop to hilltop, ridgeline to ridgeline. Whatever small plateau of land the Americans controlled at any given moment constituted their total zone of influence, and was ceded again to the enemy once they had departed.

The deadly Browning automatic rifle — the BAR — was the weapon of choice for the strongest Marines, and one of Fox

Company's BAR men was Warren McClure, a young private first class from Missouri. Just that morning, he had been introduced to his new assistant, Roger Gonzales, a reservist and private first class from Los Angeles. Gonzales had been in Korea less than a week. "Forget the flag, patriotism, and the Reds," McClure told him. "We never own any territory; we're just renting. You're out here for the fight and the adventure." Gonzales hung on the old-timer's every word. McClure was all of twenty-one.

Dick Bonelli wouldn't have argued with McClure's advice. He had been born in Manhattan's Hell's Kitchen and raised in the Bronx, and fighting and adventures were a way of life for him as the son of an Italian bus driver growing up in an Irish neighborhood. He had even beaten up one of his high school social science teachers who had dared suggest that Bonelli was descended from an ape. His truculent attitude had caught up to him sixteen months earlier, when he was arrested for "borrowing" a stranger's car and was offered two options by the Bronx district attorney: the armed forces or an indictment for grand larceny.

Bonelli was a tough kid, and the Marine Corps, which by 1950 had become America's warrior elite, was a natural fit for him.

33

The farm boys and cowhands of the Army's nascent Ranger units could still remember their origins as lowly mule skinners, the Navy's SEALs were still only envisioned by former World War II frogmen, and the Green Berets did not yet exist. But the Marines — there was an outfit.

Then, as now, it was the frontline Marine rifleman who preoccupied the strategists and tacticians at Quantico in Virginia, the acclaimed Warfighting Laboratory — specifically, how to infuse in every man in every rifle company the Corps' basic doctrine that battle had nothing to do with strength of armaments or technology or any theoretical factors dreamed up by intellectuals. Instead, according to the Marine Corps Manual, warfare was a clash of opposing wills, "an extreme trial of moral and physical strength and stamina." To its acolytes, the Marine Corps was no less than a secular religion — Jesuits with guns — grounded in a training regimen and an ethos that relied on a historical narrative of comradeship and brotherhood in arms stretching over 150 years. In short, if a man wanted to be part of America's toughest lineup, he had best join the institution that had fought at the Halls of Montezuma and Tripoli, Belleau Wood and Guadalcanal, Tarawa and Iwo

Jima. And Dick Bonelli certainly wanted to fight. He may have been pushed into the Corps by the law, but now, as he put it, he would "run through hell in a gasoline suit to find the gook party."

From the beginning of the war, American soldiers had been approached by Korean children who pointed at them and said something that sounded like "Me gook." Actually, the Korean word *gook* means "country," and the children's use of the phrase *mee-gook* was probably a complimentary reference to the United States as a "beautiful country." However, among the Americans the term *gook* soon took on a pejorative sense, meaning any Asian, especially any enemy Asian. Bonelli's constant refrain since the landings at Inchon had been, "When do we get the gook party started?" It was now Fox Company's catchphrase after every ambush and firefight: *Hey, Bonelli, big enough party for you?*

The men of the company had attracted their share of fighting. Admittedly, one month earlier they had endured a ten-day "sail to nowhere" around the Korean peninsula. They had boarded flat-bottomed "landing ships, tank" (LSTs) at Inchon on the west coast and had steamed to an unopposed landing near the mined seaport of

Wonsan in the northeast. To their humiliation, they had been beaten there by a flight carrying Bob Hope and his USO dancing girls.

Yet this peaceful debarkation at Wonsan was the exception. Almost from the moment they waded ashore, the Marines of Fox Company encountered bloody, if sporadic, resistance along their two-hundred-mile slog north. The newspaper columnist Ambrose Bierce once noted that war was God's way of teaching Americans geography, and now obscure dots on the North Korean map with names like Hungnam and Hamhung and Koto-ri were proving his prescience. The company had lost good men in each of these places, and nearly a month earlier, during a two-day firefight at the Sudong Gorge, the Seventh Regiment encountered its first Chinese. They'd beaten them decisively, but afterward Fox had buried another eight Marines.

Fox Rifle Company was only a tiny component of the First Marine Division, which was itself just part of a pincer movement organized by General MacArthur. From his headquarters seven hundred miles across the Sea of Japan in occupied Tokyo, MacArthur commanded two separate United Nations columns moving inexorably north toward Manchuria. The columns were separated by fifty-five miles of what MacArthur described as the "merciless wasteland" of North Korea's mountains. In the western half of North Korea, near the Yellow Sea, the U.S. Eighth Army, augmented by South Korean, British, Australian, and Turkish troops — more than 120,000 combat soldiers in all — was overstretched in a thin line running from Seoul deep into the barren northern countryside.

Farther east on the Korean peninsula, MacArthur's X Corps, 35,000 strong, was also marching north, with eventual plans to meet the Eighth Army somewhere along the Yalu River, the country's northern border with China. Commanded by the Army's Major General Edward M. Almond, X Corps was a fusion of two South Korean Army divisions; a small commando unit of British Royal Marines; and a regimental combat team, put together from the U.S. Army's Seventh and Third Divisions. There was also the First Marine Division, the oldest, largest, and most decorated division in the Corps. The Marines considered General Almond as somewhat too adoring of MacArthur, and there was a tacit understanding among seasoned military observers both on the ground in Korea and back in Washington, D.C., that this fight belonged to the First Marine Division.

The First Marine Division was commanded by Major General Oliver Prince Smith and consisted of three infantry regiments — the First, the Fifth, and the Seventh — which were supported by the Eleventh, an artillery regiment. Each regiment consisted of about 3,500 men: three rifle battalions, each of approximately 1,000 men in three rifle companies of anywhere from 200 to 300 men. All told, General Smith had about 15,000 of his Marines along sixty-five miles of a rutted North Korean road that ran north to an enormous man-made lake the Americans called the Chosin Reservoir — a Japanese bastardization of the Korean name, Changjin — or the "frozen" Chosin.

MacArthur's plan was to sweep North Korea free of the communist dictator Kim Il Sung's fleeing North Korea People's Army all the way to the Yalu River. He boasted to reporters that once his troops had mopped up the last stragglers and diehards of Kim's army, the American boys would be home for Christmas. This would be a nice, short little war, wrapped up in five months. But even after the North Korean capital, Pyongyang, fell to the dogfaces of the Eighth Army, the Marines of Fox Company were hard-pressed to reconcile their own reality with MacArthur's optimism.

As Fox's crusty platoon sergeant Richard Danford had muttered after the brief, brutal scuffle at Sudong, "If these are the goddamn stragglers, don't even show me the diehards." Danford, at twenty-seven, had a lot of hard bark on him, and he had learned through experience to trust little that came out of any general's mouth, particularly an Army general in Japan and away from the front line. He once heard a saying by a French politician, that war is too serious to be left to the generals. *Now, there was a guy who knew what he was talking about.* Danford figured that the Frenchman must have once served as an enlisted man.

Fox Company had caught only the ragged edges of the battle at Sudong. Other Marine companies took the brunt of the attacks by what were described as a few Chinese "diplomatic volunteers" who had sneaked across the Yalu River to aid the Koreans in the campaign against Western imperialism. Nonetheless, every American involved in the fight had been staggered by the disregard for life the Chinese displayed. Tales spread among the regiment of how an

American machine-gun emplacement could take out half an enemy infantry company, and the remaining half would still keep charging. Someone even suggested that the Corps put together a special manual for fighting the "drug-addled Oriental." Moreover, paramount in every Marine's mind that November was a frightening question: *Where were the rest of the Reds, and when were they coming?*

A month earlier, the foreign minister of the People's Republic of China, Chou Enlai, had issued a public warning to the Americans to keep their distance from the Yalu. Mao Tse-tung, the Chinese leader, backed up his minister's threats by massing several armies of the Chinese Communist Force (CCF) on the far side of the river. This actually further inflamed MacArthur's atomic ego. After the landings at Inchon, in a meeting with President Truman on Wake Island in the northern Pacific, MacArthur brushed off Mao's move as "diplomatic blackmail."

"We are no longer fearful of their intervention," he told Truman. "If the Chinese tried to get down to Pyongyang, there would be the greatest slaughter."

Perhaps. But despite MacArthur's insistence that only a few Chinese had voluntarily crossed the Yalu — barely enough to make up a division — there were rumors running through the American lines that several CCF armies had in fact begun infiltrating North Korea in mid-October. These reports were not lost on the anxious Marine general Oliver Smith. Smith, a cautious man, had never shared MacArthur's expectation of a quick victory in North Korea — privately, he scoffed at the "home by Christmas baloney." He was certain that his Marines would face strong Chinese resistance west of the Chosin Reservoir as they pushed toward the Yalu. In a private dispatch to the Marine Corps commandant general, Clifton B. Cates, in Washington — a back-channel communication that enraged MacArthur when he learned of it — Smith pleaded for "someone in high authority who will make his mind up as to what is our goal." Smith apologized to Cates for the "pessimistic" tone of his letter but explained that to obey MacArthur's and Almond's instructions to push on with the First Division's flanks so exposed "was to simply get further out on a limb."

"I believe a winter campaign in the mountains of North Korea is too much to ask of the American soldier or Marine," Smith wrote, "and I doubt the feasibility of supplying troops in this area during the winter or providing for evacuation of sick and wounded. I feel you are entitled to know what our on-the-spot reaction is."

Smith noted in his letter that about half his fighting men were young, unseasoned reservists — despite the fact that when the First Marine Division had been hastily deployed to northeast Asia all the division's seventeen-year-olds were culled from the ranks to remain in Japan. Moreover, in many cases reservists with summer-camp experience — either one summer with seventy-two drills or two summers with thirty-six drills each — were deemed "combat ready" by dint of this training, despite the fact that they had never been to boot camp.

Before Sudong, no more than a handful of Marines in Fox Company had ever seen a Chinese soldier — and the others probably wouldn't have been able to tell the difference between a Chinese and a North Korean. Corporal Wayne Pickett, who at twenty-one was another of the "old men" in Fox, was, however, one of the few. He had served a tour in Shanghai as a seagoing Marine in 1947, and he told his buddies that their firefight at Sudong was a picnic compared with what he'd seen and heard at

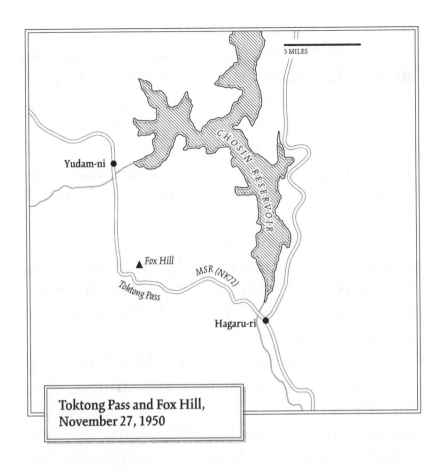

Toktong Pass and Fox Hill,
November 27, 1950

Shanghai. He added that they would sure as hell recognize a full force of "fighting Chinamen" when they met it. For one thing, the Chinese were taller, Pickett said, and a hell of a lot more robust and better armed than the human scarecrows still loyal to Kim Il Sung. Pickett also warned that the Chinese soldiers were veterans of Mao's civil war, and their fighting ability was not to be taken lightly. "And the ROKs damn well know that," he added.

As Pickett's stories spread, a few Marines in Fox Company thought back to a scene they had witnessed a couple of days after Sudong. While moving north, the outfit had passed a Republic of Korea Army unit marching south with a single Chinese prisoner. The Americans didn't have much faith in the fighting ability of most ROKs to begin with, but at the time more than a few Marines were shaken by the overt fear their South Korean allies exhibited at the mere presence of this shackled *Shina-jen,* or *Chinesu,* in their midst.

Nonetheless, by the time Fox Company lined up for its Thanksgiving dinner, they hadn't seen a hostile Chinese in the four weeks since Sudong. The Chinese had simply disappeared, and a buoyant feeling was slowly returning to the company — a sense that Christmas day 1950 might indeed be celebrated in dining rooms and at kitchen tables in Duluth and San Antonio and Pittsburgh, in Los Angeles and Miami and the Bronx.

2

During the first six months of the Korean War, its ebb and flow had pushed Fox Company to a remote, windswept tableland

210 miles north of the 38th Parallel, which had been established as the border between the two Koreas after World War II. The locals called it *Kaema-kowon,* the roof of the Korean peninsula.

In the sixteenth century, the first European missionaries and traders painted a romantic portrait of this sawtooth terrain, likening it to a sea in a heavy gale. For weeks, Fox had been traversing this knotted ground, up one desolate mountain, down the next, hiking cold and wet toward the Yalu — and these exhausted men did not compose any lyrical odes to the place. Some Marines in Fox Company had come to consider the situation a cruel game, and with nothing to lose they began playing it themselves. At dusk they would search the compass points and pick out the highest, coldest-looking hills. Then they would wager on which one they would be sent to hold for the night.

Now, on the morning of November 27, 1950, they were on the move again. The knoll Fox was abandoning after Thanksgiving rose west of the village of Hagaru-ri, which to the Americans resembled nothing so much as an old Klondike mining camp with its dilapidated houses packed close around newly erected canvas tents. The vil-

45

lage was situated atop a muddy, triangular plateau whose southern terminus was a broad field crammed with more rows of American tents, supply trains, and fuel and ammunition dumps. On the edge of this clearing Marine engineers operated five Caterpillar tractors day and night under fixed floodlights, chugging to and fro, carving a crude airstrip out of the frozen earth. Scuttlebutt had it inside Hagaru-ri's defensive perimeter that Fox was preparing to move up a winding, twelve-foot-wide dirt road the Americans had designated Main Service Road NK72, or simply the MSR.

Most of the men believed they would be traveling the fourteen miles north to another tiny village, Yudam-ni, which was in a floodplain between two rivers and the northwestern tip of the Chosin Reservoir. There they assumed they would rejoin the bulk of their Seventh Regiment and its commanding officer, Colonel Homer Litzenberg Jr., a stubborn, impatient Dutchman known as "Blitzen Litzen." Litzenberg's regiment was part of a force of 8,400 that — along with most of Colonel Raymond Murray's Fifth Regiment and three artillery battalions of the Eleventh Regiment — was the tip of X Corps' spear. Eight miles to the east, across the reservoir, 2,550 GIs who were part of two Army battalions were also positioned to storm north, locked and loaded, anticipating MacArthur's order to commence the final push to the Yalu.

But as Fox Company assembled outside the Battalion Command Post in Hagaru-ri, word filtered down that they were headed not to the reservoir, but instead to Toktong Pass — seven miles north, midway between Hagaru-ri and Yudam-ni. There they were to dig in along one of the lower ridgelines of the highest mountain in the area, the 5,454-foot Toktong-san, which overlooked the MSR where it cut through the pass. It was the only road into or out of the Chosin.

This order to essentially babysit at a bottleneck did not sit well with Fox Company. In fact, the Marines could not comprehend it. The North Koreans had been on the run for ten weeks, and by this stage in the war even Hagaru-ri was considered a safe enough rear area to have its own PX, even if its stock was limited to Tootsie Rolls and shoe polish. Moreover, Marines did not retreat, so the very idea that Litzenberg's and Murray's rear supply route needed guarding was ludicrous. The enlisted men of Fox would have much preferred to push on farther north to Yudam-ni, lest they cede bragging rights to some undeserving outfit.

Baker Company of the regiment's First Battalion was already boasting about the carpet of corpses it had left in the hilltops, gorges, and draws around Sudong. This was more than nettlesome, particularly because in Fox's opinion Baker Company wouldn't know its ass from a hole in the ground.

Naturally, the Marines blamed this strange turn of events — as they blamed most things — on MacArthur's inconceivable decision to place X Corps under the overall command of an Army general: Almond. Rivalries among the Marines themselves may have been spirited, if good natured. By contrast, there was no love lost at all between the Corps and the pogue doggies — a pejorative slang term Marines originally had applied to anyone with a soft, rear-area job but which by now was used to describe any dogface in the Army, a branch of the service that the jarheads deemed so thick with deadwood it should have been declared a fire hazard. This was another reason for Fox Company to add Almond's name to their already long shit list.

The gouged, dome-topped Toktong-san, eroded by time and Korea's bitter winters, is a southeastern spur of the ancient Taebaek mountain range. This stunted cordillera hugs the Sea of Japan from the Chinese border well into South Korea, and it reminded some of the Americans of the Appalachian range. The young Marine recruits from the East Coast on their way to Camp Pendleton in California had been particularly impressed when the troop trains had climbed the Appalachians — that is, until they glimpsed the Rockies from the flat plains of Colorado. After they crossed the Rockies, the puny Appalachians — like the scrubby piles of granite they gazed up at now in North Korea — had diminished in their memories. Compared with the Rockies, the Taebaeks seemed more hills than mountains. This impression changed when they had to climb one.

Recruiting posters showed the typical leatherneck as tall, square-jawed, powerful, and mature, but the majority of the "men" of Fox were baby-faced "boots" who had only recently started to shave. On leave they preferred malt shops to gin mills, and the opposite sex came in three flavors: Mom, Sis, and an exotic type that existed only to be lied about or ogled. Their train trips from towns and cities across the United States to Pendleton, near their debarkation point to Japan, had for most of them been their first time away from home. Now, in Korea, with their gaunt profiles reflecting the rigors of constant battle marches, they suggested not so much a picture of American samurai as a scraggly crew of teenage pirates.

The onset of the North Korean winter had been harsh; they were frozen and exhausted when it snowed, and they were frozen and exhausted when it didn't snow. An unremitting wet gale blew constantly — the Marines took to calling it the "Siberian Express" — and glazed every rock with ice. Their knees, knuckles, and elbows were covered with bloody scabs from continually slipping on treacherous slopes, and their feet and hands were always numb. Hours during the day were hardly noted, as they set their body clocks only by daylight and darkness. And aside from a vague awareness that Thanksgiving had just passed and Christmas was coming, many had no idea what date it was, much less what day of the week.

Moreover, because canteen water had to be thawed over campfires, stateside notions of hygiene had been abandoned from almost the moment they had set foot on Korean soil. A twig often had to do for a toothbrush, and they could barely lay their heads down for the night in an abandoned hootch without waking up with a scalpful of lice. Most had given up trying to wipe their runny noses with anything other than the sleeves of their filthy uniforms, and anyone who grew a mustache soon had a revolting mass of frozen mucus layered across his upper lip.

They bitched and groused, but they never shirked a command, remaining true to the Latin motto above the eagle on the Marine emblem: *Semper Fidelis,* "always faithful." And so, just past noon, while Fox Company mustered in the village of Hagaru-ri, Lieutenant Colonel Randolph Lockwood, commanding officer of the Seventh Regiment's Second Battalion, summoned his subordinate Captain William Edward Barber, Fox Company's new CO, for a trip in the company Jeep to scout Toktong Pass.

Barber was a decorated World War II veteran who had assumed command of Fox three weeks earlier at Koto-ri, after his predecessor, Captain Zorn, was transferred to Division headquarters. Barber was a tall thirty-year-old with a broad, nondescript face, an odd round nose, and thinning brown hair. In mufti he might have been taken for an actuary rather than a commander of a Marine rifle company, and few encountering him could have guessed that he'd been a star college baseball and basketball player. Yet despite his unremarkable exterior — his physical appearance reminded a few men in Fox Company of a younger version of the irascible banker Henry F. Potter in the movie *It's a Wonderful Life* — the captain carried himself with the demeanor and bearing of a hussar. This may have been a result of the long bareback rides he had taken as a child through snow-packed Appalachian hollows when he ran errands on the family's one plow horse during winters.

Barber had grown up in the rural town of Dehart, Kentucky, near the Ohio River, in a homestead hit hard by the Depression. His father, Woodrow, was a subsistence farmer and sometime carpenter; his mother, Mabel, grew vegetables in a small garden behind their house. Young Billy, the eighth of ten children, was a shy, sensitive child who devoured every book he could borrow from the local library, particularly volumes on history and current events.

He was a precocious student, the valedictorian of his high school class when he graduated at age fifteen, and early on he determined that his four brothers and five sisters needed his assistance, both educationally and financially. He always managed to find time to take his siblings aside and help them with their reading and writing, and even when he moved on to the nearby

Morehead State Teachers College he relished returning on school breaks to join his father and brothers plowing and harvesting the family's small cornfield. When the Barbers killed a hog for special occasions, such as Thanksgiving or Christmas, it was always Billy who volunteered to dress the carcass.

In the late 1930s, Barber sensed a world war approaching, and while studying at Morehead State he joined the Marine reserves — pointedly without informing his parents, who considered the military as a second-class career for such a smart young man and would have preferred him to become an educator. In 1940, following his sophomore year, he further distressed his mother and father by quitting college and shipping out to boot camp at the Marine Corps' recruiting depot on Parris Island in South Carolina. He was generous to a fault, and his brothers and sisters looked forward to his numerous letters, as he never forgot to include a few dollars — often doubling the amount when he sent birthday cards. When he returned home on leaves, he made sure to bring small mementos from his travels for everyone.

Barber was what the Marines called a "mustang," an enlisted man promoted to officer whose leadership skills had been honed in the ranks as opposed to the saddle. He proved to be a crack shot, and after boot camp he was retained at Parris Island as a marksmanship instructor. A year later, in 1941, feeling confined on the tiny base — the Marine Corps was only a small force of 18,000 men when he enlisted — he volunteered for the Corps' new paratroop service. He proved so adept at falling from airplanes that he was again ordered to stay on as an instructor, now at the Naval Air Station in Lakewood, New Jersey. From early on his superiors recognized something special in his character and marked him as a candidate for promotion.

After the Japanese bombed Pearl Harbor, Barber was transferred to the Marines' First Parachute Regiment in San Diego. It was there, at a USO canteen, that he met and fell in love with his future wife, Ione. They were married in October 1942, the same year he was promoted to sergeant. Officer candidate school soon followed, and in February 1945, having received his commission, he landed with the Fifth Marines on Iwo Jima as a twenty-five-year-old lieutenant leading a rifle platoon. Through the awful attrition of the campaign, he wound up a company commander. On Iwo he was shot in the hand and was briefly evacuated when he began bleeding from both ears. He was diagnosed with a severe concussion, but he recovered and returned to the atoll, where he rescued two wounded Marines pinned down by enemy fire. For this he added the Silver Star for Gallantry to his Purple Heart.

He remained a company commander during the postwar occupation of Japan, and in early 1946 he was posted to Camp Lejeune in North Carolina as a recruiting officer. Then he was promoted to captain and transferred to Altoona, Pennsylvania. He was living at the Marine barracks there, training reservists, when on June 25, 1950, Kim Il Sung's 90,000-man army, led by 150 Soviet-made tanks, swarmed across the 38th Parallel. Kim's forces routed the South Koreans and their American protectors and captured the capital of Seoul in three days. Halfway around the world, Bill Barber followed early news accounts of the war with a mixture of fascination, disgust, and sadness.

His fascination stemmed from a Marine officer's professional appreciation of the fighting spirit of Kim's ill-equipped but courageous and tenacious forces. The Koreans, geographically isolated, hemmed in by Russians, Mongols, and Japanese, had for centuries accepted their role as "shrimps among whales." It had actually made them tougher. They reminded Barber of the imperial Japanese forces he had fought in the Pacific. On the other hand, he was disgusted by the disorganized retreat of the unprepared U.S. Army down the peninsula. And he was saddened by the unusually high number of Marine company commanders, most of them fellow veterans of World War II, who were killed as the North Korea People's Army swiftly occupied 95 percent of the country.

By the time of MacArthur's audacious counterattack — the amphibious landing at Inchon, just southwest of Seoul, on September 15 — Barber had received his orders to report to the front. He was en route as Fox Company embarked on the long sail around the peninsula and landed at Wonsan. He caught up with them just south of the secured village of Koto-ri.

Barber did not endear himself to Fox's careworn veterans when he arrived from Japan. His uniform was starched and spotless; even his dungarees were pressed; and one Marine noted that "he was all dressed up like a well-kept grave." But he believed that a Marine's appearance should reflect combat-readiness, and he was appalled at his new outfit's slovenly demeanor; he told several fellow officers that they reminded him of one of Pancho Villa's bandit gangs. He introduced himself by directing his platoon leaders to order all the Marines in Fox to field-shave with cold water, clean their filthy weapons, and prepare for a conditioning hike at 0600 the next morning. He also spread word to knock off the fairy-tale talk about being home for Christmas.

"Just what we need," said the veteran private first class Graydon Davis, "some candy-ass captain who wants us to troop and stomp. What in hell is this war coming to?"

Nor did Barber's official introductory remarks the next morning before the hike go over well. He told his assembled company that there was a lot of war left to fight, and Fox was damn well going to be prepared to fight it. He spoke in a tangy drawl. "I may not know about strategy," he said, "but I know a lot about tactics. And frankly, I'm a hell of a good infantry officer."

As the "Old Man's" coming-aboard speech ended and the assembly broke up, Dick Bonelli remarked to a group of buddies, "Somebody ought to tell this guy that Marines are more show-me than tell-me."

Barber overheard him but said nothing. He liked grumbling Marines. The more they bitched, the harder they fought. Plus, as an enlisted man he'd been a griper himself. Fox would learn soon enough that behind the new CO's prickly and fastidious exterior was a saltiness earned on the black sand beaches of the South Pacific.

3

Although Barber had only just met his superior Lieutenant Colonel Randolph Lockwood, he already admired Lockwood's moxie. The story of how the pudgy, pink-cheeked, pipe-smoking officer had held his own during his first meeting with "Blitzen Litzen" three weeks earlier had circulated swiftly throughout the Seventh Regiment. When Lockwood, a genial graduate of the Naval Academy and Harvard, arrived at Koto-ri to assume command of the Second Battalion, Litzenberg had taken in his preppy demeanor with a thunderous stare from his big coal eyes.

"I see you're overweight," Litzenberg said by way of introduction.

"Nothing like a mountain campaign to get a man into shape," Lockwood replied. His voice was a little too cheerful.

"I'm a hard taskmaster," Litzenberg said,

glaring at him.

Lockwood smiled. "That's what I've heard, Colonel."

No one else dared talk to Litzenberg like this, and the exchange immediately elevated Lockwood's status among Litzenberg's underlings, if not with the colonel himself.

Now, as Barber and Lockwood's Jeep ascended the road to Toktong Pass, the weak sun burned the haze off mountain meadows dotted with thatched-roof huts and empty oxcarts standing nearby. This was a sudden new world — big, muscular, and edged at its margins by brooding storm clouds. It was not lost on either Marine that mountain warfare was alien territory for an amphibious force trained and accustomed to fighting on beaches. Both men had received sketchy reports of enemy contact earlier that day at the Chosin, probably involving Chinese units that had forded the Yalu, and this gave their seven-mile drive an uneasy tone.

In fact, as they snaked farther away from Hagaru-ri and up the steep slopes toward Toktong-san, two things struck them with foreboding. The first was their topographical maps. These were outdated, adapted from old Japanese documents, and nothing on the charts seemed to match the contours of the terrain. Peaks loomed high on the wrong side of the road, valleys opened where there should have been hills, and snow-covered foot trails meandered next to streams — frozen solid and marbled with blue ice — that should not have existed. More ominous was the absence of refugees. Since the landings at Wonsan the Americans had encountered emaciated North Korean civilians on nearly every road and donkey path. But this morning the MSR was deserted even by the small groups of bedraggled boys who usually begged for candy and chewing gum.

Barber had done his homework, which included reading a translated copy of *Military Lessons,* the propaganda tract the communist high command had disseminated among its troops. This pamphlet had been found in the pocket of a dead Chinese NCO at Sudong. After grudgingly noting the tactical superiority of U.S. tanks, planes, and artillery, it declared, "Their infantry is weak. These men are afraid to die, and will neither press home a bold attack nor defend to the death. If their source of supply is cut, their fighting suffers, and if you interdict their rear, they will withdraw."

Barber had also scanned intelligence files prepared by the South Korean army interpreters at HQ in Hagaru-ri. Several local farmers had been interviewed, and they reported that the area's abundant game had lately been spooked out of the narrow mountain vales around the Toktong Pass. It was as if something was moving around in there. He suspected it was a shitload of Reds.

Upon reaching the switchback where the MSR looped east to west at the apex of the pass, Barber and Lockwood dismounted before a steep, broad eminence on the north side of the road and began climbing in the shadow of Toktong-san. They were at 4,850 feet when they reached the eighty-yard-wide crest of the promontory, a shoulder of the big mountain. The effect of being cut off from the sea by mountains to the west, east, and southeast had extraordinary consequences. The raw, wet wind screaming out of the Arctic and across the Manchurian plain, and then funneling through the pass, was the fiercest either man had ever encountered. The area around the Chosin Reservoir was said to be the coldest place in Korea, and the fallow terrain was the only ground in the country where rice could not be grown. The local peasants knew to expect an average of sixteen to twenty weeks each winter when the average temperature never rose above zero degrees Fahrenheit, and Barber could not help wondering how drastically this cold would reduce his company's combat efficiency.

The hill they stood on loomed above two narrow valleys and occupied an area about the size of three football fields. At the top of the hill, on the northwest quadrant, the ground extended to form a narrow saddle — seventy-five yards wide and humped like a whale's back. This land bridge, which ran three hundred yards, fell away sharply on both sides and ended at a large rocky knoll. Above and beyond the rocky knoll a string of higher, serrated rocky ridges ran another one-third mile like a gleaming white staircase up the looming bulk of Toktong-san.

Except for the narrow saddle, the hill was well separated from the other heights in all directions by slender, snow-covered valleys. The basins to the east and west stretched a bit over two hundred yards across, with the western depression bisected by a deep ravine running lengthwise up to the edge of the saddle. The wider southern vale — level bottom ground with brown tufts of alpine grass dotting the snow like miniature haystacks — ran nearly three hundred yards. These valleys separated the hill from three similar, tree-skirted knolls to the east, west, and south.

Delineating the base of the hill, adjacent to the road, was a sheer cut bank, ten feet high by forty feet long, where the MSR had been chiseled out of the heights eighteen years earlier during the Japanese occupation of Korea. Past this steep wall, neat rows of fir trees, four to five inches thick at the trunk and perhaps forty feet tall, climbed two-thirds of the way up the slope. These immature dwarf pines, also planted by the Japanese as part of an emergency reforestation program, were spaced eight to ten feet apart. Above the tree line the crest of the hill sported small patches of gnarled brush that pushed through the hard-packed, knee-deep snow. The undulating hilltop was also broken by countless rocks and colossal boulders. Two of the largest boulders — a pair of tall, flat-faced rocks, eight feet high by six feet across — dominated the north-west corner of the peak at the beginning of the saddle. They resembled giant dominoes.

The hill's main, central ridgeline rose to 225 yards above the road at its northeast corner, and dipped to 175 yards high at the northwest peak, where the saddle began. A secondary, catty-corner ridgeline bisected the hill from the lower, southwest corner and petered out at the tree line. The entire hill was pocked and pleated with depressions, erosion folds, and a few old bivouac bunkers and foxholes that had been rocketed and napalmed by the Americans as Litzenberg had ascended the pass on his march to Yudam-ni. A shallow gully, twenty yards wide, ran straight up the middle of the hill from the road to just beyond the trees. In the lower, southeast corner, below the fir tree plantation, a freshwater spring flowed out of the mountains despite the freezing temperature.

Near the spring, two abandoned huts had been built several yards back from the road. These structures were about ten feet high, with dirt floors, low-pitched roofs, and doorless openings at either end. The larger hut, which ran parallel to the MSR, was perhaps twelve by twenty feet and was divided into two sections. It looked as if it had been a subsistence farmhouse — half of it seemed to be a kitchen. The slightly smaller hut, sitting at a right angle about ten yards up the hill behind the main house, retained a strong odor of farm animals and had a large grain storage bin at its south end, closest to the main building.

As Barber and Lockwood climbed back down to their Jeep, the new commanding officer of Fox Company was already conceptualizing his defensive perimeter. His Marines, Barber told Lockwood, would defend Toktong Pass from this hill. He would align his men up the gentler eastern grade, across the crest, and down the steep western slope in the general shape of an inverted horseshoe, the "reverse U" position taught at Quantico. The road would "close" the two piers of the horseshoe, with the breadth of the oval perhaps 155 yards wide from east to west.

After Lockwood accepted his plan, Barber asked to remain at the pass while Lockwood returned to Hagaru-ri. Lockwood reluctantly agreed and told him to expect the arrival of his company within the hour.

Back in the village, however, Lockwood could find no vehicles to transport Fox Company up the MSR. At 2 p.m. word passed among the men that they would be hiking the seven miles up the icy, muddy, glorified goat trail. One Marine noted in his journal, "Now we gripe openly and vociferously."

The footsore Marines of Fox Company were not happy to be lugging more than sixty pounds each of weapons, ammo, and gear up the road. In addition to the standard-issue Garland M1 — an eight-shot, clip-fed semiautomatic rifle that

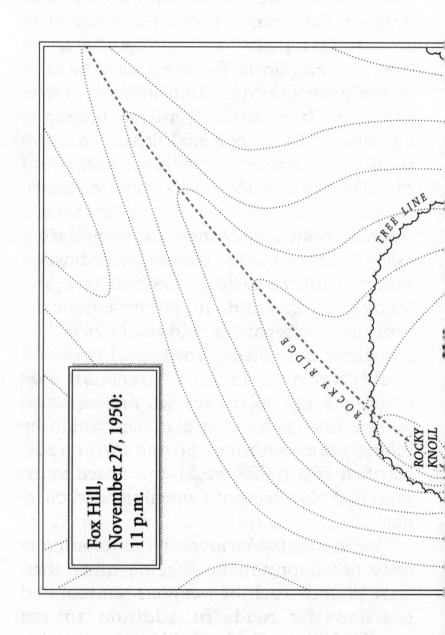

Fox Hill,
November 27, 1950:
11 p.m.

TREE-LINE

ROCKY RIDGE

ROCKY
KNOLL

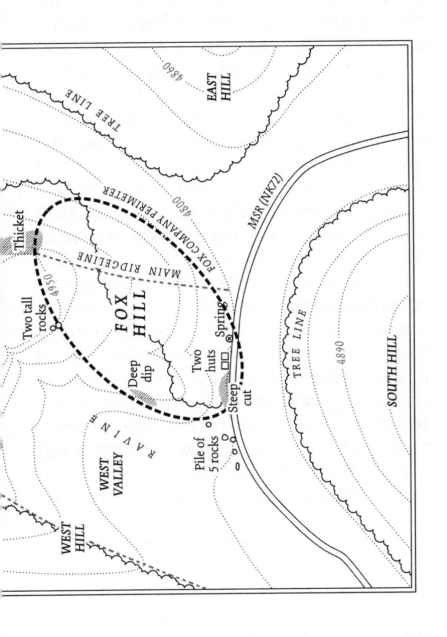

EAST HILL

4860

TREE LINE

4800

FOX COMPANY PERIMETER

Thicket

MAIN RIDGELINE

MSR (NK72)

Two tall rocks

4950

FOX HILL

Deep dip

Spring

Two huts

Steep cut

TREE LINE

4890

SOUTH HILL

RAVINE

WEST VALLEY

Pile of 5 rocks

WEST HILL

weighed about ten pounds — they carried carbines, .45-caliber sidearms, light machine guns, mortar barrel tubes and plates, bazookas, entrenching tools, boxes and bandoliers of ammunition, cartons of C rations, satchels of grenades, heavy down sleeping bags, command post and medical tents, medical supplies, a radio and field phones, half-tent covers, and personal items such as books, extra socks, souvenirs, and a bathroom kit. Some had .38-caliber pistols, gifts sent from home, in shoulder holsters under their armpits.

They were also swathed in bulky layers of winter clothing. Each man wore a pair of "windproof" dungarees over a pair of puke-green wool trousers and cotton long johns; a four-tiered upper-body layer of cotton undershirt, wool top shirt, dungaree jacket, and Navy-issue, calf-length, alpaca-lined hooded parka; a wool cap with earflaps and visor beneath a helmet; wool shoe pads and socks worn beneath cleated, rubberized winter boots, or shoepacs; and heavy-duty gloves covering leather or canvas mittens. Some men had cut the trigger finger off their gloves.

This late in the afternoon, no one was confident of reaching Toktong Pass before dark, but luck struck when the company's forward artillery observer announced that he had scrounged transport from the commanding officer of How Company, the Second Battalion's 105-mm howitzer unit based at Hagaru-ri. The "arty boys" had agreed to lend Fox the nine trucks they used to lug their big guns.

"Bring them back with the tanks full," one of the artillerymen joked, and at 2:30 p.m. the company was ordered to saddle up. As men climbed onto the open flatbeds of the six-by-sixes and squeezed into the seats of the company Jeep — some Marines riding on the hoods — more than a few freezing men wondered where their new commanding officer was.

4

If Fox Company was suspicious of its new spit-and-polish CO, he too was leery of them. Following the landings at Inchon, the company had taken heavy casualties during the Uijongbu campaign north of Seoul. Then, on the push north to the Yalu as winter set in, frostbite had become more effective at thinning the outfit than the random roadside ambushes. By the time Barber assumed command at Koto-ri nearly half the unit consisted of fresh "boots" and most of its officers were as new to Korea as

Barber was.

The company was nowhere near its full strength, and one day on the road near Koto-ri Barber watched aghast as an entire squad failed to take out three fleeing North Korean soldiers no more than two hundred yards away. On Iwo, this would have been a job for one Marine. Barber's defining character trait may have been his rigorous self-discipline, and he expected no less from the men under his command. Thereafter he instituted a routine of daily rifle practice on makeshift ranges, using cans cadged from the mess tents as targets.

This did not sit well with weary, frozen Marines who could see warming campfires and smell coffee roasting while they lay prone in the snow firing at bacon tins. Oddly, however, despite the punishment no one considered Barber a mean-spirited leader. Unlike many Marine commanders, he took pains to explain the reasons for every reprimand he issued. And in this case the regimen worked. Before long each man in the outfit had improved his marksmanship impressively.

Similarly, during skirmishes along the trek to Hagaru-ri, Barber found hands-on opportunities to teach his new line replacements how to call in close air support, register artillery rounds, and fire the mortars at night. (Sometimes, to his men's perplexed amazement, he would simultaneously break out in a full-throated rendition of the Marine Corps hymn.) All in all, Barber felt that by the time Fox Company set off for Toktong Pass his "training on the run" had not only improved his unit's fighting skills but brought the men together as a cohesive team. They would need to be.

Barber had studied Sun-tzu and was also familiar with the military writings of Mao Tse-tung, who had been strongly influenced by Sun-tzu's ancient but still practical strategies during the recent Chinese civil war. "The reason we have always advanced a policy of luring the enemy to penetrate deeply," Mao had written in *On Protracted War*, "is that it is the most effective tactic against a strong opponent."

Now, alone on a vital pass, Barber took another look at North Korea's unforgiving mountains. Who was out there? And in what strength? The Chinese had been fighting in these hills for millennia, and Barber again considered Sun-tzu, who had set down his ideas in the fourth century BC. If Mao was still following those precepts, the odds were that the First Marine Division was being lured into a trap.

And, Barber noted, his company, his first command in Korea, was right in the thick of it.

At 3 p.m. the convoy carrying most of the three rifle platoons and the headquarters staff of Fox Company left Hagaru-ri and began the climb up to Toktong Pass. Even with the nine borrowed trucks, however, there were not enough vehicles to transport the entire outfit, its equipment, and the adjunct details now assigned to it. The company had been reinforced by an 81-mm mortar section consisting of two tubes each manned by ten Marines, as well as an additional eighteen Marines from the Second Battalion's heavy weapons section who toted two water-cooled Browning .30-caliber heavy machine guns. About two dozen men from the First Rifle Platoon had to be left behind until the trucks could return for them. As drivers gunned their engines, more than a few men slept where they dropped in the flatbeds.

The MSR was wide enough to permit the passage of only a single vehicle, and the convoy's progress was delayed when it found itself in a trace to a column of slow-moving tractors towing a battery of 155-mm howitzers to Yudam-ni. Not until 5 p.m. did

Captain Barber — by now rejoined by Lieutenant Colonel Lockwood, who had transported a cameraman to the hill to record the company's arrival — see Fox's lead Jeep coming up the winding road. The Jeep, its trailer laden with gear, pulled over next to the two abandoned huts. Barber directed the convoy onward, until the entire line of vehicles was adjacent to the base of the hill. Upon orders to dismount, several Marines had to be shaken awake, including Private First Class Warren McClure, the BAR man of the First Fire Team, Second Squad, Second Platoon.

McClure had dreamed of carrying a BAR since high school, when his guidance counselor, a Marine veteran who had earned a Bronze Star on Iwo Jima, regaled him with stories about fighting the Japanese. McClure, who described himself as a hillbilly, had grown up in a small town in central Missouri near the Lake of the Ozarks. He and his friends had devoured war movies of the 1940s and reenacted famous battles of World War II almost daily in their backyard fields. When his family moved to Kansas City, he enlisted in his school's Marine reserve program and spent summers and weekends with an artillery battalion learning to operate 105-mm howitzers.

In the summer of 1950 McClure was preparing to leave for boot camp. When war broke out in Korea, he was instead ordered onto a troop train bound for San Diego. He assumed he would be assigned to an artillery outfit. Instead, to his surprise and delight, when he arrived at Camp Pendleton he was drafted into a Marine rifle company.

"We went out and threw three grenades and fired twenty rounds from a BAR, and that was my training," he would later explain to his assistant in Fox Company, Private First Class Roger Gonzales. "Then they asked for a volunteer to be the BAR man."

McClure jumped at the opportunity. The air-cooled, gas-operated BAR — the Browning automatic rifle, steady, fast-firing, and accurate to five hundred yards — was considered the finest one-man weapon in the infantry, the ultimate in battlefield efficiency. It weighed twenty pounds complete with bipod and twenty-round magazine, and it was the basis for a Marine fire team. The model for this four-man team had been developed ten years earlier at Quantico, and once again the Corps seemed to have borrowed from the Society of Jesus, for the concept was a variation of the Jesuit tenet of freedom within discipline. Its beauty lay in its simplicity.

A Marine rifle company was a vertically integrated pyramid — each company had three platoons, each platoon had three squads, and each squad had three fire teams. The fire team was an eminently sensible idea, for in the confusion of battle no one man could reasonably be expected to be responsible for more than three others. More important, in the heat of a gunfight there was a comfort in knowing that a Marine hefting a deadly BAR was no more than a few steps away.

Now McClure told Gonzales, "If the earth didn't curve, who knows from how far away I could hit a man?" The two jumped from a six-by-six onto the road, stretched, and stamped blood into their freezing feet. McClure was about to start a monologue regarding the killing power of the BAR when he noticed another Marine take a thermometer from a pack. It registered minus-twelve degrees Fahrenheit. A dark cloudbank, whipped by twenty-five-knot winds out of the north, obscured the peak of Toktong-san.

"Smells like snow," the Marine with the thermometer said.

McClure shook his head. Back in Missouri, he and his younger brother had often spent hours hunting and fishing in the forests and creeks of the Ozarks. On weekends they might bring home enough rabbits to feed the family for days. Except for the higher elevation, these North Korean hills reminded McClure of the mountains at home in winter. He felt no hesitation in correcting the other man. "Too cold to snow," he said.

A few moments later the first snowflakes began caking his helmet and plastering his wavy blond hair to his forehead.

Not far away, Captain Barber ordered the first two trucks to return to Hagaru-ri for the rest of his men, and he directed a sixteen-by-eighteen tent erected just east of the larger hut to serve as his command post. The company radio operator was setting up his communications post in and around the tent as Barber called his team leaders together. The captain was immediately interrupted by Lieutenant Lawrence Schmitt, the company's communications officer. Schmitt told him that the SCR-300 radio was already low on battery power because of the intense cold.

Both the radio — which would keep Barber in touch with the howitzer unit in Hagaru-ri, as well as Colonel Litzenberg up at the Chosin — and the company's 610 field phones, used for communication between platoon leaders, ran on batteries. Cold weather slows the chemical reaction that generates electrons to supply electrical current inside a battery. The bitter cold of Toktong Pass drained them in minutes. This was a problem that had not been anticipated by the American forces in northeast Asia, who were unfamiliar with the peninsula's fierce winter temperatures. Moreover, the Korean winter of 1950 would be the coldest recorded in thirty years.

Meanwhile, at the Hagaru-ri defensive perimeter, the six big 105-mm howitzers of How Company, which were specifically dedicated to the support of Fox, were still a full seven miles from Toktong Pass. Factoring in the effect of the cold weather on the gases that propelled the shells, as well as the effect of the elevation, this left the pass barely within their maximum firing range — another quarter mile, and the shells would have been useless. And now there was a chance that Barber might not even be able to reach the howitzer commander by radio. The captain ordered Schmitt to fix the communications problem and turned back to the briefing.

"Follow me," he said, leading his company officers and platoon sergeants on a brisk trot up the hill. At the crest the little group paused to watch the headlights of a convoy of six-by-sixes rumbling south from Yudam-ni, carrying wounded Marines. When the grinding gears of the final vehicle were only a distant echo, Barber informed his battle commanders that he had reached a hard decision. Despite the approaching darkness, the bitter cold, and the mind-numbing winds, he wanted the men dug in before any warming tents were erected.

Waiting atop Toktong Pass, his face swollen and nearly bleeding from the lash of the gale, Barber had vacillated over his choices for several hours. His men were dog-tired, and it would have been more compassionate to let them break out their entrenching tools tomorrow morning after a good night's rest. He had even checked the frost level with his bayonet; it sank to a depth of sixteen inches. Jackhammers would be more appropriate than shovels for this ground.

But something in Barber's gut told him the company needed to protect itself as well as possible as soon as possible. He would have preferred to have enough personnel to send a squad across the saddle to occupy the higher ground of the rocky knoll and the ridge behind it, but he didn't. He assumed they were being watched even now by Chinese scouts on those heights. Barber wanted to register the artillery at Hagaru-ri by asking the battery to fire a few shells, but it was too dark. He also understood, from his experience in the Pacific, that during a firefight it was psychologically harder for a man to retreat from a foxhole than from a poncho spread across the ground. He reiterated the directive to dig in — "I don't like casual compliance with my orders" — and assigned the following areas of responsibility.

The sixty-two Marines and one corpsman of First Lieutenant Elmo Peterson's Second Rifle Platoon would dig in across the steeper western slope, from just above the vertical ten-foot cut bank and up the 175 yards over the thirty-degree grade until they reached the saddle on the northwest corner. Looking at the hill from the road, this would be on the left.

First Lieutenant Robert McCarthy's Third Rifle Platoon of fifty-four Marines and one corpsman would string out across the wide hilltop, their left flank linking up with Second Platoon's right flank in front of the saddle. Barber realized that this would be the most dangerous area to defend, because when the Chinese attacked they would undoubtedly stream across that land bridge.

"Two forward squads up, one reserve back," he told McCarthy, elucidating the Marines' classic defensive V position. McCarthy nodded. *As if I don't know how to dig in for the night.*

Finally, the First Rifle Platoon — sixty-two Marines and one corpsman commanded by First Lieutenant John Dunne — would complete the horseshoe, entrenching in a 225-yard line down the gentler eastern slope, nearly to the road. Each platoon would space its two air-cooled light machine guns accordingly, with as much firepower as possible concentrated on the saddle.

The defense of the "open" seventy-five-yard space along the road would be the responsibility of the sixty-nine Marines and Navy corpsmen of the heavy machine-gun units, the mortarmen, and Barber's headquarters and staff (H&S) section, stationed near the command post. The mortar units — under the command of Lieutenant Joseph Brady and consisting of Fox Company's three 60-mm tubes, augmented by the two 81-mm tubes — were positioned a few yards east of the smaller hut. Since it was now almost dark, Barber directed his mortarmen to spend what daylight they had left firing on the rocky knoll and rocky ridge — registering their ordnance for correct distances — while a motor pool detachment erected a sixteen-by-eighteen tent just below the mouth of the shallow gully. He then assigned the company's two bazooka teams and their ammo carriers — seventeen Marines in all — to occupy the larger hut, where half a dozen corpsmen had already sacked out for the night. The bazookas were to be stored inside the hut and test-fired in the morning while the corpsmen set up their two twelve-by-sixteen med tents.

Finally, Barber ordered the leader of his heavy machine-gun section, Staff Sergeant John O. Henry, to locate the optimal sites for his two heavy Brownings. At twenty-five, Henry was a sturdy veteran who had served as an Army Air Corps turret gunner aboard B-24 bombers during World War II, cashed out after the war, and reenlisted in the Corps. With his broad oval face, bulging biceps, and blond sidewall haircut, Henry looked like the Hollywood version of a five-striper, and in keeping with that image he didn't mind being known as a place where trouble started.

Barber and Henry had hit it off immediately when they'd met in Hagaru-ri — this often happened with veterans of the Pacific war — and the captain knew he could rely on the "old" machine gunner's judgment and experience. Their relationship was strengthened because Barber immediately recognized that Henry knew heavy weapons inside and out. This was why Barber allowed Henry to select his own emplacements on the hill.

The snow was coming down more heavily now, thick dry flakes that fell like a curtain. On Henry's orders the heavy machine gunners set up about twenty-five yards above the MSR and a bit closer to the eastern slope. From these nests — twenty yards apart to prevent them from being taken out by a single mortar shell — the two nine-man crews would be able to cover movement both up and down the road as well as catch, in a daunting crossfire, any enemy attacking from across the southern valley.

At one point, just before dusk, Lt. McCarthy came down from the hilltop and ordered Henry to move his units farther up the grade, nearer to the Third Platoon Marines covering the saddle. Henry argued that his guns simply had to overwatch the road just below. McCarthy and Henry's disagreement had nearly reached the shouting stage when Captain Barber appeared out of the white mist. Barber stopped and listened, and after both men had made their cases he merely shrugged. "Bob, John knows what he's doing," he said. "Leave him be." That made Henry feel good.

It was close to 5:30 p.m. by the time the last Marines from the First Platoon who had been left behind at Hagaru-ri arrived in the returning six-by-sixes. Barber told them to complete the southeast section of the perimeter nearest the road. Behind them a six-foot-high, seventy-five-yard erosion ridge arced southeast to northwest, cutting off sightlines to the crest of the hill. These men would serve as the end of the right flank of the "horseshoe" that would tie in with the units parallel to the road, albeit slightly above them.

Several Marines could not help noticing that the company command post tent, the mortar units, the bazooka section, the two huts, the parked Jeep and its trailer, and the freshwater spring — though protected by the heavy machine gun emplacements above — were all situated about thirty yards to the southeast of and outside Fox Company's defensive perimeter. One of those who noticed this was Private First Class Troy Williford of the Third Platoon, who scanned the outlying positions and shot a quizzical glance at his partner on the fire team, Corporal Wayne Pickett.

"Old Man must know what he's doin',"

Pickett said as they trudged up the hill. "I mean, he's a World War Two vet and all."

5

Over the next few hours an aerial view of the terrain would have resembled a particularly motivated ant farm. As the sun set behind the western mountains, platoon sergeants yelled at squad leaders who in turn hollered at fire team leaders to move their Marines off the goddamn road and up the goddamn mountain. Orders were nearly impossible to make out in the heavy snowfall. Despite this impediment, light machine gun emplacements were allocated, listening posts were designated, platoon command posts were established, interlocking fields of fire were sighted and calculated to exacting degrees, and sites for two-man foxholes were assigned ten paces apart. The only sounds were those of shivering men pinging entrenching tools into the frozen earth. Occasionally the stinging vibration of metal slamming into rock would reverberate through a man's hands and up his arms and cause him to yelp. Gradually the outline of an inverted horseshoe took shape across the heights while emotional, psychological, and physical dramas played out.

Private First Class Graydon "Gray" Davis

was bone tired. Every part of his body hurt. He lagged behind his squad mates, who were scrambling over the sheer cut bank near the road and up the western slope. He had spent the first seventeen years of his life in hot, humid southern Florida, and in the two years since he'd enlisted he had never encountered such cold. He was certain he would never grow accustomed to the tricks it played. The water in his canteen, for instance, was frozen solid. Alternately blowing into his gloves and swinging his arms to regain circulation, Davis reflected on the juxtaposition of the surreal and the quotidian in this crazy land.

On the one hand, he hated most things about the country: the freezing winter, the harrowing mountain paths, the fleas and lice, and not least the North Koreans themselves. Davis was a history buff and knew well that Korea was a country forged in war. Fighting had been a way of life here for centuries, and when the various clans, tribes, and provincial armies were not trying to kill each other they were trying to kill outside aggressors, who now, apparently, included Gray Davis.

On the other hand, only a few days earlier Davis and some buddies had commandeered a heated "gook hootch" near

Hagaru-ri in order to clean, oil, and wipe dry their weapons and heat their little cans of C-rats — meatballs and string beans, hash, beef stew, ham and lima beans. Inside they found a mama-san and her two kids. As in most Korean homes, the chimneys were ducted under the kitchen floor to provide radiant heat, and during those rare few hours of God-sent warmth Davis's antagonism toward the natives had relaxed.

In fact, while the Marines were chowing down one of them had begun whistling a couple of bars of the Christian hymn "Amazing Grace." Suddenly the woman and her two children were smiling. She sent one of the kids outside to fetch her husband, who returned, headed straight for a corner of the hut, and stuck his arm into a sack of old potatoes. The Americans leaped up and leveled their rifles. But then the man retrieved a tattered hymnal left behind long ago by a missionary. The entire family then lined up and sang the hymn for them in Korean. Davis was floored. *Maybe these people were human after all.*

As he recalled this incident at the side of the MSR, Davis's reverie was broken when the company's gunnery master sergeant got up in his face and demanded to know what the hell his problem was.

"Sarge, it's just too cold to move," he said. This took stones, for the gunny was rumored to have a right hook that could stun a brick.

The master sergeant wore a lion tamer's expression as he briefly pondered this response. He then inquired if a shoepac directed up Davis's butt might possibly help to warm him. Davis double-timed it, clawing over the cut, seeking a place to dig in.

If Gray Davis had known what awaited him on this icy hill in the middle of nowhere, he might well have opted for that shoepac up his butt. Though officially the South Koreans were being assisted in their "defensive struggle" by the United Nations, in reality the war was being waged nearly exclusively by Americans like Davis. Unlike World War II, this fight was viewed by the rest of the "free world" — still emerging from the rubble of the previous war — as limited in scope. It was a problem for the United States to handle. Worse, even in the United States there was little enthusiasm for what was being officially described as a mere "conflict" or "police action."

Although Great Britain, Australia, and a few other nations dutifully sent a limited number of troops to Korea, their governments were not necessarily supportive; none wanted to see the war expanded to China. Even the usually bellicose Winston Churchill warned, "The United Nations should avoid by any means in their power becoming entangled inextricably in a war with China. The sooner the Far Eastern diversion can be brought into something like a static condition and stabilized, the better it will be."

But Churchill and other world leaders — and to that list some added President Harry Truman — had not fully taken into account what one critic called MacArthur's "deranged blood lust." The Supreme Allied Commander confided to his staff that he wanted to strangle the Communist Chinese government in its infancy, before it could accumulate more power and territory. MacArthur dreamed of reinstating Chiang Kai-shek (or some other American puppet) to leadership in Peking — if only Truman would untie his hands. To that end, he tried his best.

Beginning in early November 1950, MacArthur ordered his various air forces to turn upper North Korea into a "wasteland." Factories, cities, and villages across a 1,000-square-mile area were vaporized by air strikes. Three weeks before Fox Company climbed Toktong Pass, seventy-nine B-29s dropped 550 tons of incendiaries on the town of Sinuiju and, in the words of a British attaché to MacArthur's headquarters, essentially "removed it from the map." A week later the town of Hoeryong was napalmed, creating "a wilderness of scorched earth."

The rest of the world may not have been paying attention to this carnage, but MacArthur's tactics were not lost on Mao Tsetung. Mao intuited that it was time to face this threat and confront MacArthur before American bombers began appearing over Peking's Forbidden City.

On the northeast crest of the hill, Corporal Howard Koone and Private First Class Dick Bonelli muttered juicy oaths as their small shovels clanged off the frozen turf. Bonelli slammed his spade into the ground with all his strength and cursed as it sprang back up and nearly took off his head. He knelt in his "snow hole" and looked to his right, where ten paces away two raw boots — Corporal Stan "Ski" Golembieski and Private Bernard "Goldy" Goldstein — were experiencing similar difficulty. Golembieski and Goldstein had joined the company a week earlier, and since then they had spent most of their time pestering Bonelli with questions about how to stay alive in a firefight. He decided that now was the time for their first lesson.

"The first thing you do," Bonelli said, "is you never take your eyes off me. Everything I do, you do too. But, I gotta repeat, you watch my back all the time, real close. And you never let anything happen to me. Ever. 'Cause something happens to me, your chances of surviving drop real fast."

The two reservists hung on Bonelli's words, and Koone wondered how his partner managed to keep a straight face talking such bullshit. At one point Bonelli broke off his chatter and peered past Golembieski and Goldstein, searching for the upper left flank of the First Platoon, which would complete the "bridge" to his fire team's sector. His view, however, was obstructed by the hill's central ridgeline.

"Aren't we supposed to meet up with the First here on our right flank?" he said.

"They heard all about you and your moods," Koone said, deadpan. "They ain't coming anywhere near us."

There was a large, impenetrable thicket of brush almost directly in front of their position, and Bonelli eyed it suspiciously. "Here's hoping the Chinks feel the same way," he said.

Bonelli almost hadn't made it to Toktong Pass. On the long voyage from Inchon he'd drawn mess duty aboard one of the giant LSTs, working as a galley waiter serving Marine and Navy officers. (And helping himself to the leftovers.) When the ship anchored off Wonsan he was washing dishes in the mess hall, and because of a bureaucratic snafu he had not been issued any orders. When he finally climbed topside he saw that all his fellow Marines had disembarked on the smaller amtrac vehicles that were used for beach landings.

The Navy stewards with whom he'd become friends urged Bonelli to remain aboard and sail back with them to Japan. He took one look at Wonsan's shabby port and its oil refineries, blown to smithereens, and nearly heeded their pleas. But at the last minute his conscience got the better of him and he climbed over the side and down the nets onto the last vessel ferrying troops to the beach — although when the freezing water hit him he almost turned around and clambered back up.

Now memories of those three-course meals served on real china, as well as memories of his new Navy friends, crossed his mind. Surely by now they were all sipping hot sake in Kobe or Yokohama. "Yup," he said, this time under his breath. "Here's hoping the Chinks feel the same way."

Unlike their American counterparts, the Chinese forces entering Korea in 1950 did not advance by the leapfrogging, "fire and maneuver" tactics. Instead they relied on stealth, stamina, and the sheer volume of their superior numbers to overcome any objective. Since their defeat at Sudong they had learned to attack at night to exploit these assets as well as to reduce their vulnerability to the superior artillery and close air support provided by American and Australian pilots. Their evolving battle strategy was simple and effective: isolate and destroy.

Every Chinese Communist soldier wore a thick, two-piece, reversible winter uniform of quilted cotton, white on one side, dingy yellow on the other. In lieu of helmets the troops were issued fur-lined caps with thick earflaps. A few officers marched into battle wearing fur-lined boots — some were even seen riding shaggy Mongolian ponies — but most fought in canvas shoes with crepe soles, and the Marines would soon grow accustomed to hearing the "scritchy" approach of these "tennis shoes." (Another telltale sign was a pervasive smell of garlic.

Garlic had been a traditional cold remedy in Asia for centuries, and Chinese units had a pungent odor that carried hundreds of yards.)

The Chinese infantryman's primary weapon was the 7.92-mm Mauser rifle, which had been manufactured in China since 1918 and was reliable and effective at long range. Chinese troops also carried numerous international weapons captured after the defeat of Chiang Kai-shek's Nationalists a year earlier, and they were proficient at firing small-caliber mortars, their heaviest artillery. Each soldier was issued eighty to a hundred rounds of ammunition, as well as a few of the fuse-lit, bamboo-encased stick grenades the Americans called "potato mashers." Kitted out to move light and fast — their corn, beans, and rice balls precooked to avoid any telltale campfires — they reminded some of the more literate American officers of the ancient Norse *beserksganger,* twelfth-century warriors so fierce they fought without armor and ravaged like wolves.

For millennia Chinese warlords and emperors had relied on a considerable percentage of teenage peasant conscripts to fill their armies. So vast was the country, and so huge the population, that "fodder" may have been a better term for these fighters, and soldiering was not a career held in high esteem. This had changed somewhat by 1950. Now, at the core of the officer and NCO classes in the Communist Chinese Army there were tough, battle-hardened veterans whose fighting ability had been developed by defeating Chiang's better-equipped forces in the civil war. Many had also been at Mao's side during the "Long March" over eighteen mountain ranges and across twenty-four rivers in 1934. These experiences, combined with a culture of patriotism and ancestral honor, enabled the Chinese Communist regime to assemble a trim fighting force nearly equal to western military standards — and much greater in total size.

Chinese "Tactical Field Forces," which were the elite of the CCF's combat strength, numbered somewhere between 2 million and 3 million men. Second-line troops, or garrison armies, nearly doubled that number. Finally, a Chinese militia, which was similar to America's National Guard and from which the official CCF drew recruits, doubled the number again. All told, China had nearly 10 million men under strength of arms.

If these forces had an Achilles' heel, it was

that officers at the company level were granted virtually no latitude to adjust tactics once an order of battle had been issued. This inflexibility often resulted, as the Marines had seen at Sudong, in bloody, futile slaughter as units fought to the last man no matter what the circumstances were. This situation could be partly attributed to their communication system, which was primitive by western battle norms, relying as it did on bugle calls, flashlight signals, and the occasional flare. When the Chinese broke radio silence, it was more often than not a ruse to relay misleading intelligence to eavesdropping Americans. But by all accounts the Chinese Communists were brave fighters who rarely turned tail — owing, perhaps, to the fact that if they did try to run away, they would be shot by the politically appointed commissars who accompanied them — a field tactic Mao had learned from the Russian armies of World War II.

Finally, and perhaps most profoundly, the Chinese had enormous contempt for the American fighting man. This was evident in the captured book, *Military Lessons,* that Captain Barber had studied before ascending Toktong Pass. Soldiers were taught that the United States had surpassed Japan as the world's most exploitive colonizer, and their political tracts reflected this idea. "Soon we will meet the American Marines in battle," read another captured document circulated among all hands. "We will destroy them. When they are defeated the Americans will collapse and our country will be free from the threat of aggression. Kill these Marines as you would snakes in your homes!"

Though certainly unintentionally, this analogy fit the current circumstances well. The entire First Marine Division, as well as the GIs on the east side of the Chosin Reservoir, had been cut into five separate chunks, much as one might chop up a deadly cobra. Unbeknownst to the Americans, Koto-ri, twenty-five miles to the south of Yudam-ni, was being encircled by the Sixtieth and Seventy-seventh Chinese divisions; Hagaru-ri was being surrounded by the Fifty-eighth and Seventy-sixth Divisions; and the peaks around Yudam-ni and the Chosin Reservoir basin — including Fox Hill — swarmed with Chinese from the Fifty-ninth, Seventy-ninth, and Eighty-ninth Divisions.

A typical Chinese Communist division had approximately 7,000 men, and three divisions constituted what the Chinese called an "army" (and the Americans a "corps"). On orders from the master military strategist Lin Biao, General Sung Shih-lun, commander of the Chinese Ninth Army Group — a force of fifteen divisions totaling about 100,000 men — had taken a page from MacArthur and set in motion his own pincer movement designed to trap the 8,000-odd Marines at the Chosin from the west while taking the Hagaru-ri airfield from the east. And what about the small American outpost holding the road from the Toktong Pass? A mere annoyance. There were fewer than 250 freezing, weary Marines at this pass. Sung allocated a battalion to wipe them out.

Warren McClure and his assistant BAR man Roger Gonzales of the Third Platoon were assigned to a location in a clearing just above the tree line, halfway up the western flank of the hill. Directly across the valley from their position rose a shorter knoll that would come to be called the West Hill. McClure and Gonzales settled into a shallow ditch and studied the serrated ground below them, especially the ravine that ran up the valley's center toward the high saddle. "Good cover for anybody coming at us from across the way," McClure said.

Below them the terrain fell away to form a yawning sinkhole — the "deep dip," McClure called it — about twenty yards across by thirty yards long. McClure and Gonzales could not see the bottom of this sinkhole, and they contemplated the possibility of a squad of enemy soldiers hidden under its lip. Well to the north, somewhere near the Chosin, they watched distant flashes of artillery fire and heard what they assumed was one hell of a firefight.

The sound of the battle made both Marines anxious. They understood that, as they listened, their friends were being maimed and killed. They had little doubt that their own outfit would be next.

Four miles north of McClure and Gonzales's position, and two miles south of Yudam-ni, the 150-odd men of Charlie Company, First Battalion, Seventh Marines, were indeed fighting for their lives against an overwhelming Chinese attack. Like Fox, Charlie was an undermanned company. Still, it had been ordered to overwatch until dawn a small knoll designated Hill 1419 — the number was its elevation in meters — along the lonely stretch of road where the MSR began rising to Toktong Pass from the north. Charlie Company immediately dubbed the mound Turkey Hill because vast piles of Thanksgiving turkey bones had been dumped there by Baker Company, which had originally taken and secured the hill three days earlier. Charlie constituted a link in the strong American chain between the two Marine rifle regiments nearly within shouting distance to the north and the reinforced Fox Company guarding their southern flank. Though its strength had been nearly halved by an earlier firefight, and the company was also shy an entire platoon that had remained at Yudam-ni, Charlie's officers nonetheless felt secure in their position. They were wrong.

The outfit began earning its nickname, "Hard Luck Charlie," not long after midnight, when the first enemy assault knocked out the company's sole radio. As wave after wave of Chinese swarmed the hill, Charlie took 40 percent casualties and could not immediately contact Yudam-ni for either reinforcements or artillery fire. Platoons were overrun one by one until the Americans were forced back into a small defensive perimeter at the top of the hill.

Eventually, an enterprising Marine repaired the radio, and the survivors from Charlie Company were rescued at the last minute by the First Battalion's commanding officer, Lieutenant Colonel Raymond Davis, who would eventually lead two companies, including Baker, back from the reservoir through a screen of fire to flank the Chinese and allow Charlie to retreat from Turkey Hill. In the meantime, all Charlie could do was signal for help by mortaring off brace after brace of star shells and hope someone would come to its aid.

At the crest of their own hilltop, Corporal Pickett and Private First Class Williford of Fox Company were digging in. Aside from his knowledge of "fighting Chinamen," Wayne Pickett also knew a thing or two about cold weather.

Pickett came from the small town of Jenkins — population 225 — in northern Minnesota and would admit only to being somewhat taken aback by the speedy drop in temperature each night in Korea. Compared with the hardscrabble life he and his eight brothers and sisters had led at home, scratching out a frozen hole on a Korean hilltop was small beans. And it was nothing compared with ice fishing for dinner in the dead of a Minnesota winter. "Come home with no catch," he told Williford, "and you don't eat."

When Pickett was five years old, his

mother died in childbirth delivering twins. His father, a fireman with the Northern Pacific Railroad, tried to keep the family together but found the financial burden impossible. A year after his mother's death, Wayne was sent to live in a state-run orphanage. He was subsequently farmed out to a dairy rancher in western Minnesota, where he worked for the next two years before returning to the orphanage. At age nine he was adopted by Allan and Clara Pickett of Duluth.

Like many of the Marines in Fox Company, while he was growing up Pickett had been mesmerized by newspaper and magazine articles, movies, and newsreels about World War II. He could quote entire scenes from *Guadalcanal Diary,* and he was dazzled by the glamour and glory of the fighting Marines. Upon graduation from Central High Duluth in 1946 he enlisted, and after boot camp he was assigned to the Corps' Sea School. He traveled to China aboard the heavy cruiser USS *St. Paul* as a seagoing Marine before taking an early discharge in 1948, when the Corps' manpower was reduced dramatically from its wartime height. Pickett remained in the active reserves while taking courses at Duluth Business College, and ten weeks after North

Korea's invasion of South Korea he found himself on a crowded troopship bound for Kobe, Japan. He'd been fighting with Fox from Inchon to Seoul and had taken part in the voyage around the peninsula for the landing at Wonsan.

The names of the places where he'd fought, the places where he'd watched buddies die, were all a blur. Hungnam. Sudong. Hagaru-ri. And now here he was on a frigid hill above a place named Toktong Pass trying to crack the frozen crust of the earth with his spade. Finally, he and Williford gave up. There was a giant boulder, a nearly vertical slab of granite, a few paces from their position.

"See that rock?" Pickett said.

Williford nodded.

"That's our foxhole."

The two men gathered their kit, slid in behind the rock, and anchored one end of their pup tent to its base. They spoke of being home for Christmas.

One month earlier, on October 25, 1950 — exactly four months after the North Korean armies had poured south across the 38th Parallel — advance elements of several South Korean ROK units reached the Yalu River. They had American air support, including napalm, a recent invention, which produced some of the most fearsome fire-bombing in history. At that point it seemed as if the North Koreans' plans to dominate northeast Asia — plans backed by the Soviet Union — were finished. A bottle of water from the Yalu was even sent to Syngman Rhee, the president of South Korea. Legend has it that after the bottle had been filled, ROK soldiers lined up on the banks of the river and urinated into it as an act of defiance toward the Chinese on the other side.

General Paek Sun Yap, possibly the ablest ROK commander, was not, however, in a mood to celebrate. A few Chinese soldiers had been captured on the Korean side of the border, and he insisted on interrogating them personally. "Are there many of you here?" he asked. They nodded and replied, "Many, many." But when he reported this to his American allies, the intelligence was dismissed as fantasy — and not merely by MacArthur.

In Washington, D.C., the Joint Chiefs of Staff and President Truman's other military advisers continued to believe that the Chinese had sent only a small number of troops into North Korea, purely as a gesture to save political face, and that Mao was unwilling and unprepared to take on the

United Nations on behalf of such an ally as weak as North Korea. Still, the American brass seriously considered a suggestion forwarded from MacArthur's Tokyo war room: to bomb the Yalu River bridges and keep even the face-saving forces in China. The proposal was rejected by the Joint Chiefs when they decided that such an attack could have the effect of goading the Chinese leadership into action to save face yet again.

The Americans also believed that the CCF armies would never enter the Korean peninsula because the Soviet Union did not want to see the war extended. American intelligence, however, did not yet see that political and ideological cracks were opening between Stalin in Moscow and Mao in Peking. The Truman administration had no idea that China was bristling at being a "puppet state" of the Soviet Union. The administration also chose to overlook the fact that, in October, Chou En-lai had summoned the Indian ambassador to his ministry and told him that if MacArthur's United Nations forces crossed the 38th Parallel, China would intervene.

In the last week of November, no American official — military or civilian — had any idea that some 300,000 Chinese troops were already inside Korea, and an equal number were on alert in Manchuria. MacArthur in particular was unaware that his forces were significantly outnumbered in an unfamiliar and increasingly brutal territory centered on Fox Hill.

Private Hector Cafferata and Private First Class Kenny Benson, First Fire Team, First Squad, Second Platoon — two kids from New Jersey who had enlisted together and traveled cross-country by train to Pendleton — crawled out on the left flank of the saddle beyond the two tall "domino" rocks demarcating the northwest corner of the hill. They were about thirty yards in front of their platoon's defensive perimeter; the rocky knoll loomed above them, looking like some sinister medieval castle. The two constituted one of Fox Company's several forward listening posts. Like Pickett and Williford on the peak of the hill, they had the front lines just on the other side of their rifle sights.

Benson was shivering so much he was afraid the enemy would hear his bones rattling. "Christ," he said, "what this weather wouldn't do to a brass monkey."

Cafferata did not answer. It had stopped snowing, but the temperature had fallen to about twenty-five degrees below zero. That did not concern Cafferata as much as the wind, a strong whistling airstream blowing from their backs that lifted the snow into blinding squalls and white eddies. His parka, completely buttoned up, nonetheless whipped and fluttered like a sail. When the enemy charged down that knoll and across the saddle — a highly likely event, in Cafferata's estimation — the noise of the wind would surely cover their approach.

Cafferata did not utter a word as he and Benson shared a meager supper of frozen Tootsie Rolls. He'd been studying their situation. But finally, he turned to his foxhole buddy.

"Look at the bright side, Bense," he said. "At least we'll be the first to get a crack at 'em."

Benson shrugged. Sometimes he had a hard time figuring Cafferata out.

The two men, from neighboring small towns in northern Jersey, had first met playing for a semipro football team. Benson was a blond, six-foot, 200-pound all-around athlete who could recite all the statistics from his favorite publication, *The Sporting News*. By contrast, Cafferata had no love for organized sports. He'd signed up to play football only when the coach, impressed by his six-foot-four, 230-pound frame, had offered him ten dollars a game.

"How could you not like baseball?" an incredulous Benson had asked Cafferata during one of their Marine reservist weekends at the Picatinny Arsenal in Jefferson, New Jersey. "It's the all-American pastime, for Chrissake."

"If I carry a stick in my hand it's got to have bullets in it for shooting turkey and duck, maybe some vermin for practice," Cafferata said. "Besides, I could never hit the damn ball anyway. I'm the world's worst baseball player."

Although Cafferata, at nineteen, was only a year older than Benson, he was physically a man among boys. Nicknamed "Moose," he had a large, clomping physique topped by a face that looked like a hard winter breaking up. His eyebrows resembled thick caterpillars crawling toward his mop of wavy black hair, and with his flattened nose, creased cheeks, and jutting ears he could have been cast as a heavyweight in the classic black-and-white boxing movies he had watched as a kid.

Cafferata had been a socially awkward boy who didn't drink or date girls in high school. He preferred to spend his free time hunting, fishing, and trapping in the forests and wetlands near his parents' house in New Jersey. On his long walks home from school he would set muskrat and raccoon traps, and the next morning he'd check them on the way to class. He also carried his shotgun every day in case he spotted something edible while visiting the traps, and the high school custodian grew accustomed to the sight of "Big Hec" changing out of his waders and filthy hunting vest and storing his gun in the janitor's closet before the first bell rang. By the age of thirteen he was also earning money after school and on weekends by cutting oak and hickory trees for firewood. Although his father worked at various part-time jobs, the family often depended on Hector's catch to feed the four voracious Cafferata brothers. Anything extra Hector would sell to the neighborhood butcher or a local Jewish fishmonger, who turned the carp into gefilte fish.

Although most of Fox Company took Cafferata for an Italian-American, his father was a Peruvian immigrant who had enlisted in the U.S. Marines between the wars. When Hector was seventeen, he did the same, more out of a feeling that he had missed something important by being too young to fight the Nazis and the Japanese than from any sense of familial duty. But he described himself as a loner, and he'd hated the reservist summer camps and weekend meetings — "Nothing but drinking and card playing" — and when he quit attending he was dropped from his unit's roster. When the war in Korea broke out, he begged his way back into the Corps, pleading with his platoon sergeant to be allowed to jump on the troop train that was pulling away for Camp Pendleton. At literally the last minute Cafferata was allowed to rejoin his old unit; more than a few of his superior officers subsequently wondered over the wisdom of that decision.

On Cafferata and Benson's first night in Korea, they had both gone to sleep after shoving their shoepacs outside their tent without wiping them down. At reveille their squad leader could only shake his head in wonder and disgust as he watched the two confused reservists puzzling over their boots, which had frozen into blocks of ice. There was another legendary yarn about them in Fox Company. One night outside Hagaru-ri, Benson had decided to widen their foxhole while Cafferata went for coffee. He was still shoveling furiously upon Cafferata's return and failed to heed his buddy's warning that Colonel Litzenberg was standing above him.

"Yeah, sure, Hec," he'd said, refusing to look up and purposely heaping dirt over what he assumed were Cafferata's shoepacs. "I don't give a fuck if it's Santa Claus. I'm tired of you sleeping on my face."

"Ten-hut."

Now Benson did look up at the man whose boots he had fouled. He swore he saw steam blowing from Blitzen Litzen's ears. To make matters worse, both men were cited for having a round in their rifle chambers and their safeties off in a secure rear area.

In short, Cafferata was considered a first-class screw-up, with Benson not far behind. Perhaps, Benson thought, they were indeed better off up here on the front line, where they could stay out of trouble — if only the earth were as soft as it had been down at Hagaru-ri. He swung his entrenching tool again to no avail and turned to Cafferata in frustration.

"We'd need goddamn dynamite to make a hole here," he said. "Forget about the gooks for a minute, Hec. What say while it's still light we go chop down some of them trees and build ourselves a little nest?"

In Washington, D.C., President Truman was

busy fending off calls for much more than the use of dynamite in Korea. In late June, when North Korea initially invaded South Korea, the Joint Chiefs of Staff had immediately ruled out the use of atomic weapons in this new war zone. North Korea, with the possible exception of the capital, Pyongyang, did not offer the large targets of opportunity that Japan had in World War II. Moreover, American generals and admirals advised the president that conventional weapons were more than adequate to deal with Kim's ragged army. Why destroy a gnat with a shotgun? This came as something of a relief to Truman. Only five years after Hiroshima and Nagasaki, he knew that the United States still faced the world's opprobrium for dropping the two A-bombs.

As Mao's threats intensified, however, some people rethought the Joint Chiefs' calculations. General Curtis LeMay of the Air Force, who had directed the firebombing of Tokyo in 1945, begged to unleash atom bombs on North Korea. And several members of Congress, led by Congressman Albert Gore Sr. of Tennessee, argued that "something cataclysmic" needed to be done to stop Korea from becoming a "meat grinder of American manhood." Gore suggested using atomic weapons on the 38th

Parallel to make it a radiation belt separating the two Koreas. No one, however, argued for the atomic option more strenuously than General MacArthur.

MacArthur had disagreed with the Joint Chiefs' decision from the beginning of the war, and in mid-November he stepped up his attempts to push the atomic button. This, he said, would not only result in the complete capitulation of Kim Il-Sung within two weeks, but also end any possibility of a Chinese or Russian incursion into the country for three generations. No *cordon sanitaire* dividing North and South Korea would do for MacArthur. He wanted to separate the Korean peninsula from the rest of the Asian mainland "with a belt of radioactive cobalt strung along the neck of Manchuria." His plan was to saturate the strip of land just north of the Yalu River with thirty A-bombs. After that, 500,000 of Chiang Kai-shek's Nationalist Chinese soldiers would be used to guard the border for the active life of the cobalt — then calculated to last between 60 and 120 years.

"I visualize a cul-de-sac," MacArthur wrote to the Joint Chiefs. "The only passages leading from Manchuria and [the Russian city of] Vladivostok have many tunnels and bridges. I see here a unique use for the atomic bomb — to strike a blocking blow — which would . . . sweeten up my B-29 force."

Although MacArthur insisted that his plan was "a cinch," American civilian leaders, wary of the Soviet Union's small, if growing, atomic stockpile, rejected it — for now.

Radiation strips and cobalt zones were the last thing on Private First Class Bob "Zeke" Ezell's mind as he hauled two heavy cans of ammo for the light machine guns up the east slope of the hill. He was freezing but trying his damnedest not to let the others see how miserable he was. Ezell, who had just turned nineteen, was a tall, skinny baseball star from Wilmington, California, near the Los Angeles harbor. In his hometown he was renowned for his reckless outfield play. Here in Korea he was nothing more than an assistant ammo carrier sick of hearing the northern boys, especially the squareheads from Minnesota, boast about adjusting to the cold. Corporal Harry Burke, a bazooka man from a small town in the southwest corner of Minnesota, had even taken it upon himself to lecture the company's "California queers" on foot care after one of Ezell's buddies was evacuated with frostbite. And just a few mornings ago, in Hagaru-ri, a couple of Marines who called themselves the "Minny Gang" had made Ezell the butt of their jokes when he'd poured milk on his cereal and found a stump to sit on outside the mess tent, only to discover the milk frozen solid.

"Gotta eat your Wheaties *inside* the tent, Zeke. Don't you pretty boys from California know anything about winter?"

Ezell learned fast that if you didn't come back at them quickly they'd ride you even harder, and he gave as good as he got. But he was at a natural disadvantage. He bore an eerie resemblance to the young Tyrone Power and was forever being kidded about his perpetual smile and his brilliant white teeth. Ezell was quick to remind his tormenters that Power had suspended his acting career to enlist in the Corps and had become a Marine pilot who'd taken wounded men off the islands of Iwo Jima and Okinawa. That shut them up for a while.

Like most of the kids in Fox, Ezell had spent his youth immersed in the movies of the World War II era, and he and his buddies had enlisted in the Marine Reserves to live out these fantasies. But his first love was baseball, and he was good. He'd been all-league in high school and he'd made the all-star team in his first season in the minor leagues, playing for an affiliate of the Boston Braves. He dreamed of following in the footsteps of a fellow graduate of Harbor High: George Witt, a minor leaguer who would eventually pitch for the Pittsburgh Pirates.

In the states, Ezell's recruiting officer had seen the marksmanship medal he'd won at a Marines summer camp and immediately assigned him to a rifle company in the Seventh Regiment. When Ezell asked about boot camp, the officer had grinned. "We need riflemen on the front line," he'd said. "You're an athlete. Pretend you went to boot camp."

Now he was thousands of miles from home, trying to scrape out a machine-gun nest on a windswept hill. Boy, would he like to pretend *this* away. Although Ezell was merely an ammo carrier, each man in his unit — one of the First Platoon's two light machine gun emplacements — had been trained to take over the gun in an emergency. They constituted the right flank of Captain Barber's "horseshoe," and the first thing Ezell did when he dropped his ammo cans in the snow was study the terrain.

The gun's field of fire would cover a seventy-five-yard arc across the treeless valley that separated this more gradual slope from what the Marines were calling the East Hill, two hundred yards away. In the fading light Ezell could just make out the top of the loop of the MSR, about 150 yards beyond the East Hill, where the road bent south to Hagaru-ri. At this fork in the turnpike a trampled path — what passed for a spur road in North Korea — broke off and veered northwest toward the hamlet of Chinghung-ni. A little beyond this crossroad the MSR intersected with a dry creek bed that ran parallel to, and below, Ezell's position. Where the creek bed met the road it ran under a small culvert. Ezell noted that the depression was large enough to hide perhaps four men if they squeezed in tight. *Bet that'd be pretty toasty,* he thought.

Winter war in North Korea was like fighting inside a snow globe. Prior to the Marine landings at Wonsan, American military physicians specializing in cold-weather warfare had studied winter campaigns such as the Russo-Finnish War, Hitler's march on Moscow, and the Battle of the Bulge, one of the coldest engagements on record. The idea of outfitting U.S. military personnel in layers, as opposed to a single piece of heavier outer clothing, was one result of these analyses. Another consequence was the ill-conceived decision to issue perspiration-absorbing, wool-felt shoe pads fitted into clunky shoepacs, whose rubberized shell did not allow air to circulate.

In fairness, given the limitations of cold-weather science at that time, no medical study could have prepared the Marines for Toktong Pass, where a sleeping man could freeze to death in his own sweat. Over the past few weeks frostbite had taken more American soldiers out of action than the North Koreans, and no matter how often or how loudly corpsmen and officers warned about it, men wouldn't listen. The first way to avoid frostbite was to keep your extremities from perspiring — easier said than done in a firefight. Once a man stopped moving, his sweat would freeze into a film of ice, usually between his hands and his gloves and between his feet and the felt insole of his shoepacs. Damage to the hands could be contained. But if he didn't periodically remove his shoepacs and wool pads, massage his feet, and change his socks, frostbite would set in within hours. Needless to say, there was little opportunity for such regular salubriousness on the hill, and men and shoepacs simultaneously seemed to lose the will to stay dry.

Moreover, the temperature and the constant gale drastically affected the men's appetite. As a rule human beings are genetically programmed to eat more as the temperature drops. But just as these Marines had little or no time to care for their feet, they had few opportunities to build fires, boil snow, and melt their rock-hard C-rations. The chow tasted like dog food to start with, and everyone in Fox recalled the result of eating the frozen Thanksgiving feast. Now, with those stomach disorders fresh in their minds, the Marines limited themselves to the dry items in their C-rations. The icy beef stew, beans, and congealed hash were all avoided in favor of a steady diet of crackers, biscuits, and candy. This diet made the men miserable and weak, and the more miserable a man was, the less he would eat. The less he would eat, the less he *could* eat. As a result of this cycle, the stomach shrank. Many Marines were losing four to eight pounds a day. Captain Barber worried that if he had to spend too many days on this hill he would end up commanding a company of scarecrows.

Barber and his officers, most conspicuously the Second Platoon's Lieutenant Peterson, constantly impressed on the Marines the necessity of changing their socks as often as possible. Peterson had carried only two pairs of socks with him up to the pass, yet on his inspection rounds he made a point of demonstrating how he kept his spare pair hanging from his belt and down the inseam of his pants leg. It was the best — in fact the only — place to dry them out, he said.

When Peterson had trudged up the hill he discovered a small cave no more than ten yards behind the juncture of his First and Second squads on the western slope. He could hardly believe his good fortune. He directed his platoon sergeant, Richard Danford, to convert the snow-free grotto into his platoon command post, and he ordered William McLean, the corpsman attached to his platoon, to dig in nearby. Both kept a watchful eye on their new platoon commander as they complied.

Peterson was the Second Platoon's third CO since it had arrived in Korea five months earlier, and he was by far the most handsome man in the outfit — "prettier" even than Bob Ezell. A twenty-eight-year-old North Dakotan with a square jaw, broad shoulders, and wavy black hair, Peterson was the one Marine in the outfit who could have been on recruiting posters. He had enlisted at eighteen after finishing high school, had seen action on Guam and in China during World War II, and had cashed out at the end of that war. Like most of his contemporaries, he'd remained in the reserves while he went back to school — in his case, to earn a BS in civil engineering from the State University of Montana and a master's degree from the University of Iowa. He was teaching at Oklahoma State University when war broke out in Korea. Called back to active duty, he breezed through officer candidate school and was posted to Fox. Naturally, the men called him "Prof" behind his back.

Peterson had caught up with the company in Hagaru-ri, and he barely knew the names on his platoon roster when they left for the Toktong Pass. But his experience as an enlisted man in World War II lent him more authority, particularly among the veterans, than a shiny new second lieutenant might normally have received. His credibility increased when, leaving his sergeants to stand up his platoon command post in the cave, he made his inspection rounds.

Peterson was one of the few Marines who had any kind of experience with cold weather — he recalled several weeks during one winter in Montana when the temperature never rose above twenty below. So as he stopped by each foxhole he not only demonstrated his socks trick, but also imparted whatever other ideas he knew to ensure that his men were squared away as well as possible. He instructed them, for instance, to tuck in only alternate layers of their multiple shirts and jackets, as the circulating air warmed by body heat would act similarly to the insulating sheen of water trapped in a wet suit. He also showed them how to buddy up by combining their mummy bags so one man's free foot rested in the warmth of his partner's crotch.

Similarly, he knew that the best way to keep water in a canteen from freezing was to add a few drops of rubbing alcohol or, in a pinch, a dollop or two of hair tonic. And he advised his Marines to periodically take as many deep, diaphragmatic breaths as possible to keep the body flooded with oxygen at this elevation. Finally — and this was a surprise — he told them to try to wash their hair as often as possible.

"Clean hair retains heat," he said, "dirty hair doesn't." His men wondered where the lieutenant expected them to find even tepid water for shampooing. But they knew Peterson's heart was in the right place, and that he cared about their survival. This went a long way with them — whether or not a shampoo was feasible.

The rifleman Private First Class Bob Kirchner of the Second Platoon was certain he was burrowing into an old cemetery. He was near the top of the west slope, settled into an eerie, grave-like depression, and those were surely not rocks his entrenching shovel was crunching. He wondered whose bones he was disturbing.

The twenty-one-year-old Kirchner was used to mountainous terrain, but he'd never seen anything so desolate as North Korea. The steep, pointed peaks, tiers and tiers rising as far as the eye could see, reminded him of inverted ice cream cones. At home in Pittsburgh, the hills and hollows had at least some color, even in winter, with strong, thick stands of conifers and spruce shining green and verdant even during blizzards. But these were the barest damned mountains he'd ever seen, like a moonscape. He wondered what the Korean words for "Old Baldy" were.

Kirchner had dug no more than a few inches when Lieutenant Peterson, making his rounds, dropped by his hole. "Remember that kid I caught you wrestling with back in the village?" he said.

Kirchner nodded.

Peterson made a dramatic show of taking in the rolling heights in every direction. The sun was low in the sky and he thought the view was, in a way, soothing — the rolling swell of the mountains kissed by a bluish haze the color of cigarette smoke. "I'm thinking he's probably somewhere up there, and you might have to shoot him tonight."

When he'd first arrived in Hagaru-ri, Kirchner had spent a night in an impromptu warming station, a house his squad had confiscated from a North Korean family. They hadn't thrown the locals out into the cold, and the old mother, her teenage son and daughter, and a young girl of about three or four had huddled in a corner against the glaring white light of a Coleman lantern as the Marines had warmed themselves and rested. The little girl reminded Kirchner of his own baby daughter at home, and as the hours wore on he began playing with the Korean girl, cooing silly little songs and tickling her under the chin. This seemed to lighten the family's mood, and by daybreak you would have thought everyone had known everyone else for years. The woman had even pulled out a frying pan to beat with a stick, and the little girl did a few step dances to the tune.

Kirchner was a skinny kid of average

height, with black hair slicked back from a broad forehead. He had a prominent, aquiline nose and powerful thighs and calves. In the morning, he and some of his buddies had started Indian leg wrestling to break the monotony. The teenage Korean boy watched them for a while and finally got up the gumption to challenge Kirchner to a match. Kirchner had been taught to raise his leg three times to signal the start of the action, but the boy did not know any such formality. As Kirchner was raising his leg for the first time the boy jumped him, caught him off balance, and nearly broke his back.

Everyone got a big laugh out of it, including Kirchner, who demanded a rematch. This time, prepared, Kirchner lifted the boy clear in the air and threw him right through the door — where he landed on top of Lieutenant Peterson.

Peterson came rushing into the hootch with his sidearm drawn, and it took the Marines a moment to explain that they were only playing. Two nights later, out on patrol east of Hagaru-ri, Kirchner and his squad were ambushed. During the firefight he recognized the same boy, who was about to heave a grenade when Kirchner shot him dead. He hadn't told anyone about the incident.

Now he set down his spade and gazed up at Lieutenant Peterson. "I don't know, sir," he said. There was a hint of sadness to his voice. "I don't think we'll be seeing that kid again."

6

Howard Koone and Dick Bonelli, having dug no more than twelve inches into the rocky, frozen ground, gave up. They placed their backpacks on the forward lip of the shallow depression to use as parapets for their rifles. They also piled more snow around the edges of their half-assed foxhole, fully aware that as hard-packed as it might be, it would not stop a bullet. Before sunset Bonelli had been able to look down from his elevated position and glimpse, between cloud banks, the black-ice contours of the southern arm of the Chosin Reservoir as it snaked behind the crevassed inclines of Toktong-san. Now the snow clouds had dispersed, the stars had not yet risen, and in the clear night sky Bonelli could see orange flashes of artillery fire up near the reservoir.

Their fingers numb from the cold, Bonelli and Koone tore scraps of paper from their

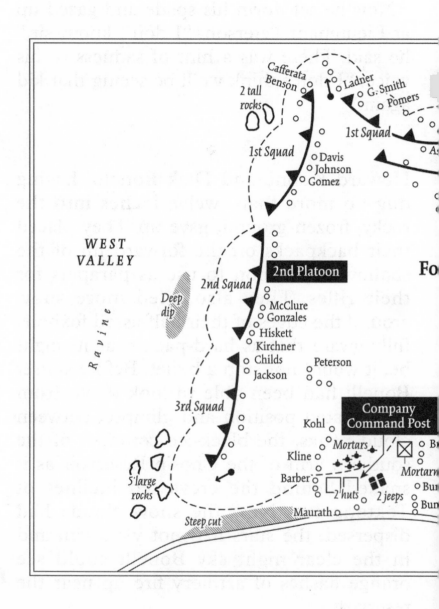

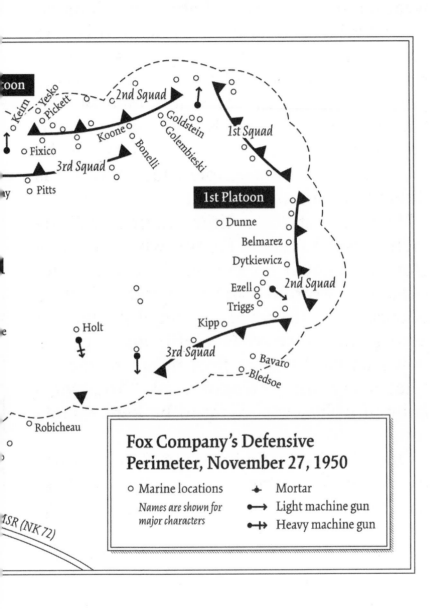

oon

Keim
Yesko
Pickett
2nd Squad
Goldstein
Golembieski
1st Squad
Fixico
Koone
Bonelli
3rd Squad
Pitts

1st Platoon

Dunne
Belmarez
Dytkiewicz
Ezell
2nd Squad
Triggs
Kipp
Holt
3rd Squad
Bavaro
Bledsoe

Robicheau

**Fox Company's Defensive
Perimeter, November 27, 1950**

o Marine locations   ✦ Mortar

*Names are shown for
major characters*   ●—→ Light machine gun

              ●—↦ Heavy machine gun

ISR (NK 72)

C-ration boxes. Before being shipped over-seas Bonelli had participated in cold-weather maneuvers in Labrador, Canada. That was Tahiti compared with this. He removed a mitten and lit a waterproof match, but the wind blew it out. He tried to pull another match from the folder, but his bare fingers were already so frozen and stiff he couldn't detach it from the pack. In the bitter cold even the simplest task became as difficult as boning a marlin.

He held out the solitary match, still at-tached to its folder. Koone whipped off a glove and got it lit. He put it to the paper while they both blocked the wind with their bodies. They sheltered the small flame, and across the crest of Fox Hill and up and down its flanks more fires began to flicker. "Eat everything," Koone said. "You don't know if we're even going to be here tomor-row."

One of the new boots asked Bonelli about the Uijongbu campaign, in which Bonelli had fought after the landing at Inchon six weeks earlier. Bonelli snorted.

"Like a Marx Brothers movie," he said. "One time I'm out on a listening post all by myself, cleaning my rifle, when out of nowhere this North Korean soldier walks right up to me. 'Who the hell are you?' I said. 'And what the hell you doing here?' 'Strolling,' the guy tells me. Perfect English. *Strolling!* So I whipped my bayonet around and caught him in the thigh. He half-runs and half-gimps away. But I chase him down. Dove and caught him. Was about to give it to him good when a South Korean patrol comes by and nails him. Only time I ever saw a ROK do anything worthwhile."

He continued. "See, what the gooks did, they had these big mortars, and they had good maps. They would drop a shell in your lap before you could blink. And this guy was their spotter."

By now the two boots were mesmerized, and Bonelli couldn't help himself. "Ever tell you about the time I robbed the Korean bank?" he said.

It made for a good bedtime story for "the kids," Bonelli thought. He began to reminisce about how, during the Uijongbu campaign, his patrol had run across a bombed-out bank and blown the safe with grenades. They thought they were rich and would come back and buy the country after the war was over.

Bonelli looked at Koone. For once the Indian smiled. "Thousand-dollar bills," Bonelli said. He drew his gloved hands apart. "Stacks of them. Filled a duffel bag."

Stan Golembieski leaned in. "What did you do with all the cash?"

Bonelli could feel the anticipation build as he made them wait for the kicker. Then he said, "Used 'em to make a fire the next morning. Brewed the best pot of coffee I ever tasted with that money."

A spectral winter fog stole up the valleys of the Toktong Pass at 6:30 p.m. as the Third Platoon commander Lieutenant McCarthy and his platoon sergeant, John Audas, inspected their dug-in positions along the crest of the hill. They informed their riflemen that earlier in the day the Seventh and Fifth Regiments at Yudam-ni had made contact with Chinese units. When Bonelli heard this he decided to move the knapsack he had placed on the parapet of his hole so it sat between him and the worrisome thicket. It had frozen solid to the snow.

At 7 p.m. a bonfire was started at the base of the hill near the company command post tent. The mortarmen, the heavy machine gun crews, and the headquarters unit moved close. Because of the rises, depressions, ridgeline contours, and fir trees, the flames could not be seen by Marines at the top of the hill. Stories around the fire tended, as

130

usual, toward past conquests in love and war, some of them true. There is no sincerity like that of a soldier telling a lie. Soon the conversation came to be dominated by one question: *Think we'll be home for Christmas?*

At 9 p.m. Captain Barber's three rifle platoon leaders informed him by field phone that they had secured their positions for the night. Fox Company was strung over the hill like a pearl necklace. Barber ordered all fires extinguished, and the men were given passwords. They were placed on two-hour, fifty-fifty watches: one man would sleep while the other stood sentry. Ten minutes later several Marines near the road heard the last convoy of trucks from Yudam-ni coughing soot as they rolled south on the MSR en route to Hagaru-ri.

A four-day-old moon, nearly full and glowing as white as a spotlight, rose at 9:30 p.m. from behind the South Hill across the MSR. Thousands of stars lit up the sky. The temperature hovered near minus-thirty degrees Fahrenheit.

Just before midnight, Captain Barber radioed Lieutenant Colonel Randolph Lockwood in Hagaru-ri. He informed his superior officer that the 234 Marines, twelve corpsmen, and one civilian interpreter of Fox Company, Second Battalion, Seventh Marines, were ready, able, and effective.

■ ■ ■ ■

The Attack

■ ■ ■ ■

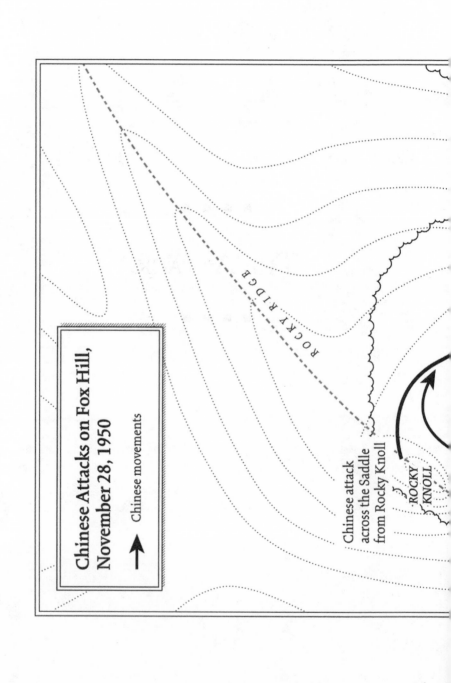

Chinese Attacks on Fox Hill, November 28, 1950

→ Chinese movements

ROCKY RIDGE

Chinese attack across the Saddle from Rocky Knoll

ROCKY KNOLL

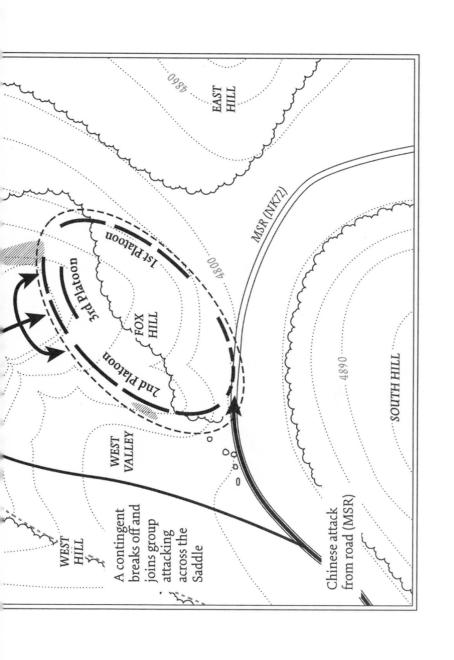

EAST HILL

4860

MSR (NK7)

4800

4890

SOUTH HILL

1st Platoon

3rd Platoon

FOX HILL

2nd Platoon

WEST VALLEY

WEST HILL

A contingent breaks off and joins group attacking across the Saddle

Chinese attack from road (MSR)

DAY TWO

NOVEMBER 28, 1950
TWELVE MIDNIGHT TO 6 A.M.

1

Lieutenant Bob McCarthy had been only mildly upset about losing his argument with Sergeant John Henry about the positioning of the heavy machine guns. Now he was livid. Less than an hour earlier he'd reconnoitered the Third Platoon's perimeter across the hilltop. Half the men had failed to challenge his approach. He had been forced to "chunk" a few helmets with his rifle butt. He didn't care how cold and tired the men were. *Anything to make them mad, even if they're mad at me. Angry men are alert men.*

Now, at 1:15 a.m., he was back in his command post, or CP, reaming out his squad leaders. McCarthy had established the Third Rifle Platoon's CP in an old enemy bunker that his staff sergeant, Clyde Pitts, had discovered about thirty yards below the crest of the hill. The dugout

137

wasn't much more than a pit, and its roof planks were rotting, but at least they would keep out most of the snow, which had again begun falling lightly. Despite his ill humor, the lieutenant thanked God for Pitts. He was a Marine lifer, a veteran of numerous Pacific campaigns during World War II, and a world-class scrounger. Like Captain Barber, McCarthy was new to Fox Company, having arrived in Koto-ri only a day after the new commanding officer. He'd been the skipper of a weapons company in the States, and he knew guns.

One morning after the outfit had reached Hagaru-ri, McCarthy had ordered a snap weapons inspection. Of the nine fire teams in his platoon, only one had a working BAR. The remainder were so old and sluggish, with recoil springs that failed to react in the cold, that they were practically useless. He immediately summoned Pitts.

"Staff Sergeant, I don't know where they're coming from, or how you're going to do it, but I want eight working BARs here by sundown. Do you understand, Sergeant?"

Pitts nodded, spit a thick wad of tobacco juice in the snow at McCarthy's feet, and responded — well, responded with something that appeared to be an affirmative.

138

McCarthy was barely able to understand the sergeant's words through his cotton-thick Alabama drawl. But he came through. That night McCarthy distributed eight new BARs to his fire teams. He never asked Pitts where they had come from.

Now Pitts was perhaps the most red-faced of all the noncoms seated in a semicircle around McCarthy as he voiced his displeasure over the company's lack of alertness before sending them out to square away the problem. Fifteen minutes later, McCarthy pulled another surprise inspection. Password challenges rang out loud and clear in the thin, crisp air.

On the way back to his bunker McCarthy lingered to talk with Edward Jones, the Navy corpsman assigned to his platoon. McCarthy liked Jones, and the two spoke long enough for Jones to wonder about the lieutenant's familiarity with medical terms. Jones thought that McCarthy — with his stocky torso, Celtic features, and short, brushy dark hair — actually looked like an emergency room doctor, or at least the Hollywood kind. Lew Ayres as Dr. Kildare, maybe.

McCarthy liked the analogy so much that he confided to Jones a personal irony. If he had uttered the word "yes" five years ago, he said, he just might be in that foxhole instead of Jones.

At twenty-eight, Bob McCarthy was one of the oldest Marines in the company. He had enlisted in 1940, after his sophomore year at Oklahoma A&M, where he'd studied to become a veterinarian. The son of a pipe-fitter in Tulsa, he'd been such a gifted child — according to his score in a national intelligence test — that the principal of his grammar school recommended he skip second and third grades. His mother liked to boast about that. She was the only woman in her bridge club whose child had been jumped two classes. When McCarthy's father was laid off during the Depression, the family used their small savings to buy a farm on the outskirts of the city. The senior McCarthy explained to his family that growing their own food might well be the only way they would eat.

In high school and college McCarthy felt a natural affinity for the sciences, and he excelled in biology, chemistry, and psychology. His mother was still thinking of her son as a future veterinarian when she discovered by chance that Bob had dropped out of college to join the Marines. He explained to her that he felt he owed service to a nation that had allowed him to move so effortlessly up the educational ladder. Much like Captain Barber's family, McCarthy's parents were distraught. Nothing, however, could change his mind.

McCarthy became a seagoing Marine, and by a stroke of good fortune he sailed from Pearl Harbor one day before the Japanese sneak attack in 1941. He subsequently saw action across the Pacific theater from Midway to the Philippines. He was promoted to corporal in 1943 when his platoon leader — again, much like Barber — noticed something special in this intellectual young man and urged him to apply for a slot in an experimental Naval College program being taught at the University of Notre Dame. He scored so high on the entrance exam that he was only one of two enlisted men chosen for the course. After three semesters at Notre Dame he received his college degree and was selected to attend St. Louis University's medical school on a Navy scholarship.

This was where he made his fateful choice. There were — and are — no Marine corpsmen. The Marine Corps is technically a branch of the Department of the Navy, but it is as fiercely self-sufficient as possible. The Corps trains its own engineering units, attorneys, military police, and pilots, and even journalists, weather forecasters, and musicians. The two career options closed to Marines, however, are medicine and religious vocations, as the Navy serves these functions with its own doctors, nurses, medics, and chaplains.

When McCarthy learned that in order to attend medical school he would have to trade in his Marine blues for Navy whites, he politely declined and enrolled in Marine officer candidate school instead. Now, as he hunched next to Jones's foxhole and took in the scene around him, he was certain he had made the right decision. Although Marines bristled at the notion of being mere "adjuncts" to the U.S. Navy, not a leatherneck alive had anything but the highest regard for the Navy corpsmen who risked their lives on the battlefield. But Bob McCarthy knew, deep down, that he would rather lead a charge than clean up after one.

It was 2 a.m. when McCarthy returned to his bunker from his second inspection. He handed his field phone to Corporal Thomas Ashdale, the leader of the Third Squad — who had once studied for the Catholic priesthood — and told him to awaken Sergeant Audas for the 4 a.m. watch. He crawled into his bag in the back of the bunker and was asleep within seconds.

At the same time, near the base of the hill,

the company's forward air controller noted faint flares, soft as starlight, bursting in the sky several miles to the northwest. The snow had stopped falling, the clouds were gone, and a bright moon had risen. Unknown to the air controller — unknown, in fact, to everyone else at the moment, including the regimental commander Colonel Litzenberg at Yudam-ni — the illumination shells he was watching were Charlie Company's desperate cry for help.

Earlier, the air controller had managed to raise a weak signal on his own radio, and after watching a second barrage of flares burst in the same area in the northwest sky he contacted the howitzer battery at Hagaru-ri and requested several precautionary rounds, to be dropped on the little West Hill, the knoll two hundred yards opposite the Second Platoon's dug-in positions on the west slope. Captain Benjamin Read, the artillery outfit's commanding officer, replied that because ammunition was scarce he was under orders to fire his six big guns only if Fox Company came under direct attack.

The air controller replaced the radio receiver, uttered a mild oath, and kept his eyes fixed on the night sky for the next five minutes. At 2:05 a.m. he was startled by the rumble of a Jeep climbing the road from

Hagaru-ri. This was the second Jeep to break the moonlit hush that had fallen over the pass. The first, a bit after midnight, had rolled down from the north with a five-man wire crew stringing a communications line between Colonel Litzenberg's regimental command post and Captain Barber's tent. The noisy unspooling of the wire had awakened several Marines on the lower slopes, but most of the men stationed above never heard it.

An enlisted man jumped from this second Jeep, threw a large bag of mail over his shoulder, and disappeared into the smaller of the two huts, where the mortarmen and corpsmen were sleeping on the dirt floor. After a few seconds the enlisted man returned to the Jeep and began grappling with one of the other canvas mailbags on the backseat. Twice more the Marine returned to the vehicle to tote bags into the small hut. He was about to enter the hut for the third time when he spun around at the sound of a voice issuing a challenge.

Above him, on the secondary ridgeline about forty yards west of the hut, a Marine from the Second Platoon, his outline partially hidden by a thicket of trees, was yelling at something, or somebody, coming down the road from Yudam-ni. Simultaneously, Staff Sergeant William Groenewald, standing watch in Captain Barber's company command post tent, picked up his buzzing field phone. Lieutenant Elmo Peterson of the Second Platoon informed him that in the bright moonlight he could clearly make out a large group of "natives" emerging from the shadows behind the West Hill and marching down the MSR. Groenewald shook Captain Barber awake.

"Captain, Second Platoon says there's natives coming down the road."

"What time is it?"

"Just past oh-two-hundred, sir."

"Hold 'em until we can question them."

Barber sent his staff sergeant to find Mr. Chung, the Korean interpreter, who was sleeping in one of the huts. Barber's first thought was that this was a stray South Korean unit, or perhaps a group of civilian refugees. He recalled the deserted road on the trip up to the pass. *So that's where they all went.*

Like Barber, the Americans on the western grade of the hill had no way of knowing that the line of soldiers moving toward them, four men to a row, belonged to the first of five companies in a Chinese battalion of the Fifty-ninth CCF Division. As this point column emerged from behind the West Hill

145

and approached Fox's southwest perimeter, the Marines on the lower west slope could hear them chattering among themselves and their white canvas sneakers shuffling on the dirt road. Seconds later they were surprised to also hear bolts racking on automatic weapons and the tapping of potato mashers on the frozen ground to activate their fuses.

2

At precisely 2:07 a.m., an anonymous Marine from Fox Company's Second Platoon, his password challenge unreturned, emptied the twenty-round clip of his BAR into the forward ranks of the approaching soldiers. The Chinese returned fire at the same instant.

Corporal Ashdale, on watch near Lieutenant McCarthy's command post bunker, wheeled and shouted, "Here they come!"

The next four hours were a hellbroth of bugles, gunfire, whistles, explosions, clanging cymbals, acrid smoke, and frantic war cries, destined to be recorded in Marine Corps annals as the onset of the Battle for Fox Hill.

Corporal Jack Page, the gunner manning the most westerly heavy machine gun, opened up with several long bursts into the enemy point company, elevating and lowering his aim for maximum effect. Chinese soldiers fell across the road as if scythed. Page guessed that his sweeping gunfire had wiped out nearly two dozen men. The rest scattered to either side of the MSR in small groups, and kept coming.

Private First Class Billy French, the Marine who had delivered the mail from Hagaru-ri, dropped the third mailbag and ran to his Jeep. He grabbed his carbine and ducked under the vehicle as the red tracer bullets of Page's heavy machine gun arced over him, over the two huts, and over Captain Barber's tent command post. French fired at anything that moved on the road while bullets thudded off the frozen ground and grenades exploded around him. He watched one particular tracer from Page's machine gun ricochet off a rock and head straight for him. He pulled his head into his parka like a turtle. The bullet winged over his head and snapped into the backseat of the Jeep. He wondered if you ever saw the round that killed you.

Two privates first class — Lee Knowles and Bob Rapp — sleeping in the trailer hitched to the company Jeep, woke to an unnerving cacophony of shepherds' horns, whistles, rhythmic war chants, and Page's screaming machine gun. These two First

Platoon Marines had arrived on the last truck that had chugged up to the pass from Hagaru-ri, and the first thing they spotted, on dismounting, was the empty trailer pulled to the side of the road. They trudged past it toward the hill, searching for a place to dig in, but when Rapp spat and his saliva froze as soon as it hit the road, they had glanced at each other, turned in place, stowed their gear, and climbed in to bed down.

Now, as bullets cracked past their ears, Rapp yelled to Knowles that they had to get out. Knowles threw a bear hug around him and whispered, "Lie doggo, they're all over us." He could see their faces across the road, not ten feet away. An instant later, the First Platoon's Sergeant Kenneth Kipp popped his head up behind Knowles and Rapp on the Fox Hill side of the trailer. From his position on the east slope, Kipp had seen their predicament and led his four-man fire team down to cover their escape.

As Kipp's team poured bullets down the road, Rapp and Knowles grabbed their rifles, heaved themselves over the side of the trailer, and ran fifty feet up the hill. They fell into two empty foxholes, stood up, and turned to fire. Kipp was leading his men back up to their original position when

Rapp was shot through both forearms.

As the first slugs ripped through his canvas tent, Captain Barber pushed himself out of his sleeping bag and ordered Lieutenant Schmitt to contact Colonel Litzenberg at Yudam-ni, using the landline laid by the wire team two hours earlier. Barber and the other nine men in the tent scrambled for their weapons and shoepacs — Barber and his executive officer, Lieutenant Clark Wright, put each other's on in the confusion. The captain sensed that the Chinese knew exactly where his CP was situated. Barber was the last man to bolt through the rear flap, and as he clawed his way to higher ground he turned and saw enemy infantrymen pouring down the MSR, already climbing over the cut and beginning to surround the two huts. He heard Schmitt yell that the wire to Yudam-ni had been severed.

The Chinese reached the smaller hut first. Lieutenant Brady, the mortar unit's commanding officer, leaped from his bag and tackled the first enemy soldier through the front door while his mortarmen and Marines from the headquarters unit grabbed whatever weapons and gear were close at hand. They all ducked out the back doorway leading up the hill. At a spot about thirty feet from the hut they gathered with the other mortarmen who had been billeted in the mortar section tent.

Lieutenant Brady was the last out of the hut, and as he joined the group their position was hit by a fusillade of hand grenades. Brady tried to concentrate his men in a defensive perimeter. A grenade exploded, and he was wounded in the hand and back. He dropped to his knees, stunned by the fragments. The two Marines on either side of him were killed, and one of the 60-mm tubes was damaged.

The mortarmen regrouped behind and above the smaller hut. Lieutenant Schmitt and his radioman ran by carrying Captain Barber's SCR-300 radio and a 610 field phone. Schmitt stopped and ordered the surviving mortarmen to haul their tubes, shells, and wounded up to the shallow culvert, no more than a few feet wide, that climbed two-thirds of the way up the center of Fox Hill. One crew had difficulty loosening the baseplate of an 81-mm mortar from the frozen ground. Covering them with a BAR, Sergeant Robert Jones, the 81-mm unit's forward observer, emptied a full twenty-round clip into a squad of Reds running at them from the southeast corner of the larger hut. Schmitt finally pried the baseplate from the ground with an entrenching tool and carried it away.

When the mortar teams reached the bottom of the culvert their section leader, Staff Sergeant Robert Kohls, directed them to move all mortar tubes and ammo to the top of the little draw where it ended just above the tree line. Although greatly exposed, the mortars had to be set up with unimpeded fields of fire. This meant there could be no tree branches hanging overhead. As soon as Kohls turned to cover his unit's retreat, a potato masher exploded between him and Private First Class Richard Kline, one of the 81-mm gunners. Kohls's throat was slashed by grenade fragments; Kline suffered wounds in his right arm and both legs. Kohls dropped to the ground; Kline picked him up; and together they limped up the culvert.

The mail carrier, Billy French, firing his carbine from beneath his Jeep, heard voices above him. He rolled out from under the vehicle, jumped to his feet, and shot two Chinese soldiers who had crawled into the backseat. He turned, emptied the remaining bullets in his clip at the charging white-clad figures across the road, and ran up the hill. Somewhere near the tree line he found an empty foxhole and fell into it face-first.

The bazooka gunner Corporal Harry Burke stayed low in the larger hut while he hurried to get into his winter gear and shoe-pacs. He noticed that the Navy corpsman Mervyn "Red" Maurath was already dressing the wounds of two Marines. Automatic weapons fire punched holes in the flimsy walls of the building. This so concentrated Burke's attention that he realized only belatedly that he had jammed the wrong feet into his shoepacs. He didn't stop to change them, and after stuffing his sleeping bag into the large cooking pot in the kitchen area of the hut, he grabbed his bazooka and ran through the easternmost door. The Chinese were no more than eight feet away. He emptied his .45-caliber pistol.

Six hours earlier Burke had thought it pretty fortunate that he had managed to secure a sleeping space in a warm hut while the rest of the company went away, cold and griping, to dig in among the rocks. Out in the field you didn't get a roof over your head every day. Now Burke, the heavy machine gunner Jack Page, and several Marines who had also sacked out in the large hut laid down covering fire as Maurath and three more Marines carried the two wounded men up the hill and into the trees. Burke followed them.

When he'd climbed perhaps thirty yards he stopped to look back. A Chinese soldier was peeking out of the hut Burke had just abandoned. The bastard was taunting him, daring the Marines, in English, to come back and retrieve their warm winter gear. With a laugh he assured them that they would not be shot. Burke and the men around him emptied their weapons at him.

Below and to Burke's left corporals Robert Gaines and Rollin Hutchinson scooped up their weapons and stray pieces of gear and scampered up the hill. They were from the First Platoon's Third Squad, and they had arrived on the last truck with Rapp and Knowles. It had been so dark that instead of digging in they had merely chucked their sleeping bags to the ground on the lower, southeast corner of the hill between the erosion ridgeline and a jumbled column of rocks the size of large headstones. They had wordlessly agreed to dig foxholes in the morning, spread their canvas ground cover on the snow, and fallen asleep.

Now they were stumbling blindly through the pine trees when they heard someone yell, "Get the hell over here!" They moved right and took up positions behind Private First Class Jim Holt's heavy machine gun. When Page on the other heavy gun had begun raking the Chinese, Holt also had a clear field of fire. But his water-cooled gun jammed, the water frozen to ice, and it remained jammed. Gaines and Hutchinson dropped in behind Holt and racked the bolts of their M1s.

Private First Class Phil Bavaro, a cook with Fox Company, jumped up from the grain storage bin in the small hut where he'd been sleeping. He caught a glimpse of his fellow cook, Private First Class John Bledsoe, hotfooting it out the northern entranceway and up the hill. Bavaro, still in his skivvies, snatched up his parka and his M1.

He and Bledsoe had been among the last Marines to arrive on the hill, and upon spotting the smaller of the abandoned huts, Bavaro had made a beeline for it, with Bledsoe behind him. Inside, Bavaro had stripped off his outer clothing, spread his sleeping bag inside the large wooden grain storage bin at the downhill end of the structure, crawled into the bag in his long johns, and nodded off. He was used to sleeping in confined places. His bunk on the troopship had been a gun tub.

Now, as bullets cracked past his head, Bavaro barely reached the door when somebody yelled, "Grenade, Cookie!" Bavaro dropped facedown in the doorway. A potato masher exploded to his left. The shrapnel opened a deep cut on his right thumb and peppered his rifle.

The same voice yelled, "Now, Cookie!" Bavaro dodged to his left, tripped over a fallen tree trunk, and backflipped down behind it. Beside him the supply sergeant, David Smith, whose warning he had heard, was firing his M1 into a dozen Chinese coming toward them. Automatic weapons fire split the tree trunk, and Bavaro and Smith scrambled farther up the hill. But they were caught between the crossfire of the advancing Chinese and Jack Page's heavy machine gun behind them. They rolled and flopped into a slight depression, so narrow and shallow Bavaro wished he didn't have to share it, even with the man who had just saved his life. A second later the corpsman Red Maurath and three Marines carrying two wounded men squeezed in beside them.

Near the center of the base of the hill the shot-up remains of two Chinese squads regrouped with the intention of taking out Page's heavy machine gun. They knew exactly where it was — the red-phosphorous-coated tracers it fired every fifth round gave away the gun's position.

The enemy infantrymen climbed to within yards of the emplacement before the Marines surrounding Page decimated them with M1 and BAR fire. Staff Sergeant John Henry shot three men point-blank with his .45-caliber pistol, then picked up a Thompson submachine gun from one of the dead and shot three or four more. Killing people this close, he realized, was a lot more intimate than spraying them from the top turret of a B-24.

The mail carrier, Billy French, thought something was wrong with his carbine. It wasn't knocking anyone down. Despite its smaller round, the lighter carbine was the preferred weapon of officers and platoon leaders, and French had counted himself lucky to have scavenged one back in Hagaru-ri and not to be lugging an M1. But now he and other Marines firing the carbines noticed, to their amazement and chagrin, that their bullets barely penetrated the white quilted uniforms of the advancing Chinese. They just kept coming. Word spread among the Americans on the hill, not for the last time, "Men with carbines, aim for the head."

The Chinese point column on the MSR had once consisted of nearly 150 soldiers. Now, perhaps half still stood. Their number continued to shrink as Marines from the Second Platoon on the lower west slope poured rifle and light machine-gun fire into their rear. Gray Davis and his BAR man, Private First Class Maurice "Luke" Johnson, were among these. Davis was fascinated by tracers. He felt they should be issued to riflemen as well as to machine gunners to help sight the enemy at night. To that end he'd scrounged a clip to save until the time was right. His foxhole mate, Johnson, thought this idea insane. *Why don't you just put up a billboard showing them where we are?*

Nonetheless, to Davis the time was now right. He had left the tracer clip perched on the parapet of their hole before the fighting started. But now he couldn't find it. He turned to Johnson and stared.

"Damn right," Johnson said. "Threw 'em away when you weren't looking. Get killed on your own time."

A few Chinese tried to avoid the murderous enfilade by taking shelter under the base of the cut bank — the sheer ten-foot wall where the hill met the road. Lieutenant Peterson, running up and down behind his platoon's lines, ordered the Marines closest to the road to roll hand grenades over the precipice. The Chinese were being beaten back, but the Americans were running low on ammunition. Peterson ordered all men to fix bayonets.

Farther east of the cut bank a dozen or so Chinese ducked behind a pile of five large rocks a short distance up the slope from the southwest juncture of the hill and the road. Using the rocks and surrounding brush as cover they maneuvered up the hill toward the tree line. It was an obvious attempt to take out the lower of the Second Platoon's light machine guns. They, too, were zeroing in on the gun's tracers. Finally the Chinese burst into the open. They were met — and cut down to a man — by fire from the machine gun as well as the rifles and BARs on either side of it.

By 2:15 a.m., eight minutes after the first, unidentified Marine from Fox Company had issued his password challenge, the wounded mortarman Richard Kline and his assistant gunner had set up their 81-mm tube above the tree line at the top of the shallow culvert. The company's second 81-mm team hacked out an emplacement a few yards behind them. Captain Barber, his runner, and most of the headquarters unit had also made it up the gully by now. Barber set up a temporary command post in the top row of trees just below the mortar emplacements. The communications officer, Lieutenant Schmitt, joined him. Schmitt and his assistant dumped the company 610 field phone and the SCR-300 radio on the ground next to Barber and began cranking the handles in desperation.

Because the mortar team leaders, including Lieutenant Brady and Sergeant Kohls, had been wounded, Barber directed Private First Class Lloyd O'Leary, the most senior member of the 60-mm team remaining, to take command of the combined mortar units. Barber had had his eye on O'Leary since the company's first night bombardment on the road from Koto-ri. The kid had exhibited a natural ability to acquire targets in a hurry, account for his ammunition, and calculate advance firing zones. Barber had also noticed that O'Leary possessed a streak of leadership.

Now O'Leary ordered the three 60-mm teams to dig in about thirty yards east of Kline's position while Kline scrambled around the emplacement putting out luminous aiming stakes at different compass points.

While the Chinese point company was being slaughtered down on the road, the four remaining companies of the enemy battalion broke off the MSR and began a flanking maneuver. This was what CCF military training manuals called "assembly on the objective" — the apparent ability to materialize on enemy positions from different directions at the same time. A flying buttress of 500 to 600 soldiers raced up the valley separating Fox Hill from the West Hill. The Americans never saw them reach the saddle. In fact, because of Fox Hill's rugged contours and multiple ridgelines, most of the Marines on the upper slopes and across the eastern grade had not even heard the sounds of the firefight below.

The Chinese assembled at the far end of the land bridge beneath the rocky knoll. A column of grenadiers formed into a skirmish line and began creeping toward the crest of the hill, where the right flank of the Second Platoon met the left flank of the Third Platoon. Behind these 100 or so close-combat breachers were about 400 regulars armed with assorted rifles and automatic weapons. They moved out in silence in rows of forty, spaced ten yards apart. Just as Captain Barber had anticipated, their immediate objectives were the two light machine-gun emplacements covering this corner of the heights.

At 2:20 a.m., at the pinnacle of the hill, the grenadiers sprang from the ground, stumbling into the holes occupied by the Third Platoon's forward fire team. Sergeant Johnson McAfee was bayoneted in his sleeping bag. Corporal Wayne Pickett and Private First Class Troy Williford, off watch and asleep in their bags behind their rock, were dragged like squirrels in a sack back across the saddle toward the rocky knoll. Private First Class Daniel Yesko, on watch in an adjacent hole, leaped to his feet and emptied his M1 clip. He was shot in the hip and crumpled to the ground. Five Chinese soldiers jumped him, clubbed him into submission, and carried him off as well. As he was being dragged away Pickett heard Yesko's muffled screams, "I've been hit! I've been hit!"

Yesko's firing and cries also reached the corpsman Edward Jones. Jones leaped from his hole and began running toward the commotion. He was shot and killed before he was halfway there.

Private Hector Cafferata caught the scent of garlic before he saw them. He and Private First Class Ken Benson were hunkered down in their listening post well out in front of the American defensive perimeter. Cafferata was on watch, his stocking feet stuffed into his sleeping bag, while Benson dozed. He was trying to melt frozen peanut butter in his mouth when he thought he heard gunfire down by the road. Or was it just the wind playing tricks? He was about to wake his foxhole buddy when he saw scores of white-clad figures flashing past their foxhole about thirty yards to his right.

"Bense," he whispered, "they're coming. Wake up. Get your boots on."

Benson had barely gotten to his knees and was struggling with his shoepacs when a satchel charge landed in their hole. He picked it up and heaved. The explosion shook them both. His eyes still ice-crusted from sleep, Benson exchanged a quizzical look with Cafferata. They were kids, albeit tough kids, and this was the first action either one of them had seen. It struck them as a game of some kind. It certainly couldn't be real.

Benson shouted, "Home by Christmas, Hec?"

Benson emptied his BAR clip and Cafferata let loose a salvo with his M1. It was like being back in the woods in New Jersey, picking crows off a tree limb. The Reds were so close he didn't even have to aim. Within moments he had taken down more than a dozen.

The firing alerted Sergeant Meredith Keirn, the crew leader of one of the Third Platoon's two light machine guns near the crest. He opened up at the same time as Corporal Hobart Ladner, who manned another light machine gun twenty paces to his left. They lit up the saddle, the guns' red tracer rounds casting a crimson tint on the faces of the charging enemy.

Having lost the element of surprise, the remaining Chinese rushed forward with a series of heart-stopping bugle blasts, chants, and whistles. They were on top of Keirn in an instant. His machine gun dropped them so close that the dead began to pile up before his emplacement, face-first, like sandbags, impeding his field of fire. His four ammo cans held 250 rounds each. Within moments he was down to his third, the last few rounds inching toward the loading breech.

As the enemy swarmed over the hilltop the thirty-five men who constituted the two forward squads of the Third Platoon were hard hit. Corporals Harvey Friend and Norman Johnson and privates first class Peter Tilhoff, Paul Troxell, Richard Stein, Dan

Stiller, and Charles Stillwell were killed almost immediately. Private First Class James Umpleby, the only surviving member of his fire team, was wounded in four places but continued to fire his weapon until he ran out of ammunition. He then collapsed, unconscious.

Behind and slightly down the hill from Cafferata and Benson, corporals Oma Peek and James Iverson of the Second Platoon were also in trouble. Several squads of Chinese, caught in the crossfire between the two light machine guns, were funneled directly toward their foxhole. Iverson and Peek were inundated by hand grenades and automatic weapons fire; their position was overrun. Iverson was mortally wounded and Peek was knocked unconscious.

Holes were opening all over the American perimeter. Hundreds of Chinese poured through the gash in the broken flank between the Second and Third platoons, and Cafferata and Benson were surrounded. Two enemy riflemen reached the lip of their hole; Cafferata clubbed them with his shovel. One of them dropped a Thompson submachine gun. Cafferata picked it up and emptied it into another approaching squad. Benson, reloading, elbowed him. "Time to go, Hec."

Go? Go where? It had been so dark by the time Fox Company reached the hill that the two Marines had no idea where the rest of their platoon's foxholes were. Then, at the same time, they both remembered a slit trench they had passed on their sortie to cut tree branches for their "nest." It was about twenty-five yards behind and above them, closer to the top of the hill. They grabbed their weapons and ammo, rolled out of the hole, and fought their way back, Cafferata still in his stocking feet. They fell into a trench occupied by privates first class Harrison Pomers and Gerald Smith.

Pomers, a regular Marine, was one of the Third Platoon's fire team leaders. He was a tough kid who had once been a linebacker for the Corps' amateur football team. He was also a former scout swimmer with a seagoing squadron based in the Caribbean. Right about now, he was wondering how the hell he had wound up here, surrounded by Chinese and about as far away from that warm blue water as a man could get. Pomers had met Smith, a raw reservist, just a few hours earlier as he was scoping out the abandoned trench, four feet deep and eight feet long. He'd been so overjoyed at not having to dig out a foxhole that he'd promptly forgotten the new guy's name. He remembered it now, although he had no idea who these two Second Platoon Marines falling into his trench were.

Pomers had removed eight clips from his cartridge belt and lined them up on the lip of the trench. He was already through half of them. After he was joined by Cafferata and Benson, the four stood shoulder to shoulder, firing into the enemy flanks — particularly those now closing in on Corporal Ladner's machine-gun emplacement. It was no use. Ladner and his three-man crew disappeared in a sea of smoky white figures. Ladner and privates first class Benjamin Hymel and Jack Horn were killed. Private First Class Bill Boudousquie was wounded and left for dead. Two Chinese infantrymen trampled over his prone body as they dragged Ladner's light machine gun down into the ravine that ran up the valley between Fox Hill and the West Hill.

A concussion grenade exploded in the slit trench and kicked Pomers into the wall. Another bounced off his helmet and exploded just outside the trench, nearly knocking him out. He could move nothing but his left arm. He wiped his head, saw the blood on his left hand, and frantically reached for his helmet. Miraculously, he found it and slapped it back on. A voice was calling his name. A face came into focus. He recognized a Navy corpsman. "You'll be OK," the corpsman said.

After watching Ladner's machine-gun nest fall, Cafferata, Benson, and Smith let loose a torrent of covering fire as the Chinese surrounded another Third Platoon fire team. The hill itself seemed to tremble. But privates first class John Stritch, William Fry, John Bryan, and Arnold Vey died in the holes where they stood and fought.

The Chinese continued to concentrate their attacks on the machine guns. On the hilltop Sergeant Keirn's nest was finally overrun. Four Marines in Keirn's crew died around him as he knocked six enemy soldiers down with his forty-five-caliber sidearm. He threw his empty pistol at another charging soldier just before his left arm was blown off by a fragmentation grenade.

With the capture of the two light machine guns the Chinese had effectively taken the northwest crest of Fox Hill. They now divided and attacked down the west slope and across the top of the hill. Private First Class Bob Kirchner, out of ammunition near the top of the west grade, bayoneted one man charging his hole, and then another. Still more came. A bugle blared from behind a large rock not ten feet away. Kirchner wheeled and a stray shot took off the tip of the little finger on his left hand. He stared blankly at the bloody stump; the hand seemed to belong to someone else. The squad leader Sergeant Joe Komorowski came flying by his hole hollering for a grenade. Kirchner tossed him one as if lateraling a football. Without stopping the big sergeant pulled the pin, climbed halfway up the rock, and dropped it on the bugler's head.

In the hole next to Kirchner, Private First Class Fidel Gomez and Private Harold Hancock raked a solid wall of charging infantrymen. Neither had been to boot camp, but both had qualified in advance combat training, including marksmanship, at Pendleton. There the targets had been far more distant. The enemy was now no farther than thirty feet away. The Chinese fell like bowling pins. His adrenaline churning, Gomez at one point turned to Hancock to ask for more clips. His foxhole buddy was frozen into his firing position. Gomez pushed him. He fell backward, dead, a bullet hole through his left eye. Gomez, a devout Catholic, said a quick prayer for his soul.

Over on the Third Platoon's right flank, at the northeast corner of the peak, Howard

Koone saw what looked like red fireworks off to his left. He kicked Dick Bonelli's sleeping bag. "They're coming," he said. Bonelli sprang up, grabbed his M1, and glanced over his right shoulder. "Ski" Golembieski and "Goldy" Goldstein were already in firing positions. The Chinese crashed through in waves.

"Jesus Christ, it's a New Year's Eve party!" Bonelli hollered as volleys of potato mashers trailing their glowing cloth fuses filled the air. All four Marines in Koone's fire team stood to meet them — and all four of their weapons misfired, including Koone's BAR. The firing pins had frozen solid.

"Fix bayonets and throw hand grenades," hollered Koone. He was the first to toss one. Three Chinese soldiers sailed through the air. Bonelli pulled grenade pins and threw as fast as he could, tossing short while Koone threw long. Bonelli bit off one pin and part of his lip stuck to the frozen metal. Koone jumped from the hole and stood on the edge raging like a madman, waving his shovel over his head. "C'mon motherfuckers!"

A Chinese soldier emerged from the dark and Koone plunged the point of the entrenching tool deep into his throat. *Jesus!* Bonelli thought. *Fuckin' Cochise we got here.*

169

All around him Bonelli could hear the gurgling death cries and anguished yelps of the shredded enemy. He did not speak their language, but even in this horrific clamor he was instinctively able to distinguish between those who were yelling for help and those who were offering their final prayers. He turned around. Golembieski and Goldstein were gone, vanished. He swore and pulled another pin. As he let the grenade fly Koone tumbled back into him, hard, knocking him over. The corporal had been hit in the ankle by a burst from a burp gun.

Koone screamed. He felt as if someone had chopped at his leg with an ax. He saw stars, and a hot taste of aluminum seared the back of his throat. He felt like vomiting, but he couldn't get the bile to rise. He tried to get to his feet, but the sudden rush of blood to his brain sent him into a dizzying spiral. He screamed again and again. He wailed so loudly that he scared Bonelli. "Jesus, you tryin' to bring every Chinaman in Manchuria down on us!" Bonelli said.

Alone and desperate, fearful that Koone's shrieks would attract half the Chinese army, Bonelli half-carried and half-dragged Koone out of the hole and down the hill. After a few paces he stumbled across Golembieski and Goldstein, frantically working their rifle bolts. He started to curse them. They cut him off.

"New perimeter," Golembieski said. He was panting. "Lieutenant says all Third Platoon re-form thirty yards down the slope."

Bonelli had no way of knowing that Bob McCarthy had burst from his dugout at the first rifle reports and rallied his reserve fire teams to plug the gaps in the line while ordering the hilltop perimeter pulled back. As Bonelli passed through this new line he thought that it seemed to be holding.

"Back up in a minute!" he yelled to no one in particular and continued dragging Corporal Koone down the hill. Koone felt as if his leg were made of lead and thought his foot was about to tear off. Bonelli was oblivious. He continued to holler: "Back up in a minute!"

Private First Class Ernest Gonzalez did not hear Dick Bonelli's cries, although he was less than twenty yards away. The whizzing, subsonic boomlets snapping over his head reminded him of "pulling butts" — marking targets on the rifle range at Pendleton. But there was one difference: the enemy's gunpowder had a peculiar stench. Gonzalez had been told that the Chinese lubricated their guns with whale oil to keep them from freezing up. It smelled more like whale shit to him.

He wiggled out of his sleeping bag in the slit trench on the center-right flank of the Third Platoon's perimeter. For some reason he checked his watch. It was 2:22 a.m. He squirmed into the foxhole to his right, raised his head above the lip, and saw scores of white-clad "phantoms" running across the ridgeline.

Gonzalez was an assistant BAR man, Third Squad, Third Platoon, Third Fire Team, and he had been cold and angry from the moment he ascended to the top of Fox Hill. Now he was cold, angry, and frightened. A few hours earlier his squad had huddled at the base of the hill, halfheartedly digging in for well over an hour before finally being assigned positions all the way up at the eastern edge of the crest. Gonzalez was only seventeen and weighed barely more than 100 pounds; he was so thin that, people joked, he was nearly invisible when he turned sideways. When he turned up to face the hilltop and judged the wind he realized that the gale would cut him in half. His nose and cheeks were already affected by mild frostbite, which he had picked up at Hagaru-ri, and a deep gash on his left index finger, the result of a woodcutting accident a week earlier, was refusing to heal. Now they wanted him to act as a human wind sock?

"Fuck it," he'd said to his BAR man at the bottom of the hill. "I'm staying here."

"Get your skinny ass up there," the BAR man said.

Gonzalez muttered a curse, but he moved. It was the murals that got him going.

A year earlier Gonzalez and three friends from East Los Angeles had ventured down to the Marine Armory in Chavez Ravine, where the Los Angeles Dodgers would one day play. They had lied about their age and tried to enlist in the reserves. All four boys had failed the written entrance test, and they then talked about visiting the local Army recruiting office. But Gonzalez was determined — his extended family included veterans from both world wars — and the next day he persuaded his best friend, Charlie Rivera, to join him in giving the Corps one more try. The same recruiting officer who had administered the previous test was again passing out the entrance exam, but he didn't appear to recognize the two boys from the barrio. They passed, and they were assigned to Able Battery of the Second Howitzer Battalion.

Before leaving the recruiting center Gonzalez had studied the murals at the armory — dramatic, heroic depictions of the island-hopping Marines of World War II. The seriousness of the commitment he had just made became etched in his mind.

Gonzalez's unit had been called up on July 18, when President Truman activated the reserves, and on reaching Pendleton he was transferred from the Howitzer Battalion to Fox Rifle Company. He was shipped to Yokahama, Japan, where he trained for nearly a month before arriving in Wonsan on November 7. (That was his saint's day, commemorating Saint Ernest, a medieval German Benedictine abbot who joined the Crusades, preached in Persia and Arabia, and was tortured to death in Mecca.)

"Should have known right then that this wasn't going to turn out well," he said to his buddy Private First Class Freddy Gonzales, another Marine in Fox Company. Freddy Gonzales was not a relative, although he told Ernest that their aunts knew each other. In fact, when Ernest Gonzalez had caught up to Fox just south of Sudong he discovered that there were many Hispanics in the outfit, including three more Gonzaleses in addition to Freddy. Ernest was the only one whose name ended in "z."

Something of a rivalry emerged between the southern California branch and the Texas branch, and as a show of independence Ernest and each of the Gonzaleses began responding in a more individual way during morning roll call. "Here," one would say. Another would answer, "Present." A third might merely say, "Yes." Ernest decided his response would be "Hoo," a variation of the Marines' "Hoo-yah."

Near the top of the hill Ernest Gonzalez's fire team had found two abandoned foxholes connected by a slit trench about eight feet long. Gonzalez scooched down into one hole, barely a stone's throw from the southwest corner of the same gnarled thicket Dick Bonelli had eyed with suspicion. His BAR man took the other hole. Their team leader jumped into a third, ten feet to Gonzalez's right. Only then did Gonzalez realize that their fire team was one short. He would have to serve as both assistant BAR man and rifleman.

Now, with the Chinese seemingly surrounding their position, Gonzalez thought, fleetingly, of that man their fire team was lacking. *Could use that extra gun now.* He knelt in a firing position. His BAR man was already emptying clips into the enemy columns from his hole on the left side of the trench. His fire team leader was doing the same with an M1 from a hole to the right. Gonzalez lifted his own M1. He had butterflies in his stomach. He had never been in combat before. He was about to squeeze off his first round when he was knocked to the bottom of the hole by a retreating Marine. The American, whom Gonzalez did not recognize, tossed him his rifle. He shouted that it had jammed. He picked up Gonzalez's gun and started firing. Then he jumped the back lip of the hole and took off down the hill.

Gonzalez unjammed the firing pin on the M1 and rose to shoot again. He saw a squad of Chinese soldiers, outlined by the moon, crossing the terrain laterally to his left. He fired and a man dropped — his first kill. He wanted to cheer, but something told him not to act like an idiot. He was aiming again when a grenade exploded near his BAR man and knocked him down. Gonzalez started to crawl on his belly and was halfway across the slit trench when the BAR man popped back up. He hollered, "I'm OK!" Gonzalez could see blood gushing down his face.

Again Gonzalez spotted a small cluster of Chinese moving laterally to his left. Again he sighted by the moonlight. He fired and watched another man fall. Out of the corner of his eye he saw flickering white sparks an instant before he heard the shots: a burp gun. The flashes reminded him, incongruously, of summer fireflies back in East Los Angeles. The bullets danced across the lip of his foxhole.

The Chinese sniper had camouflaged himself deep in the tangled thicket on the northeast crest of the hill. Crouching low in his hole, Gonzalez pulled the pin on a grenade, watched its spoon fly over the lip, silently counted to three Mississippi, and heaved it in a high arc. He was fired on no more from the corner of the thicket.

Within seconds two more Marines tumbled into the slit trench next to Gonzalez. One was bleeding profusely from his forehead and mouth. As the second tended to his buddy a potato masher landed between them, wounding them both. Gonzalez felt the shock wave of the concussion pass through his body, but he didn't go down. The two men crawled over the downhill side of the lip and staggered off.

Movement flashed to Gonzalez's right. Two Chinese soldiers charged the foxhole of his fire team leader, dropped grenades, and hit the ground. Following the explosions they jumped back to their feet and raced across the hill, leaving the American for dead. Gonzalez shot at their fleeing forms. He did not know if he hit either one. Now, again to his right, he saw a man crawling from behind a huge boulder not ten yards away. He raised his M1, fired, and missed. The man — possibly an American; Gonzalez could not tell — sprang from his knees and loped down the east slope of the hill.

4

The combined fire of the Second Platoon higher on the west grade and the re-formed Third Platoon line slowed the Chinese advance. Gunfire and grenade explosions slackened, and standing targets became scarce. Though the enemy held the crest of Fox Hill, there remained small islands of Marines scattered within the Chinese ranks. In one of these pockets, the slit trench on the left flank, Private First Class Pomers regained consciousness. He crawled the eight feet to the west end of the trench and found Hector Cafferata peering over the lip, searching for something to shoot.

"You know, Hec," said Pomers, "I was praying while I was shooting, praying to God that if I had to die, please don't let me shit in my skivvies."

Back down the hill, lost in the trees, Dick Bonelli had no idea where the aid station was. He figured it had to be close to one of those huts he'd seen by the road. As he crashed through the fir trees with Koone on his back he heard a thrashing sound on his right. A figure staggered out of the dark. Bonelli dropped Koone and wheeled, bayonet-first, stopping just short of gutting Private First Class Amos Fixico. Bonelli recognized Fixico as another one of the outfit's Indians, a Ute from Arizona. His left eyeball was hanging near his cheekbone, glistening like a peeled hard-boiled egg. He was one of the ammo carriers in Sergeant Keirn's light machine gun unit, and he told Bonelli about being overrun. He, too, asked for the aid station. Bonelli could only shrug and point his chin down the hill. The three took off, Bonelli and Fixico supporting the now unconscious Koone.

They had gone only a few yards when a challenge rang out. Bonelli answered. "I'm a Marine. With wounded. We need the aid station."

"Gooks down on the road," the voice said. "Better get your ass over here."

It was Private First Class Holt's heavy machine gun unit. Holt's water-cooled gun was still frozen solid. Bonelli was stunned

179

to learn that the bottom of the hill was in Chinese hands. From up on the crest he had not even heard any gunshots. Several Marines from the headquarters unit pulled Koone and Fixico into the emplacement. Bonelli headed back up the hill.

The mayhem all around Ernest Gonzalez's slit trench suddenly eased. Each side seemed to be catching its breath and, as one Marine noted, "waiting for the other to start something."

Gonzalez scanned the horizon for darting figures. He saw none. The gunfire, in fact, had abated to the point where Gonzalez was able to hear snoring — *snoring!* — coming from a foxhole several yards away on his right flank. He hollered, "Wake up, man! Wake the fuck up!" The snoring continued.

A moment later a bullet slammed into Gonzalez's helmet. He felt light-headed, as if he'd smashed his head on a curb playing street football back home. He drifted into unconsciousness.

Bob McCarthy's re-formed defensive perimeter had held. At 2:25 a.m. his dazed Marines listened as a Chinese bugler far up on the saddle blew a signal to regroup.

By now, at the base of the hill, the Chinese

point company's attack had also been thoroughly repulsed. White-clad corpses were strewn across the MSR and the area around the two huts. To the bazooka man Harry Burke they resembled white birch trees turned up by their roots. The occasional moan or whimper from a wounded man, a hideous sound, was the only noise to puncture the crisp night air.

Throughout the fight Captain Barber had been a ghostly whirlwind, roaming the front lines from the road to the hilltop, firing his carbine, rallying his fire teams, hollering instructions. Two of his runners had been wounded following him up and down the hill. He was now back at his temporary command post just below the upper tree line, checking on their condition, when he was handed a partial casualty list.

Most of the scattered wounded were still being identified, but Barber saw the names of the two Marines on either side of Lieutenant Brady who had been killed instantly in the fight at the bottom of the hill: Sergeant Glen Stanley and Private First Class Ronald Strommen. Of the thirty-five Marines in the Third Platoon's forward foxholes on the hilltop, fifteen were dead, nine were wounded, and three were missing. Barber knew the list would lengthen greatly when

Lieutenant McCarthy could account for his entire platoon.

Because of the extraordinary acoustical barriers across Fox Hill — the many gullies, depressions, and boulders and the two ridges bisecting the granite hulk (three, including the six-foot-high erosion fold) — practically all of the First Platoon strung out down the eastern grade had no idea that a battle had even been fought. The platoon leader Lieutenant Dunne and Master Sergeant Arthur Gruenberg had established their command post slightly behind their forward squads in a small depression near the top of the tree line. The batteries in Dunne's field phone had gone dead, and he was at a loss regarding the source of the muffled echoes emanating from the other side of the hill.

Farther up the east slope, however, Sergeant Charles Pearson and Corporal Kenneth Mertz of the First Platoon knew something nasty was up when several stray bullets punctured their makeshift pup tent. But where the shots had come from, or who had fired them, neither could tell. The two men had been delighted the previous evening when they had stumbled across a rare level patch of turf just above the tree line on the upper third of the slope. They had shoveled snow to form a small "fort" and tied their large shelter-half tents together to make a flimsy roof. Watching the Marines digging in around them, Pearson had remarked to Mertz that he had "the luck," and said to stick close by if things got hot. Now, peering through the bullet holes in their canvas shelter, Mertz was certain that things were hot. He just didn't know where.

Similarly, the First Platoon's light machine gun ammo carrier Bob Ezell, dug in just above Pearson and Mertz — only one hundred yards away from the right flank of the Third Platoon — had been screened from the pandemonium by Fox Hill's tall central ridgeline. Ezell had heard muffled sounds that might have been gunshots, and he had seen plenty of tracers arcing over the hilltop. Even though he didn't know exactly what was happening he was fairly sure that, whatever it was, it was heading his way.

At the far end of the saddle, behind the rocky knoll, the captured Marines Wayne Pickett, Troy Williford, and the wounded Daniel Yesko were held in a small cave. For Yesko, this was ironic. One week earlier he had been granted a hardship discharge —

"marital problems" was all he would say —
and he had been scheduled to fly home to
the States via Japan that morning. He had,
in fact, been offered an opportunity to
remain at Hagaru-ri when Fox Company
had left for Toktong Pass. At the last minute
he'd opted to spend his last night in Korea
with his buddies Pickett and Williford on
the hill. He figured he'd catch a ride down
to the airfield when the supply trucks arrived in the morning. Now Pickett looked
him in the eye, placed a finger to his lips,
and thought of his own fiancée in Duluth.

None of the Americans could speak Chinese, but from the tumult about them they
sensed the general drift of the rapid-fire
conversations. The Chinese regulars wanted
to shoot them. They were dissuaded by a
tall, elegant captain menacingly waving a
Thompson submachine gun. Their shouts
echoed off the rock walls of the small cave.

Pickett's mind reeled. It was a given that
in any war a soldier might "catch" a wound.
He had even calculated the smaller likelihood of being killed. But taken prisoner?
The thought had never entered his mind.
He was, however, one of the few Marines in
Fox Company who'd had prior contact with
hostile Chinese. In 1947, when he'd been
berthed off China's east coast aboard the

cruiser USS *St. Paul* for four months as a seagoing Marine, the war between Chiang Kai-shek's nationalists and Mao's Communists was still raging. One day during war games two of the fleet's Marine Corsair fighter-bombers had run out of fuel and crash-landed miles from the American airfield at Tsingtao, at the time still held by the Nationalists. Both pilots had bailed out, and one was able to make his way back to the base on foot.

Pickett's thirty-man Marine detail had been sent out to rescue the other. A brief firefight with the Communists had ensued, though no one was killed. The American pilot was eventually recovered through diplomatic negotiations, but not before Pickett's unit found itself on a strand with its back against the East China Sea, facing an overwhelming Chinese force.

"Believe it or not," he now whispered to Williford and Yesko as the arguing continued around them, "they warned us to get out of there or we'd be flooded when the tide came in. And they were right. So we got out of there, no questions asked. You never know with these people. Sometimes they can be friendly, and sometimes they'll just cut your throat."

As if to prove Pickett's point, the Chinese

officer who had prevented their execution suddenly ordered a squad of his men to march the confused Marines back across the saddle toward the American lines. Halfway there a light machine gun on the west slope opened up on the little group. The squad retreated, dragging Pickett, Williford, and Yesko back to the cave with them.

5

Stationed halfway up the western slope, near the center of Second Platoon's line, Warren McClure and Roger Gonzales had been cut off from the Chinese assaults not only by the hill's secondary ridgeline, but also by a wall of large boulders that ran parallel behind their position to the tree line. They could only guess at the cause of the muted ruckus taking place seventy-five yards above them. Nor had they any clue that there had been a fight down on the road.

Before settling into their depression they had fretted for some time over the probability that enemy troopers might use the sinkhole in front of them as cover. But they had finally shrugged off their apprehensions and constructed a shelter by lacing three half pup tents together. When McClure squirmed into his mummy bag he put on a knee-length, alpaca-lined vest that he'd "secured" at the Hungnam supply depot by means he preferred not discuss with Gonzales. McClure suspected that the vest may have been intended to warm the imposing torso of Colonel Litzenberg.

McClure left his bag unzipped and dragged his BAR in after him, the muzzle wedged between his untied shoepacs, the stock resting on his chest. He had adopted this sleeping position since seeing the four Marines bayoneted on the hillside overlooking the Sudong gorge, their sleeping bags turned into body bags when their moist last breaths froze the zippers closed. The new man Gonzales, studying McClure, did the same with his M1. Every so often he would grasp the slide of the rifle and work the action back and forth to keep it from freezing up. Neither man could sleep.

It was just past 2:30 a.m. when word spread among the Marines who had not been involved in the firefights that the Chinese had already attacked Fox Hill from two directions, and were probably coming back for more. McClure and Gonzales were feeding rounds into the chambers of their weapons when they were summoned by their squad leader, Sergeant George Reitz. Reitz ordered them to establish a forward listening post overlooking the western valley.

The two crept out in front of the Second Platoon's perimeter and crawled for twenty-five yards before settling in behind a large rock that, if they knelt, provided cover enough for both. The West Hill now loomed less than two hundred yards away. Peering straight down over the rock, they could spit into the sinkhole, McClure's "deep dip." But they still could not see its bottom. Beyond the hole was the narrow valley with the ravine running up to the saddle.

Voices unobstructed by ridges and folds carried well in the still night air, and as McClure and Gonzales sighted their weapons and rechecked their spare clips they heard their fire team leader, Private First Class Robert Schmidt, request permission to toss a precautionary grenade out in front of his position. McClure did not hear Sergeant Reitz's response, but a few seconds later an explosion rocked a small shelf of rock perhaps twenty yards to the right of their listening post. Shrapnel skittered off their covering rock, and McClure turned and hollered. He said that if Schmidt threw another goddamn hand grenade it would most certainly be the last goddamn hand grenade he ever threw. Schmidt did not reply.

At 2:35 a.m. McClure spotted a Chinese squad of nine men crawling out of the ravine and making for the sinkhole directly below him. The point man, creeping crablike, rose to his knees just as he reached the far lip of the sinkhole. McClure lined him up in the sights of his BAR. He squeezed the trigger. Nothing happened. His firing pin was frozen. He grabbed Gonzales's M1 and fired. The Chinese point man, hit in the chest, toppled backward. The rest dived into the hole.

Next McClure saw two more enemy soldiers, hunched over and loping down from the saddle. As they neared the deep dip he shot both with Gonzales's rifle and watched them drop over the lip. He handed the M1 back to Gonzales, removed his gloves, and untied the five hand grenades he'd fastened with spare shoelaces to his BAR belt harness. The grenades were freezing, like dry ice to the touch. He laid them out on the ground in front of him, put one glove back on his right hand, and shoved his bare left hand into his field jacket for warmth.

A moment later the remaining eight soldiers from the enemy squad crawled over the far edge of the sinkhole. They took off toward the West Hill, loping low to the ground in single file, each man gripping the coattails of the man in front of him. McClure pulled the pin on a grenade, counted to four by thousands, and let it fly. It exploded among them at knee height. As the few survivors scattered, Gonzales popped up from behind the rock and picked them off one by one. Every Chinese soldier they had seen to this point was now down, dead or wounded. McClure studied the large swath of his skin that had stuck to the metal pin of the grenade. It was that cold.

The two Marines decided to let Sergeant Reitz know what the hell was going on out here. McClure turned and "covered" Gonzales with his inoperative BAR, watching him all the way as he crawled back and dropped into the foxhole occupied by Reitz and the fire team leader, Schmidt. He wheeled to look out again over the western valley and barely caught the heels of four canvas sneakers slithering over the far lip of the sinkhole. Although the bottom of the hole remained obscured, he was in a position to see the upper chest, shoulders, and head of any man who stood up. Incredibly, this is what both Chinese did.

McClure pulled another grenade pin — losing more skin in the process — counted slowly to four, and rolled it down into the hole. Seconds before it exploded he saw the Chinese bend over as if they had dropped something. Now he reached for his left glove — enough flesh had been lost to these frozen grenades — and, stretching out to grasp it, accidentally kicked his BAR down into the sinkhole. *Jesus, what an idiot.* He spotted yet another enemy soldier staggering over the far edge of the deep dip. The man looked as if he had been wounded — his hands were hanging at his side and balled up into the sleeves of his padded jacket. But McClure's gaze quickly moved from his hands to the Thompson submachine gun strapped across his chest.

This time he used his teeth to pull the pin on a grenade, tossed it, and hit the Red in the chest. The grenade bounced off him and failed to explode. The soldier lunged forward as if he had not even felt the impact. McClure tossed another, again using his teeth to pull the pin. He hit the man on his padded earflap. Another dud. The Chinese climbed out of the hole and charged him.

McClure's thighs were as thick as tree trunks, and in Missouri he had been a defensive lineman on the Bigger Diggers, a local semipro team. Now he squatted in his meanest football stance, preparing to tackle this lunatic. But suddenly the man snapped out of whatever trance had swept over him. His eyes met McClure's, and he turned and ran, scrabbling back through the sinkhole and across the ravine.

Without his BAR, and "not knowing just how dead" the Chinese in the deep dip might be, McClure pulled the pin on his last grenade, held the spoon down, and zigzagged back through the American lines in search of another weapon. Working his way up the hillside, scavenging for a working rifle, he ran into his platoon leader, Lieutenant Elmo Peterson. Aside from several perfunctory inspections McClure had never engaged in any conversation with him.

"Where you heading, son?" Even in the heat of battle Peterson resembled a recruiting poster.

"Find a weapon, sir."

"Should be plenty lying around."

McClure's search took him up the west slope and nearly to the top of Fox Hill. About thirty yards away he could make out the two tall, flat-faced rocks that demarcated the northwestern crest. Star shells popped and squeaked overhead, their artificial light throwing the shadowed scene into horror movie relief. Somewhere beyond the rocks a red flare was burning on the ground, covering the terrain where the hilltop met the saddle in an eerie orange glow. The smell of cordite hung in the air, and ten yards beyond the flare McClure spotted a dead Chinese soldier, frozen in a sitting position. He asked Peterson's permission to run out and grab the slain man's gun. He couldn't see a weapon but one had to be there. Before Peterson could answer a bugle call shrieked across the saddle, and the Chinese attacked.

"Here they come again!" Peterson yelled. It was 2:45 a.m.

The Chinese battalion commander had thrown his last reserve company of more than 100 men into the fight, mixed in with the survivors from the first attack. With much whistling, bugling, and beating of drums, about 250 Chinese soldiers again streamed across the saddle in rows, albeit this time, as one Marine noted, "with much less élan."

Peterson snaked on his belly up the hill and hollered over his shoulder for McClure to run down to the company's mortar positions and tell the commanding officer — "whoever the hell's in charge now" — to begin lobbing rounds up onto the saddle. Peterson turned back from McClure and saw a Chinese soldier leveling a Thompson submachine gun at him. Then he pulled the trigger.

Peterson felt a bullet go through his left shoulder and also felt a rush of adrenaline. He lifted his carbine and drilled the Red through the eye.

McClure hesitated when he saw Peterson hit. The handsome "Prof" waved him on. "You hear me, son?" he urged McClure. "Get a move on."

Private First Class Fidel Gomez and the corpsman Bill McLean dropped into the snow on either side of Peterson. Both had M1s, and Gomez had picked up a Thompson submachine gun from a dead enemy soldier. Gomez was wide, powerful, and compact, built like a fullback, a position that had earned him all-county honors in San Antonio, Texas. As the three lay prone, awaiting the second attack, Peterson informed them that the left flank of the Third Platoon had been overrun during the first firefight. They needed to hold fast, right here, and plug this gap in the American line.

McLean smiled and pulled a small bottle of brandy from his field jacket. "Well, in that case," he said.

Gomez, who was nineteen, had never tasted brandy. Before enlisting he had tried only beer. In fact, his older brother Anacleto, a veteran of World War II who had fought with the Third Marines through Bougainville, Guadalcanal, and Iwo Jima, had attempted to bribe Fidel with beer into giving up the Corps and going to college. Anacleto, who had been Fidel's father figure since their real father abandoned the family when Fidel was four years old, couldn't stand the thought of his kid brother, the youngest in the family, being killed in Korea. Fidel had ignored him, but he sure had enjoyed the beer.

He took a small swig of McLean's brandy. "Man," he said, "I like this stuff."

Meanwhile, McClure double-timed it through the trees and found the mortar unit at the top of the shallow gulley. He noticed an 81-mm's bipod set atop two industrial-strength C-ration bean cans, its tubes pointed nearly straight up for short-distance bombardment. He relayed Peterson's orders to an 81-mm gunner, pointing toward the saddle for effect, only to be met with a sorrowful stare. "We've only got three rounds left," the gunner said.

McClure pondered this answer — *Where the hell had all the mortar rounds gone?* — before deciding he had done his job and it would be best to return to his position on the hill's western slope. He turned to take off and nearly ran over Captain Barber and Barber's runner.

"What's your name?" The commanding officer's voice could have scoured a stove. If it was physically possible, McClure thought it sounded octaves lower than on the afternoon of his coming-aboard speech. McClure had never been face-to-face with Barber before. The captain's uniform was no longer starched and pressed — it was tattered. Barber had been out fighting with the men.

"Private First Class Warren McClure, sir. First Fire Team, Second Squad, Second Platoon." Nearly under his breath he added, "BAR man, sir."

He thought he saw a flicker of confusion in Barber's eyes, as if the captain were seeking this lonesome BAR man's missing weapon. But the captain merely said, "Keep it up, son. Keep it up. Get back to your people."

Barber nonchalantly turned up the hill, yelling for his artillery forward spotter Lieutenant Donald Campbell. He planned to radio How Company in Hagaru-ri to ask for a howitzer bombardment of the rocky knoll. That's where the Chinese seemed to be gathering for these attacks.

McClure took off to rejoin the Second Platoon.

6

The Chinese raced across the saddle with the intention of hitting Fox Company just as they had done thirty minutes earlier. This time the Marines were ready. The Chinese hadn't reached the halfway point before Private First Class O'Leary was directing the company's 60-mm mortars, which still had plenty of shells, to tear into their ranks. Marines liked to joke that the 60-mms were the ultimate "weapons of opportunity" — a play on the wording of tactics in the Corps manual — and was this ever an opportunity. There is no defilade from a 60-mm, and the notes from a lone bugle sounding the charge were cut off abruptly as its owner was blown to pieces.

In the slit trench at the top northwest corner of the hill — still thirty yards beyond Lieutenant McCarthy's new, re-formed defensive perimeter — Hector Cafferata, Ken Benson, Harrison Pomers, and Gerald Smith were again standing shoulder to shoulder, emptying clip after clip into the Chinese right flank with murderous effect. Twice Cafferata caught potato mashers in midair and tossed them back into the advancing throng. At one point he heard a *spang* — the sound of his M1 emptying — so the self-proclaimed "world's worst baseball player" grabbed his entrenching shovel with two hands and swung it like a baseball bat, knocking an incoming grenade back into the enemy ranks.

Another grenade landed on the lip of the foxhole connected to the trench. Cafferata lunged backward for it and heaved, but it exploded as it left his hand. The big man cursed. His left hand was bloody and gashed, the fingers shredded. His reaction was simply to reload and continue firing.

Now the night sky seemed to be blotted out by hundreds of hand grenades. Pomers turned to Cafferata. "Where the fuck do they carry them all?" he said.

A flash grenade dropped with a thud on the lip of the trench. Benson reached out and flicked it way. It exploded a few feet from his face, shattering his glasses. He rubbed his eyes with his gloves. He could feel small pieces of bamboo shrapnel in his face. A dull red glow veiled his vision. "Hec, I can't see," he said.

Blind or not, he'd been trained well, and now he squatted in the bottom of the trench and with the efficiency of an assembly-line worker proceeded to reload rifles. Cafferata would empty a clip and drop the M1 down to Benson, who would have a fully loaded rifle at the ready. With each new clip Cafferata would repeat the same question.

"Can you see yet, Bense?"

"Nope, not yet."

Cafferata, Benson, Pomers, and Smith were all that prevented the Chinese from again splitting the defensive line of the two Marine platoons at the northwest peak of the hill. They held, and Cafferata alone was credited with killing almost forty enemy soldiers during the night. The rest of his fire team, as well as the Marines below him, took care of the rest. The second Chinese charge was turned back. Scattered fighting continued among Americans and stragglers, but the major offensive was over.

Twenty minutes later a runner appeared at Lieutenant Bob McCarthy's dugout command post carrying orders from Captain Barber. The lieutenant was to form a detail to clear the crest of the hill. A dozen men were assembled under the command of Sergeant Audas and ordered to "drop their cocks, grab their socks, and go kick some Chinese ass." Among them was Dick Bonelli.

"What we got going here, Sarge?" Bonelli ducked automatic weapons fire coming from the top of the hill. Several squads of Chinese had dug in along the boulders and brush at the crest, and they would need to be rooted out like weeds.

Audas was a professional Marine, a street fighter from Chicago who had experienced his first military action as a rear gunner aboard a dive-bomber over Guadalcanal. The sergeant looked at Bonelli as if he were mental. "We're taking back the goddamn hill, whattaya think?"

Bonelli spotted Captain Barber trudging up the slope, with McCarthy and his aide Sergeant Pitts. Pitts had a through-and-through bullet hole in his helmet. The three were completely exposed to the gunfire from the crest.

"Engage!" Barber shouted to the small squad. "Engage up this hill!"

It was as if the theater, not the play, excited the CO. Sergeant Pitts suggested it might be expedient for Captain Barber to take cover.

"They haven't made the bullet yet that can kill me," Barber declared.

Dick Bonelli's jaw dropped.

Sometime just before 3 a.m., near the bottom of Fox Hill, Private First Class Gray Davis — the kid from Florida who narrowly escaped getting Gunny Bunch's shoepac up his butt — saw a squad of Chinese reinforcements angle off the MSR near the base of the West Hill and begin trotting up the western valley. The moon was so bright he could see their shadows on the snow. They were perhaps 150 yards across from his foxhole, and they were headed for the saddle.

He sighted his M1 on the last man in the file and fired. He saw a tuft of snow kick up fifteen yards short. He made a mental note to adjust his rifle's battle sight to compensate for the misleading distances — at night in the mountains the enemy always seemed much closer — and fired again, this time aiming along the rifle barrel four or five inches above the muzzle. He dropped the man with the second shot.

Davis watched as two soldiers from the group stopped to pick up their wounded comrade. As the three struggled to keep up with the main file, Davis fired again and knocked down one of the good Samaritans. The other bolted to catch up to his squad, leaving the two shot Chinese where they fell. Before Davis could sight and squeeze off another shot the cluster disappeared into the ravine that ran up the middle of the valley.

Watching this scene play out, Corporal Jack Griffith realized that they were going to need more ammunition. Griffith was new to Fox Company. He, Davis, and Luke Johnson had all received their baptism by fire in the earlier gunfight when the Chinese charged from behind the five big rocks and tried to take out the nearby light machine gun. They were all running low on bullets.

Griffith shimmied out of the hole and crawled over the low, secondary ridgeline separating their position from the old command post tent sixty yards down the hill. Dead Chinese were everywhere. He found a cache of ammo, gathered as much as he could carry and drape over his shoulders, and crawled back over the ridge. At the top of the fold he shouted to Davis and Johnson — "Make a hole!" — and took off running as fast as he could. He had just planted his feet on the lip of the foxhole when several Chinese soldiers jumped out from behind the same pile of five rocks — *Where the hell did they come from?* — and shot Griffith through both knees. He fell backward. Davis and Johnson scrambled to haul him back in.

Luke Johnson returned fire while Davis slit the three layers of Griffith's pants legs with his K-bar. The puncture wound in the

202

corporal's right knee was not bleeding badly, and the frozen blood had already begun to clot — the Marines on Fox Hill were learning that the cold could work in their favor in this regard. But the bullet in Griffith's left leg had severed an artery and, cold or no cold, blood was spurting with each heartbeat. Davis knew the loss of blood was going to send Griffith into shock and probably kill him. The human body has approximately one and a half gallons of blood, and it can lose 30 percent — about half a gallon — before its hydraulics fail. Lose a gallon and that's the end. Davis looked at Griffith's blood pooling in the snow and tried to guess how much he had left.

Johnson continued to exchange fire with the Chinese while Davis formed a tourniquet out of Griffith's belt. This slowed the blood spurting from the artery somewhat. But they needed a medic. Both Marines began hollering for one.

A corpsman appeared from nowhere. Bullets pocked the snow at his heels as he flew past the three men and tossed a morphine syrette into the foxhole. "I'll be back," he yelled. The Chinese fusillade increased, and Davis and Johnson could not help wondering when.

The morphine syrette was frozen solid.

Davis debated for a second whether it would thaw faster under his scrotum or in his mouth. He popped it under his tongue, and when it melted he injected Griffith in the left biceps. As a dark cloud blotted the moonlight a stretcher team emerged, belly-crawling over the secondary ridge behind them. One of the corpsmen said he'd heard a rumor that the Chinese sharpshooters were aiming for the legs, looking to cripple instead of kill, as it took two able-bodied Marines to care for a wounded man. The men on the stretcher team were dragging Corporal Griffith from the hole when he held up a hand to stop them.

Wounded but still lucid, perhaps a bit too happy from the morphine, Corporal Jack Griffith confessed to his fire team partners that he had been holding out on them. Considering the circumstances, he said, they were welcome to the six pairs of new, heavy ski socks hidden in the bottom of his pack.

7

As Captain Barber directed the fight to retake the crest of Fox Hill, he had little idea that the battle was about to enter a second phase on his left flank. A fresh company of Chinese had climbed the West

204

Hill from its back slope, and these men were now entrenched on the ridgeline and in the crenulated folds opposite Peterson's Second Platoon. Staccato incoming fire ensued. "Slow-motion firefights," one Marine called it. These firefights were no less deadly than any others.

Midway up the west slope, Roger Gonzales was frightened and alone. He had no idea where Warren McClure had disappeared to, but he intended to find out. Shortly after 3 a.m. Gonzales jumped from his foxhole, trotted up the hill, and spotted a familiar, if sullen, face: Bob Kirchner was emerging from the trees. He waved to Kirchner. Kirchner barely nodded back.

Kirchner was returning from the command post, where he'd just finished the grim task of identifying the body of his friend Corporal John Farley — by his belt buckle. Farley's face had been blown off during the firefight. A week earlier Farley had shared a delightful secret with his squad, a sort of Thanksgiving surprise. His wife had sent him a mason jar of olives along with a separate letter that read, "For God's sake, Johnny, don't throw away the juice." Of course it was gin, and Farley and his buddies, including Bob Kirchner, had toasted their holiday meal with "Korean martinis." Now his brains were spread about somewhere down in the west valley.

Gonzales knew none of this as he weaved along the edge of the pine tree plantation toward Kirchner. He had nearly reached his position when a sniper's bullet tore through his neck. Kirchner hit the ground and crawled to Gonzales. Gouts of blood spurted from his carotid artery. Kirchner pulled him into his foxhole, cradled him on his lap, and applied snow to the wound. Roger Gonzales asked for water, cried for his mother, and died in Bob Kirchner's arms.

From his position ten feet down the slope Kirchner's fire team leader, Corporal Walt Hiskett, had watched Gonzales drop like six feet of chain. Already stung by his dear friend Johnny Farley's death, now he was enraged.

Hiskett, a twenty-year-old from Chicago, was in the Marines because he had nowhere else to go. When he was six, in the depths of the Depression, his father had walked out on the family. Nine years later, when Hiskett was fifteen, his mother died at age forty-five. He went to live at a YMCA and dropped out of school. Joining the Marines at seventeen was a step up. Hiskett was nearly finished with his three-year commitment when war broke out in Korea. He was sent to Camp Pendleton and assigned to a "spare parts" company, which is where Marines were put until the officers figured out what to do with them. From there he moved to Fox Company, eventually becoming a fire team leader in the Second Platoon. His two best friends in the company were John Farley and Charlie Parker.

He stood to return fire, using a scrawny tree as cover. From somewhere on the West Hill a Thompson submachine gunner zeroed in on his muzzle flashes and opened up. Hiskett took a slug in his left shoulder. He slumped to the ground while Marines about him blasted the West Hill and hollered for a medic. A corpsman, Bill McLean, burst from the woods and knelt over Hiskett. He spit a morphine syrette from his mouth and jabbed it into Hiskett's arm. It took only moments for the narcotic to work. Suddenly, Hiskett felt like the luckiest man alive — "alive" being the operative word. Unlike poor Johnny Farley and Roger Gonzales, he was still breathing, and by tonight he would surely be medevaced off this hill and sleeping on clean sheets in a warm hospital bed with hot chow in his belly. He hadn't had a bath or a shower in six weeks. He wondered how long it would take the ambulances to arrive from Hagaru-ri.

Down near the road the Marines who had been caught in the firefight around the two huts began stealthily making their way up the hill. The two heavy machine gun emplacements twenty-five yards above the MSR had become the company's new southern perimeter — although Jim Holt's gun was still out of action — and many men had been trapped between the Chinese and Jack Page's nest. "Cookie" Bavaro and his savior, the company supply sergeant David Smith, who had warned him of the grenade when he'd fled from the hut, were among them. They hollered up to the machine gunner, Page: "Hold your fire, we're coming in!" When they arrived Bavaro found his fellow cook, Private First Class Bledsoe, digging a hole on the southeast corner of the gun emplacement. He borrowed an entrenching shovel and joined Bledsoe.

At the same time the corpsman Red Maurath thought it safe enough to bring in his two Marines from the small depression where he was patching their wounds. Maurath, Corporal Harry Burke and his bazooka, and the three Marines from the headquarters unit who had helped Maurath drag the wounded out of the large hut all climbed up the hill.

Sometime between 5 and 6 a.m. a wan gray light began to spread over the crest of Fox Hill, but the false dawn also brought a new cloud cover that obscured the terrain across the hilltop. Thick snow began to fall as the dozen Marines with Sergeant Audas scanned the crest for enemy soldiers. At one point Audas's patrol froze in its tracks as a Chinese bugler somewhere quite near blew taps. The trumpet echoing through the snow and fog made the experience all the more eerie. At the first mournful notes, Dick Bonelli turned to the Marine next to him, Private Walt Klein. "Just how crazy are these fuckin' gooks?" he said.

Klein ignored Bonelli — he was busy sighting his M1 on an enemy straggler making for the safety of the rocky knoll across the saddle.

All over the hilltop Chinese soldiers lay dead and dying, the wounded pleading for help, praying, moaning, crying, singing their death songs, or quietly freezing to death. Bonelli nearly tripped over an enemy infantryman whose white quilted jacket had been perforated by more than a dozen bullet holes. The man was still alive. Sheer curiosity led Bonelli to slit open the jacket with his bayonet. He was stunned. Beneath his outer layer the man wore a ropy goatskin vest. *So that's why the carbines aren't penetrating.* Additionally, the man's arms and legs were fitted with tourniquets. *Crazy bastards keep coming until they get a death wound.*

He called to Sergeant Audas, and word began to spread yet again: men with carbines, aim for the head.

Twenty minutes later several trapped and wounded Chinese diehards, including the bugler who had blown taps, decided to put up a final fight near the spot where Sergeant Keirn and his light machine-gun crew had been overrun. Bonelli, Klein, and several other Marines made short work of them. One enemy soldier, barely in his teens, rushed at Sergeant Komorowski with a knife fastened by rawhide strips to the end of a long bamboo pole. The sergeant clapped him on the head with the butt of his rifle and took him prisoner.

Walt Klein was the first to reach Keirn's light machine gun post. The gun was gone and four dead Marines were sprawled at the bottom of the nest. Incredibly, Keirn, his left arm missing, was still alive. He sat on his haunches behind where his weapon should have been, as if firing an imaginary machine gun. He looked up at Klein with cloudy eyes and asked for a cigarette. Klein lit one and placed it between his lips. A corpsman appeared and unspooled a roll of bandages. Klein thought the corpsman's job was impossible, like trying to plant cut flowers. He stuck another smoke in Keirn's field jacket pocket just before two stretcher bearers carried him down the hill. Keirn died the next morning in the med tent.

When Audas's squad bent to lift the bodies of the four dead Marines in Keirn's foxhole, two wounded Chinese soldiers leaped out from beneath the corpses with their hands in the air. Their ticket out, Audas thought. Military service, no matter how heroic, was traditionally held in low esteem in Chinese culture. Foot soldiers were merely disposable pawns to be used when negotiations broke down, and there was no provision in the CCF for discharge, honorable or other. Once a peasant was swallowed up in the Chinese Army, that is where he stayed until he was killed, was captured, or grew too old to fight. Audas sent the prisoners, including the kid who had wielded the makeshift bayonet, down to Captain Barber.

Here and there random bullets, like the first light raindrops falling on a calm lake, kicked up divots of snow around Audas's patrol. The Chinese were firing from the rocky knoll and, behind it, the rocky ridge running north up to Toktong-san. Unlike the snipers much closer on the West Hill, they hit no Marines. Out of the corner of his eye Bonelli saw a Chinese soldier who was playing dead at the top of the hill rise up from a pile of frozen corpses and point an automatic weapon. Before Bonelli could react another Marine cut him in half with a BAR.

For Captain Barber, this presented a moral dilemma. He was aware that Chinese battlefield strategy included playing dead in order to lure a Marine into proximity and then kill him, and he considered this premeditated murder. But did this tactic give him the right, in order to protect his own men, to summarily execute wounded enemy soldiers? His company was taking a severe beating on this hill, and he could not afford to lose even one more Marine in this way. If the enemy surrendered, that was one thing — although how many men he could spare to guard prisoners was another complicating factor he'd have to figure out later. For now, however, he issued orders to put all "dead" and wounded Chinese out of their misery. Such were the exigencies of war and the burden of command in combat.

Despite having taken back the hilltop, Barber ordered Lieutenant McCarthy of the Third Platoon to maintain his defensive perimeter where it had re-formed down the slope, about ten yards above the tree line. This would give McCarthy's men some cover from the snipers on the rocky knoll and high ridges of Toktong-san. Barber also realized that the Third Platoon was too depleted to dig in again and hold the entire crest. Preliminary casualty reports coming in to his command post indicated that McCarthy's outfit had been nearly halved.

8

Private First Class Ken Benson, wounded in the face by grenade fragments, groped blindly on his hands and knees.

"You passed out for a minute," said Hector Cafferata. "Nothing but dead Chinks is all you can see." He told Benson how he had noticed an enemy soldier's hand move in a pile of corpses not far from their hole and had bellied out to investigate. "Thought the guy was croaked by the time I get there. So I turn and I'm halfway back here and what's the bastard do? Heaves a grenade at me. Jesus. Thank God it was a dud. Went back out and put two in his head."

Benson was only half-listening. He knew

he needed to get to the aid station. Ignoring Cafferata's offer to help, he started off on his own, crawling across the hill. He might have crawled all the way to Hagaru-ri had he not fallen into Private First Class Bob Ezell's foxhole near the First Platoon's light machine-gun emplacement on the upper east slope.

Ezell stuck a lit cigarette into Benson's mouth while Benson related the story of the "battle of the slit trench" in which he, Pomers, and Smith had emptied their rifles and sidearms into the Chinese charging across the saddle until their ammo was nearly gone. He described how Cafferata had batted grenades back with his entrenching tool, and how after being blinded he himself had squatted at the bottom of the freezing fucking foxhole reloading Hector's M1 while what sounded like cannons blasted in his ears.

"It's really true," Benson told Ezell. "You lose one sense and the rest pick up the slack. After I couldn't see, everything else became so goddamn loud. My nose, too. Because I tell you, I smell coffee brewing somewhere."

Ezell stared at Benson in disbelief. He could smell no coffee, but the man was obviously not lying about being blind. Frozen blood caked both his eyes. Ezell wanted to rip off the bloody scabs but dared not. He was no corpsman. But batting potato mashers back in mid-flight with a shovel? Ezell had to wrap his mind around that one. Back in the States he'd been a pretty good hitter. But grenades? Well, he guessed it could be done.

Captain Barber, making rounds across the hill, happened by Ezell's post as Benson was relating his incredible story. For a moment the CO listened, rapt. He then instructed Ezell to help Benson down to the new aid station, the old mortarmen's tent at the bottom of the hill. Ezell, who like most of the First Platoon had missed the fight, was aghast at the number of dead Chinese he passed while guiding Benson down to the corpsmen. Halfway there Ezell picked up the scent of coffee brewing, too. When they reached the med tents someone handed Benson a steaming cup of joe. He didn't know whether to drink it or dip his freezing hands in it.

While Benson drank coffee, Barber ordered Ezell's light machine-gun crew, commanded by Sergeant Judd Elrod, to pack up and move all the way over on the northwest crest, to the old emplacement between the Second and Third Platoons where Corporal Ladner's gun had been overrun and captured. This new experience — fighting the Chinese at night — had taught him a lesson. When they came again, Barber sensed, they'd come by the same route.

Where was everybody? Ernest Gonzalez awoke to bad thoughts, insane thoughts. His mind raced. He was alone on this hill. Everyone else was dead. He too would be dead soon enough. Should he fight? Surrender? Most of Fox Company had heard stories about the commie prison camps. How they bent your mind with drugs, or sleep deprivation, or maybe even the Chinese water torture. No, he decided, he would fight. He sat up and crawled from the slit trench. He heard gunfire down the hill, a bit to his left. A lone BAR, he thought. Somebody was shooting at something. He grabbed his M1, checked the clip, and took off in that direction.

He edged over scores of dead Chinese soldiers, keeping low. Someone had defecated on the face of one of them. He half-ran, half-stumbled toward the sound of the gunfire. Bursting through a clearing in the trees he saw men. Marines. Alive. The shots he'd heard were from his own BAR man tearing up the saddle, shooting at stragglers. The BAR man turned toward Gonzalez.

"Like qualifying on the range," he said.

Gonzalez thought of the rifle practice Barber had insisted on. Then, in a row of wounded Americans on blankets outside an aid tent, he spotted his fire team leader. Blood was leaking from both of his ears. Gonzalez did a double take. He was positive he'd seen this man die in his hole. No, he was alive too, all right — blown up from the two grenades, but alive. Jesus.

"We need ammo. Got any ammo?" A Marine was talking to him. Gonzalez snapped out of it.

Yeah, ammo, sure, back up in the slit trench. He turned and began climbing. He reached the trench and felt around under his sleeping bag. One lousy grenade. He searched the hole, and then the entire trench, for spare clips. There were none.

On his way back down Gonzalez fell in behind Sergeant Audas's detail clearing the crest. He stepped on a lump of — what? It was a Chinese soldier, curled into a fetal position facedown in the snow. The man had a wedge the size of a large slice of pie missing from the back of his head. Gonzalez could see his brain. He rolled him over and saw his eyelids flicker as irregular puffs of steam escaped his mouth. Gonzalez shot him in the chest. This was the last wounded man he would ever kill. He knew it wasn't exactly murder, but it was powerful, bad *joss*. He'd heard somewhere that *joss* was what the Chinese called luck.

Catching up to Audas's mop-up detail Gonzalez now came across a bloody Marine-issue sleeping bag at the bottom of a shallow foxhole. He unzipped the bag and discovered the body of Sergeant McAfee, bayoneted where he slept. Not far away he found the frozen body of the corpsman Jones, kneeling, with his hands between his knees, as if he had been executed. For some reason this sparked a memory: the snoring Marine, the fucker who had slept through the firefight. He wheeled and ran, hopped over his old slit trench, and found the foxhole. At the bottom of the ditch was a dead man with a gaping hole in his chest. *So he wasn't snoring after all. The poor guy had been breathing through his sucking chest wound.* The safety on the man's rifle was still on.

On his way back across the hilltop Gonzalez nearly stepped on another wounded Marine, still in his sleeping bag, bullet holes stitched across his stomach. He hollered for help and a corpsman appeared with a stretcher. They carried the man down to the new CP in the trees. Ernest Gonzalez gave the guy a pat on the head, turned, and took off up the hill searching for the Third Platoon's re-formed lines.

All night on the upper, northeast corner of the hill Corporal Eleazar Belmarez and two privates first class — John Scott and Lee D. Wilson — could only listen in frustration to the sounds of a firefight close by, just over on the far side of Fox Hill's main ridge. Their foxhole constituted the ultimate high left flank of the First Platoon's defensive line, separated from the right flank of the Third Platoon by the ridgeline's solid wall of gnarled granite and the tangled, impassable thicket.

Wilson was a decorated veteran of World War II, and at first he had not been happy to be paired with Belmarez, a new boot from San Antonio. From the moment they had begun digging in eight hours earlier Wilson grasped the tactical problem inherent in not being able to see their Third Platoon linkup, Corporal Koone's four-man fire team. It could make things dicey, and though Wilson knew and trusted Scott, he had no idea what size *cojónes* Belmarez brought to the situation.

As they'd struggled to make a hole in the frozen ground, Wilson's ire rose when he saw his squad leader, Sergeant Daniel Slapinskas, along with Corporal Charles North, jump into an abandoned foxhole about ten yards down the slope to their right. The hole was chest-deep and must have been dug by the North Koreans during the summer, when a man could sink a shovel into this turf.

"Lucky bastards," he'd said aloud.

"Maybe, maybe not," Belmarez said as he'd jammed his spade into rock-hard turf like a jackhammer. "I'd rather be at the top. Higher ground, better fighting ground."

Maybe, thought Wilson, this kid will be OK. His black mood dissipated when Belmarez showed no sign of panic as they listened to the adjoining firefight.

Now, sometime just before 6 a.m., the snow had lightened to a fine white mist as Belmarez strode down the slope to Sergeant Slapinskas's hole and requested a recon mission. Slapinskas nodded and told him to take along the fourth member of their fire team, Corporal North.

The four Marines edged over the snowy ridgeline, keeping the thicket to their right. They were dumbfounded at the mounds of Chinese corpses. Belmarez and Wilson were the first to spot a Chinese soldier pop up from a snowhole and begin running, a light machine gun cradled in his arms. They had no way of knowing it had once belonged to Sergeant Keirn. All four fired and the man fell over. He was dead when they reached him. Wilson test-fired the machine gun. It worked fine.

As the four inched over the crest of the hill another Chinese soldier jumped from a pile of bodies. Wilson cut him down with the machine gun. At the rapid report of the gun, more Chinese began hopping up from scattered heaps of corpses and taking off toward the saddle. Wilson sprayed them, too, until each hit the ground. Were they dead? There was no sense in taking a chance. From that instant the First Platoon fire team administered a coup de grâce to every prone body.

Not far from where Wilson had shot the first enemy soldier with the machine gun, three more Chinese rose to their knees, their hands in the air. Belmarez patted them down, noting that they were no more than kids. He ordered Private First Class Scott to take them back to Sergeant Slapinskas's hole. While they waited for Scott to return, Belmarez drew up a plan. They would circle the forty or so yards around the tangled thicket and emerge on the opposite slope of Fox Hill. This, Belmarez said, would give them a clear field of fire to the enemy bunched together on the rocky knoll. When Scott rejoined them and all four moved out, however, they discovered that even at the far corner of the thicket they still did not have a clear sight line to the rocky knoll, which was about 275 yards away.

Belmarez and Wilson, carrying the light machine gun and its bipod, crawled another fifty yards out. North and Scott covered them from the corner of the brush. Once out in the open, Wilson set up the machine gun and began raking the rocky knoll while Belmarez fed the belt. The Chinese at the base of the knoll fell or scattered. But the enemy soldiers on the higher ridgelines soon had a bead on Wilson and Belmarez, and a heavy volley of automatic weapons fire scorched their position.

Belmarez and Wilson dived into a shallow depression, sucked in air, counted to three, and sprinted back toward the thicket, still carrying the recaptured machine gun and its bipod. They fell in behind North and Scott, out of breath, laughing uproariously. Soon all four were convulsed in laughter. Wilson had seen this before, during the last war. It was a form of nervous release.

The caps of the lonely, undulant mountains

glowed ruddy one after the other as the angled sun rose slowly on the eastern horizon, its rays reflected blindingly off the snow. Gray Davis could hear wounded Chinese soldiers moaning and praying in the valley separating his hole from the West Hill. At least he thought some were praying — they sounded very different from the yelping cries of the men who still wanted to live. He and Luke Johnson were almost out of ammo again. In covering the stretcher bearers who had dragged Jack Griffith away, they had used most of what Griffith had retrieved. Davis told Johnson he was going to go scare some up.

He crawled over the lip of their foxhole and out into the valley close to where it met the road, trying to keep in among the scrub that ran down to the pile of five big rocks. He was struck — as were so many Marines on Fox Hill — by the grotesque forms of the frozen dead. He was also impressed by the efficiency with which the Chinese had policed the battlefield. He couldn't find a gun or a box of cartridges to save his life — and now that he thought about it, that had become more than just a cliché.

Then Davis heard whimpering beyond a small, two-foot hump farther out in the valley. He "breast-stroked" about thirty yards through the foot-deep snow until he was face-to-face with a wounded enemy soldier. He was out in the open now, closer to the West Hill than he preferred. Through half-lowered eyelids the dying man — such a little guy — looked at Davis and attempted to extract a potato masher from his quilted jacket pocket with fingers that were frozen and swollen. Davis rose to his knees and shouldered his M1. The snow around him exploded with bullets from the West Hill.

Davis hit the ground and watched for another long moment, almost hypnotized, as the man continued to fumble for the grenade. Then he spotted a Belgian-made automatic rifle and a box of bullets a few yards away. He stood and ran, zigzagging at top speed back to his line, barely breaking stride to scoop up the rifle and ammo. Slugs snapped past his head and thudded into the snow around his feet. Luke Johnson laid cover fire across the slopes of the West Hill. Davis fell into the foxhole, broke open the cardboard box, and began divvying up the cartridges.

9

Up at the Chosin Reservoir, Colonel Homer Litzenberg had concluded that the Seventh Regiment's best chance for survival was

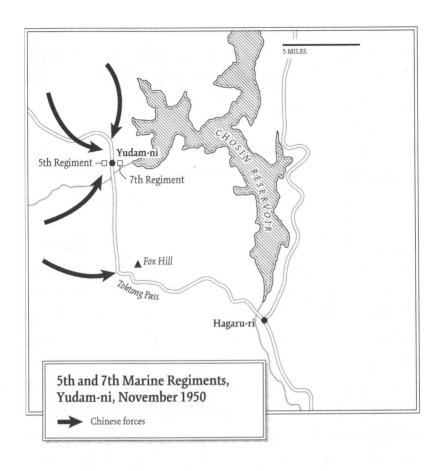

5th Regiment

Yudam-ni

7th Regiment

CHOSIN RESERVOIR

▲ Fox Hill

Toktong Pass

Hagaru-ri

5th and 7th Marine Regiments, Yudam-ni, November 1950

➡ Chinese forces

5 MILES

strength in numbers. Twelve hours earlier he had had eighteen rifle companies at his disposal, ready to push on to the Yalu. They were now down to a battered fifteen — with two of those surrounded on hills several miles away, their future effectiveness in doubt. Litzenberg had to find a way to reunite Fox with his remaining forces at Yudam-ni.

He reached Barber by radio as the captain

was overseeing the erection of the new company command post tent about fifty yards east of the shallow gully that ran up the center of Fox Hill. Litzenberg asked Barber his thoughts about quitting the hill and fighting his way north.

Barber had been worrying this bone for a while, and he considered the idea impractical in the extreme. He had taken too many casualties to move anywhere, and his ammunition stores had nearly run out. Lieutenant Peterson reported that his Second Platoon was down to between three and six bullets per man. Moreover, his small band of Marines was the only obstacle holding open the back gate from the Chosin. If the Chinese took these heights there was little chance Litzenberg's troops would get out alive.

The captain kept that thought to himself, however, and without explicitly citing the number of his wounded, lest any Chinese monitoring their radio frequency overhear, he indicated to Litzenberg by mentioning "tactical necessities" that he could not abandon his position.

Litzenberg's cryptic reply signaled that he understood Barber's meaning and intent, and before signing off Barber ended the exchange on an upbeat note. Just get us some airdrops, he said, ammo and food, especially grenades — and we'll hold this piece of real estate until the enemy drops from exhaustion.

Litzenberg could do better than that. Following his conversation with Barber he immediately radioed Lieutenant Colonel Lockwood in Hagaru-ri and ordered the formation of a composite force from the Marines remaining in the village — cooks, bakers, clerks, drivers, and communications and intelligence people. He wanted every soldier in Hagaru-ri with the exception of the artillery gunners and a small rear guard to get up that road and reinforce Fox. It was time to implement the Corps rule "Every Marine a rifleman." He called Barber back to tell him that relief was on the way.

After dropping Ken Benson at the aid station, Bob Ezell returned to his light machine-gun emplacement on the east side of the hill. The crew was gone. He asked around and learned that Captain Barber had ordered the gun dug in between the Second and Third Platoons on the northwest crest near the two tall rocks. Ezell had never been on that side of the hill, and it took him several minutes to orient himself and crawl across the crest. He used the scores of Chinese corpses as cover from the constant sniping; there were so many they reminded him of sagebrush in the desert.

He had just spied the two giant domino-like rocks a little above him when someone came tumbling down the hill. Sergeant Judd Elrod practically rolled into his arms. He had been shot in the same hip that had taken a Japanese bullet seven years earlier at Tarawa. But the force of the impact had been blunted by his binoculars case. Elrod, who had also been wounded in the fighting around Seoul, handed Ezell his smashed binoculars. "Ain't gonna do me any good," he said.

Ezell noticed that one of the glass eye-pieces was shattered. He bent to help Elrod up, but the sergeant waved him off.

"Get your ass up to the emplacement," he said. "I can get down to the med tents by myself."

By the time Ezell reached the light machine-gun nest yet another Marine was down. Private First Class Dick Bernard, an ammo carrier, had been hit twice within ten minutes by sniper fire. The first bullet grazed his right leg. The second broke his left femur. Ezell barely had time to take in the situation before someone yelled, "Duck

— he's got a grenade."

Ezell wheeled and spotted a Chinese soldier emerging from a depression thirty yards away, where the deep ravine running up the west valley met the saddle. The man had a long, stringy mustache that fell below his chin; he reminded Ezell of the evil mastermind Fu Manchu in the movies. He instinctively put three slugs into the man's chest. It was the first time Ezell had fired his rifle since Camp Pendleton. A moment later, two full enemy squads charged from the same depression. The machine gun knocked over about half of them and the rest dropped their weapons, threw up their hands, and surrendered. Ezell figured they must have been short a political commissar. One Marine wanted to shoot them, but another didn't like that plan: "If we shoot 'em, nobody else will ever surrender."

So the prisoners were rounded up and led down to Captain Barber's tent. Once again the Americans were struck — and disgusted — by how young the Chinese seemed. *Who the hell is sending fifteen-and sixteen-year-old kids out to fight a man's war?*

A corpsman, carrying a rolled stretcher, passed the enemy prisoners and their Marine guards as he ran up the hill. Ezell noticed that the sniping trailed off considerably while the Chinese were in the open area between the two tall rocks and the tree line. As soon as they disappeared into the woods, however, it picked up again. If he'd known that was how their minds worked he would have made the Chinese carry Dick Bernard down to the med tents. Instead, using the rocks as cover, the light machine-gun crew rolled the private onto the litter and Ezell joined the corpsman and two more Marines at the corners. They counted to three and took off, running as fast as they could and nearly bouncing Bernard right off the canvas stretcher.

Near the command post Ezell bumped into Freddy Gonzales. Freddy was Roger Gonzales's cousin, and Roger and Ezell had played summer ball in San Pedro. But Roger's real forte had been track and field. He was a thirteen-foot pole-vaulter and a low-two-minute half-miler. Before the war Ezell and Roger Gonzales had shared their secret hopes: making the major leagues and competing in the Olympics, respectively.

"What do you hear from Roger?" Ezell said.

Freddy Gonzales lit a cigarette and scuffed the snow with the toe of his shoepac. "KIA during the night."

■ ■ ■ ■

THE SIEGE

■ ■ ■ ■

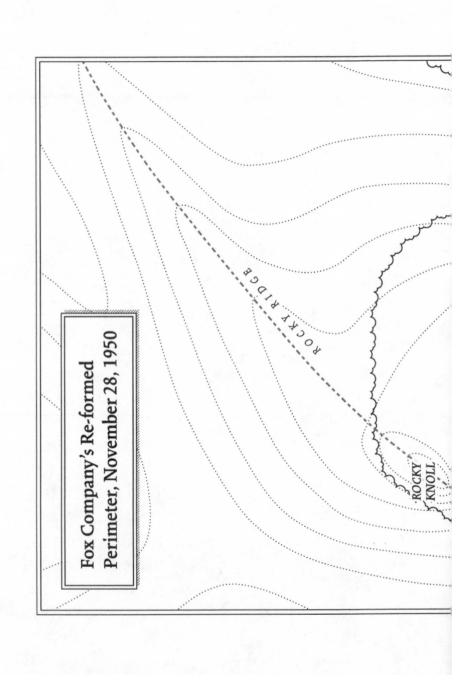

Fox Company's Re-formed
Perimeter, November 28, 1950

ROCKY RIDGE

ROCKY
KNOLL

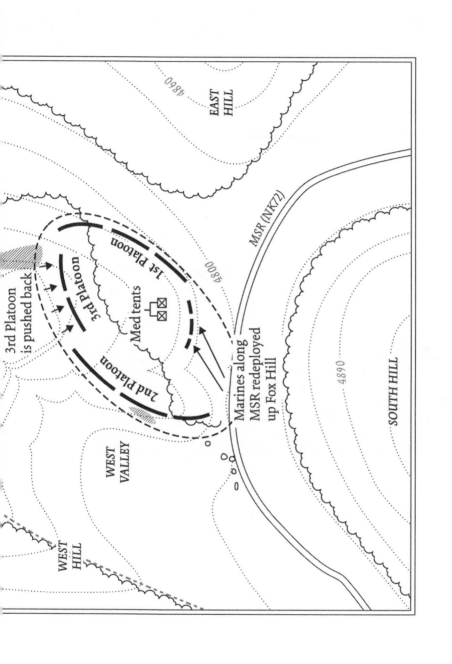

4860

EAST
HILL

4800

MSR (NK72)

3rd Platoon
is pushed back

3rd Platoon

1st Platoon

Med tents

2nd Platoon

Marines along
MSR redeployed
up Fox Hill

4890

SOUTH HILL

WEST
VALLEY

WEST
HILL

DAY TWO

NOVEMBER 28, 1950
6 A.M.–MIDNIGHT

1

At 6 a.m. the Marines strung up and down the hill unofficially declared the first night's battle for Fox Hill over. The action at the Sudong Gorge had been a vicious skirmish, but still only a skirmish. Now Fox Company had engaged in a full-scale firefight with Chinese Communists for the first time and had held their own.

The snow had stopped falling and pale sunlight streamed through the smoky scene as now and again another "dead" enemy soldier would rise like a ghost and scamper back across the saddle toward the rocky knoll. Sometimes a Marine would pick him off; sometimes he would make it. Intermittent sniper fire from the ridges and folds of the West Hill and the ridges of Toktong-san continued, and two Americans were wounded by a burst of automatic fire at 6:07 a.m. But for the most part both sides

235

were content to use the daylight hours to lick their wounds and regroup.

Men hopped from their foxholes and began dragging Chinese bodies to use as sandbags. Although there were fewer enemy dead on the west slope of the hill, Bob Kirchner managed to find half a dozen corpses to pile in front of his hole, including the two men he had bayoneted and the bugler Sergeant Komorowski's grenade had beheaded.

To his everlasting sorrow, he also dragged Roger Gonzales's body out of his hole and added it to the stack. He was sure the dead Marine would have understood; Kirchner certainly would have if the tables were turned.

Up at the two tall rocks Captain Barber directed Bob Ezell's machine-gun crew, now down to four men, to register several white phosphorous rounds — "Willie Peter" — lofted toward the rocky knoll and the rocky ridge by the 81-mm mortars. The shells were not very effective because the small mushroom clouds, with their white, spindly spider legs, did not contrast with the snow. Meanwhile, Marines across the hill began scrounging among the enemy corpses. They were amazed to find U.S. Navy–issue field glasses and American-made Palmolive soap,

Colgate toothpaste, and Lucky Strike cigarettes. Many of the captured packs and knapsacks also held small picks and shovels. After the firefight the Americans, who now understood the danger they faced, found it miraculously easier to dig into the frozen ground.

But the most stunning discoveries were the guns and ammunition. They ran a global gamut, and the recovered weaponry flabbergasted the Americans. There were a dozen or so Thompson submachine guns, the "Chicago typewriters" that the United States had shipped to Chiang Kai-shek by the boatload during World War II and the Chinese civil war. To these were added aluminum Russian burp guns, Japanese automatic rifles, British Lee-Enfields and Stens, American Springfields, and several ancient wooden rifles of indeterminate origin. Numerous khukri blades, knives carried by generations of Ghurka infantrymen, were also turned up, and the late Corporal Ladner's light machine gun was discovered half-buried in the snow near the lip of the ravine running up the west valley. Finally, Lieutenant McCarthy ordered his men to take the weapons and ammo from any dead Marines, a particularly unpleasant task.

At 8 a.m., Ezell was one of the Marines

sorting through the captured weapons on the hilltop when he saw Hector Cafferata crawling in his socks out onto the saddle toward the listening post he had escaped six hours earlier. Ezell could only imagine how awful the big man's feet must have felt as he slithered into the hole and bent down to gather his gear and shoepacs. As soon as he stood he was knocked down again by a sniper bullet. Ezell dived into a trench and called out to him, but Cafferata merely let loose a torrent of curses and oaths. *Shit-shit-fuck-shit. Fucking goddamn sniper. Mother-fucking fucker.*

Ezell yelled again. "Hector! Is it bad?"

Between curses Cafferata waved at him to keep down. "I can make it!" he hollered.

Cafferata had no way of knowing that the bullet had pierced his right shoulder, ricocheted off a rib, and punctured his lung. What he did know was that he was in agony — the pain was so great that he did not even know where, or how many times, he'd been hit. His chest felt as if it had been run through by a spear, and his groin was on fire. He assumed they'd also gotten him in the balls. When he reached down with his good right hand his underwear was pooling with blood. He could not feel his testicles. *That's it,* he thought. *No kids for me.* A wave

238

of remorse washed over him as he undid his web belt, fashioned a sling, and lurched down the hill.

The Americans down near the road were also stirring from their foxholes and defensive positions. Corporal Robert Gaines was venturing down from Private First Class Holt's heavy machine-gun nest — the gun was finally unfrozen — when he heard a combination of voices and moans from the large hut adjacent to the MSR. He peeked through a bullet hole in the planking and saw at least a squad of wounded Chinese on the dirt floor. He pulled the pins on two grenades, tossed them inside, and ran back up the hill.

Not long afterward Corporal Harry Burke of the bazooka section and a corpsman arrived at the same hut. Burke was hoping to retrieve the sleeping bag he'd stowed in the large cooking pot when he'd first arrived on the hill. Gaines's grenade had left two Chinese still alive, though badly torn up. The light brown color of their frozen flesh reminded Burke of wax dummies. He and the corpsman put them out of their misery with sidearms, and Burke found his bag right where he had left it. Everything else, however, was gone. Shoepacs, parkas, and packs had been carried away in the night.

Burke had mixed feelings. The parkas were long and bulky, and their hoods impaired your vision and hearing; they were more suitable for standing watch aboard ship than for long mountain hikes. But they sure kept you warm. As for the shoepacs — well, don't get Harry Burke started on shoepacs. Nothing more than glorified rubber duck hunter's boots, an invitation to frostbite. But now that they were gone he felt a chill run through his entire body. He looked to his left. The three mailbags had been torn open, and the floor was littered with empty food and candy wrappers, presents from home that the Marines would never see.

When Burke stepped outside he nearly tripped over a dead Chinese sergeant lying in a red puddle of ice between the two huts. He took the man's whistle from around his neck and found several pamphlets in his jacket pocket. One had a photograph of Mao Tse-tung printed on the cover. He pocketed them and climbed back up to the foxhole he had found on the southeast slope. When he blew the whistle it made a sound like a platoon sergeant's on the parade ground.

A bit lower down the east slope the assistant company cook John Bledsoe wondered aloud if his partner, Phil Bavaro, planned to dig to China. Their hole was less than two feet deep. "Can't dig to China," Bavaro replied. "That's right over there." He lifted his chin toward the north without pausing in his shoveling. "I guess I'd be digging to . . ."

As Bavaro tried to imagine what country was on the other side of the globe from North Korea, Bledsoe hopped out of the hole and walked over to the sixteen-by-eighteen tent erected by the mortarmen the afternoon before. It had been taken over by the corpsmen and turned into the med tent. The entire canvas floor, corner to corner, was covered with wounded Marines. He spotted his buddy Howard Koone, with whom he had served in China before the war. A corpsman was cutting the boot off Koone's left ankle while another jabbed a morphine syrette into his thigh.

Bledsoe brewed a pot of coffee, mixed water from his canteen with orange juice powder, and gave Koone a swig of each. Koone vomited it back up on Bledsoe's boots and passed out. Bledsoe limited the remainder of his juice and joe to the corpsmen.

Now feeling guilty, Bledsoe walked back to their foxhole and told Bavaro that he would take a turn with the spade. Bavaro headed down to the small hut, hoping to find his clothes (he was still wearing his skivvies under his parka). No such luck. His pack with its spare socks, thermal insoles, and spare underwear was gone. Worse, so was his dungaree jacket with the small flask of whiskey hidden in its pocket. To add insult to injury, in the corner of the hut he saw the box from a birthday cake his mother had sent him. He had carried that cake since Thanksgiving. Nothing was left but a few crumbs trailing across the dirt floor.

On his trek back up the hill Bavaro passed by the med tent and was dragooned by a corpsman into assisting in a field operation. He held a Marine down as the corpsman tried to dig a bullet out of his chest. Soon Bavaro's gloves were soaked with blood and frozen stiff.

Sometime after dawn, with the sun well up and the sniping well down, Barber's executive officer, Lieutenant Clark Wright, ordered the 81-mm mortar gunner Private First Class Richard Kline and the heavy machine gunner Corporal Jack Page to recon the road and take a body count. Below the cut bank, in the middle of the MSR, they came upon two Chinese soldiers sitting back to back. One was dead, the other mortally wounded. Page could tell from the dying man's white armband that he was a noncom. As Page and Kline approached him he lifted a finger to his temple and made a trigger-pulling motion. Page obliged him with his sidearm. Kline found two pearl-handled 9-mm Luger pistols on his body.

Page and Kline, not straying too far past the cut-bank, figured they could count about 100 enemy dead up and down and on either side of the road. Remarkably, most of the corpses seemed to be officers and NCOs. They carried large flashlights powered by five battery cells, with a canvas cover over the globe-like bulb. A red star was cut out of the canvas, and an officer's or NCO's insignia was etched into the metal casing. One man was apparently a paymaster; his pack was crammed with paper yuans and what looked like Chinese bonds.

Kline looked to Page. "Sure can't accuse them of hiding behind their enlisted men," he said.

On the northeast corner of the hilltop, Corporal Belmarez was the first to hear the thrum of the planes. He looked up and saw several formations of camouflaged, gull-winged Marine Corsairs heading north. As the aircraft and their payloads of rockets and napalm canisters passed overhead, all sniping from the Chinese ceased. To reduce its risk of facing better-trained American and Australian pilots, the People's Air Force of China had played no part in the war to this point. But in the short time since the Red armies had crossed the Yalu River, their soldiers had developed excellent discipline under American air attacks. Troops in foxholes learned to stifle their natural instinct to flee and instead remained hunkered down, and any caught out in the open would often freeze in their tracks and stand stock-still with arms outstretched or squat into a ball for long periods of time in an attempt to resemble a tree or a bush.

But evasion techniques that may have worked in warmer months proved futile in winter. For one thing, any attempt to remain motionless for any length of time could be just as deadly as gunfire or bombs in the subzero temperatures. And though the white quilted Chinese uniforms afforded some camouflage against the snow, Marine pilots had become adept at swooping in low and following broken trails leading to enemy emplacements, even to the point of zeroing in on a single set of footprints.

Watching the planes come into range, the

Americans on Fox Hill anticipated a slaughter. But the cheer that rose across the hill died quickly when the planes overflew them and continued on toward Yudam-ni.

2

The enlisted men of Fox Company had no idea that six enemy divisions — more than 40,000 Chinese soldiers — were now encircling the bulk of the First Marine Division. Nor did they know of the dire circumstances facing Litzenberg's and Murray's men at Yudam-ni as another 100,000 Reds approached; nor of Charlie Company's near annihilation on Turkey Hill; nor of the Army's calamitous situation on the east side of the reservoir, where the GI forces were being cut down. Nor did Barber and his officers know that two days earlier, across the Taebacks, the panicked Eighth Army had been routed and was fleeing south following a disastrous defeat north of Pyongyang. The situation, however, was certainly becoming clear in Tokyo, where Vice Admiral C. Turner Joy, commanding officer of all U.S. naval forces in the Far East, summoned the commander of his amphibious forces and directed him to begin making plans for a large-scale evacuation of Marines from North Korea.

However, as soldiers have always done, the men of Fox Company somehow intuited their fate, though without speaking of it. They also knew there was not a thing they could do about it. The wind was blowing from the north, and the reverberations of distant Corsair cannons and rocket fire carried on it were audible up at the frozen Chosin.

At 7:45 a.m., shortly after the Corsairs disappeared over the northern horizon, Lieutenant McCarthy edged up to the saddle to attempt a body count. He could barely move without stepping over an enemy corpse. He estimated the total as close to 350, with at least 150 dead between the site of Corporal Ladner's light machine gun emplacement and the slit trench from which Cafferata, Benson, Pomers, and Smith had fought. Most of the rest lay piled before the original site for the two forward squads of the Third Platoon, particularly where Sergeant Keirn had set up his nest. McCarthy, like Page and Kline down on the MSR, was struck by the disproportional number of officers and NCOs among the dead. He figured that was why most of the prisoners were so young: the veterans were fighting to the end.

Upon his return to the company command post tent McCarthy handed Barber his own casualty report. Of the fifty-four Marines and corpsmen of the Third Rifle Platoon, sixteen were dead, nine wounded, and three missing. Fox Company in total had twenty-four dead, fifty-four wounded, and three missing. Almost a third of the company had become casualties in one night. In addition, men who were still effective were running out of ammunition. Barber turned to the huge stacks of enemy weapons and ammo the Marines had collected, cleaned, and test-fired. There was a similar stack at the bottom of the hill.

"See what we've got here," he told his communications officer Lieutenant Schmitt. "And start handing them out."

Sometime during the night Corporal Wayne Pickett and Private First Class Troy Williford had been roused from their cave and forced by their captors to carry Private First Class Daniel Yesko up over the rocky ridge and down to a dilapidated farmhouse beneath the opposite slope of Toktong-san. As they were shoved into a cattle shed behind the house, Pickett saw several Chinese and North Korean officers assembling near the main building's front door. He guessed that he and the other Marines had been moved to a temporary enemy battalion command post.

Their wristwatches had been stripped off them, but the three Americans could tell from the sun's position that it was still early morning. Before long a guard flung open the shed door and pointed with his rifle barrel toward a small grove of trees one hundred yards away. *Firing squad* was Pickett's first thought. Instead they were led to a slit trench latrine. The Marines were relieving themselves there when a squadron of Australian Mustangs flew in low and rocketed the farmhouse and the shed, obliterating both buildings.

Their captors were furious, and Pickett was certain that this time they would be executed. But again they were merely marched, unbound and carrying Yesko, four miles to another farmhouse. There they were led into an adjoining corral where seven or eight more Americans were huddled. The prisoners were all Marines captured at Yudam-ni. One had been shot in the shoulder.

The Americans did what they could to treat their wounded comrades until sometime late in the afternoon, when a North Korean ambulance arrived. Yesko and the second wounded Marine were loaded inside and driven away. Pickett would have preferred to see Chinese markings on the ambulance; the North Koreans were known to be less gentle with captives. He steeled himself to enter the rice culture as a prisoner of war, and he wondered if that would include ever seeing Dan Yesko again.

3

By midmorning Fox Company was again a bustling hive, gearing up with an intensity, born of combat, that would have been all but unimaginable the day before. The bright sunshine provided some needed warmth, though the Marines guessed that the temperature had risen to only ten below zero. The lubricating oil on all weapons had been turned to sludge by the cold, so every carbine, M1, BAR, sidearm, and light and heavy machine gun was wiped of excess oil and test-fired. Every bullet of every clip of every gun was also removed, wiped down, and replaced.

The machine gunners, remembering the Chinese suicide charges on their emplacements, laid out their belts and substituted standard cartridges for the red tracers on every fifth round.

The forward artillery officer contacted

How Company's 105-mm howitzer unit, using the dying gasps of the SCR-300's frozen radio batteries, and requested that they register their shells for distance on the East Hill, South Hill, West Hill, and rocky ridge surrounding Fox Hill. Within moments, explosions ringed the company's position. The artillery observer marked them on his topographic maps. When new batteries were air-dropped, he would contact Captain Ben Read, How's commander, to tell him where the rounds landed.

Barber ordered a detail to be formed to take the company Jeep as well as the mail carrier's Jeep back to Hagaru-ri for supplies. But the vehicles' batteries were dead, and at any rate the Jeeps themselves were so badly shot up that nobody believed they would start, or run, even with fresh batteries. The same detail, led by Sergeant Kenneth Kipp, the NCO whose fire team had rescued Lee Knowles and Robert Rapp from a Jeep trailer, set off on a recon patrol east and south — the two directions from which the Chinese had not yet attacked.

Kipp returned an hour later with news Barber had anticipated: Fox Hill was surrounded. Kipp had encountered enemy snipers from both directions. Fox Company was completely cut off from any other units of the First Marine Division. Thousands of Chinese were out there, perhaps tens of thousands, and Barber's company was down to two-thirds of its strength.

There may have been a lull, but the Chinese let Fox Company know they were still watching. At 9:40 a.m., Private First Class Alvin Haney, out collecting abandoned weapons near the eastern edge of the hilltop, was knocked over by a sniper's bullet fired from the rocky knoll. Private First Class Billy French, the mail carrier, saw the shooting and bolted from his foxhole. He reached Haney and began dragging him back to cover.

But Haney was a big man and the rescue was slow. Halfway to the tree line Haney was hit again, by a bullet that lodged in his back. French persevered and had nearly made it to safety when he, too, was shot, in the foot. Corporal Gaines and Private First Class Hutchinson, the two Marines who had arrived late and had dug in near the erosion ridge, managed to pull both Haney and French to safety.

Farther northwest, near the saddle, the four Marines manning the light machinegun unit were using the two tall rocks as an improvised fort. Crouching behind the forward rock were Bob Ezell and Private

251

First Class Ray Valek. They had been joined by two other privates first class: Charles Parker and David Goodrich of the Second Platoon. A sniper on the rocky knoll — Ezell was certain it was the same bastard who had gotten Haney — just missed Goodrich's head. The slug struck the rock an inch from his ear, and the impact of the rock fragments knocked Goodrich into the open. Valek, lunging to pull him back in, was grazed in the head just below the helmet.

Gushing blood, Valek took off for the aid station, trying to keep the two rocks between him and the rocky knoll until he reached the tree line. Goodrich, meanwhile, was semiconscious and had a nasty-looking gouge in his neck from the ricochet. While Ezell treated the wound with sulfa powder and bandaged it, Parker leaned out from behind the forward rock. "I'm gonna find that son of a bitch," he said.

Earlier, in Hagaru-ri, Lieutenant Peterson had tried to confine Parker to sick bay with a bad case of the flu, but Parker refused. He truly believed Fox Company was going to be home by Christmas and was terrified of being stranded in a military hospital in Japan while his buddies left. Now, as he scrutinized the rocky knoll for the sniper who'd nailed Goodrich and Valek, he suddenly grunted. Bob Ezell turned and Parker fell into his lap, a hole in his stomach. Ezell hollered for a corpsman. Two arrived, with a stretcher. The medic examining Parker told Ezell he wouldn't need it. Parker was dead.

Ezell and the three medics carried Goodrich down the hill, intending to come back for Parker's body. Outside the med tents Ezell ran into a friend, Sergeant Clarence Tallbull, a Blackfoot Indian who served as the company's unofficial barber. Tallbull hated the North Koreans, and his buddies surmised that this was because he looked just like one. He was small and wiry and had Asian facial features; whenever he walked near a POW enclosure, the prisoners would rush to the wire to talk to him. That pissed Tallbull off. Now he had a thick, bloody bandage wrapped around his neck and shoulders.

"What happened, Chief?"

"Hit in the back of the neck. Take a look, willya, tell me how bad it is?"

Ezell bent over Tallbull and removed the dressing. He gently skinned off a glob of frozen blood the size of a small snowball. He could see the Indian's exposed shoulder bone. A day or two earlier he would have been horrified. Hell, a couple of hours ago he had been afraid to mess with Kenny Benson's crusted eyes. Not now.

"Aw, that's OK," Ezell said. "You're gonna be fine."

Tallbull smiled and gave him a thumbs-up.

When Ezell returned to the two tall rocks, Private First Class Jerry Triggs was waiting for him. Triggs, who was only seventeen, was another ammo carrier with the First Platoon's light machine-gun unit. Several paces to the east, Corporal Alvin Dytkiewicz and Private First Class William Gleason had taken over the gun and emplaced it in the same broad notch that Corporal Ladner had previously occupied, between the Second and Third Platoons. Ezell told Triggs that on his way back up he had passed close enough to the company command post to hear Captain Barber chewing out Mr. Chung, the Korean interpreter. Barber was incensed because Mr. Chung couldn't speak Chinese.

"Guess all those smart guys back at Division really didn't have any idea they were crossing the Yalu," Ezell said.

"Home for Christmas, my ass," Triggs said.

Unknown to Ezell, the interpreter had nonetheless found out, through a combination of sign language and linguistically related Korean and Chinese words, that the prisoners were from a regiment of the Fifty-ninth CCF Division, and that several of them had fought against Mao in Chiang Kai-shek's Nationalist Army before being conscripted by the Chinese Communists.

Barber had stood over the prisoners listening to the interpreter's report and noted that their uniforms reeked of garlic. To Barber they were a pathetic bunch, rocking on their haunches with their backs to the wind, shivering, frostbitten. Even the few tough, battle-hardened fighters were tiny and looked beaten, and their skin seemed to have been cured by the wind, like beef jerky. He wondered what the hell was happening up at the Chosin Reservoir.

The unflappable Lieutenant Colonel Randolph Lockwood was in his usual good mood when, at 9:45 a.m., his composite "cooks and bakers" company started up the MSR from Hagaru-ri. In the van were three tanks from Company D's First Tank Battalion; several hundred Marines followed on foot. Lockwood wore a 35-mm camera attached to a strap around his neck.

The relief detail had reached the top of the first rise, barely a mile beyond the northern perimeter of Hagaru-ri, when Lockwood saw a burning Sherman tank lying on its side ahead. The disabled tank was in a small vale where the road dipped before again rising toward the pass through a series of steep gorges. These gateway hills were studded with a string of abandoned gold mines.

Lockwood halted the column and swept the heights with binoculars. He was encircled. On hilltops in every direction he saw rows of enemy soldiers. No sooner had he moved his men off the road than they began taking rifle and mortar fire. He ordered several flanking maneuvers, but the Chinese mirrored his movements. It would be impossible to get around them.

Soon, more Chinese riflemen poured out of the gold mines. A squadron of Corsairs passed overhead, but Lockwood didn't carry a radio with the frequency to contact them. He may have had tanks, but without mortars and heavy machine guns this was suicide.

He lit his pipe and told his radioman to contact Litzenberg.

Warren McClure gave up on the idea of retrieving his BAR from the "deep dip." There were too many snipers. He had just learned of Roger Gonzales's death from

Bob Kirchner. He couldn't believe the new boot had been killed in the short time he'd been gone. Christ, he barely knew the kid, but nevertheless this death hit him hard. A foxhole buddy was, after all, a foxhole buddy. However, before he had time to think, much less grieve, his squad leader, Sergeant Reitz, again asked him to establish a forward listening post, this time by himself.

McClure surveyed the entire west slope of the hill before deciding on a small, rocky outcropping farther up the grade that jutted out, nearly hanging, over the ravine that ran up the west valley. Finding some sparse scrub for cover, he shoved the vegetation into his BAR belt, crawled out onto the ledge, and settled into a prone position behind a little rock knob that reminded him of a wart on a witch's nose. He knew that an enemy sniper would find his scrub camouflage laughable and prayed that his filthy uniform blended into the granite.

Marines behind him passed him a carbine and an M1. He was about 150 yards distant from the top of the West Hill, and at eye level with it. He was also 250 or so yards away from, and well below, the snipers on the rocky knoll. At 10:15 a.m. he heard the drone of the planes.

McClure looked up to see eight Australian Mustangs barreling down toward the west valley. He hollered for the Second Platoon's multicolored air panels. They were passed out to his little ledge, and he laid them out in the snow about ten yards to his right, pointing them toward the rocky knoll. Sniper slugs ricocheted off the rocks around the panels as he dived back behind the witch's wart.

The Royal Australian Air Force was based at the snow-covered airstrip in Yonpo, just north of Wonsan, and was famous for its officers' club, which sold beer and whiskey. Everybody said that those Aussies knew how to fight a war. For days the pilots had been peering down from their cramped cockpits while supporting the retreating Eighth Army in the west. Now they were watching the same thing happening to the U.S. Marines in the east.

In a moment the planes were directly in front of McClure over the west valley, flying so low that their propellers could have chopped kindling. He was at eye level with the pilots, and he gave one a thumbs-up. One Aussie, who had a full blond mustache, returned the signal. Half a dozen Chinese stood up on the rocky knoll and actually shot *down* at the incoming aircraft with automatic weapons. They did no damage. The P-51s plastered the rocky knoll with bombs, rockets, and 20-mm cannon rounds.

One Mustang loosed a napalm canister from its cradle near the top of the east side of the knoll, but it failed to ignite. McClure watched the twenty-two remaining Marines of the Third Platoon near the hilltop stand in their holes and fire like madmen. He knew they were aiming for the napalm. Another Mustang pounded the hill with more cannon fire and simultaneously dropped a second napalm cylinder. The two exploded at the same time, sucking the oxygen out of the air and turning the knoll into a vaporizing orange inferno. Flaming quilted uniforms toppled from it like melting candle wax. Ezell's light machine-gun crew up at the two tall rocks felt the hot wind wash over them as they burrowed into the snow.

It was over in a minute. Before heading home, for good measure, the Mustangs strafed a roadblock the Chinese had set up between the West Hill and Yudam-ni. Then the Aussies pulled up, backtracked over Fox Hill, and waggled their wings. A cheer rose to meet them. Bob Ezell felt so good about life that he broke out crackers, frozen jelly, and a roll of Charms hard candies from his

C-rats and handed the snacks around. His companions took the crackers and jelly but passed up the Charms. Marines considered (and still consider) eating Charms bad luck.

McClure's smile evaporated. He could still hear the fading whine of the P-51 propellers when he saw five Chinese soldiers rise from a fold in the West Hill directly across the valley. They jogged down the slope, performed a left oblique as if they were walking parade-ground duty, and raced toward the ravine. McClure lifted his carbine, aimed for the head, and took two of them out. The others disappeared into the deep gash in the valley.

Now four more Chinese jumped up and followed their exact trail. McClure sighted his carbine but it jammed. He lifted his M1, sighted, and picked off another Chinese. He squeezed again but then the M1 also jammed. *Goddamn rifles frozen at ten-thirty in the morning.*

He yelled for another weapon and a second carbine was passed out to him. By then, however, the second group of Chinese had been swallowed up by the ravine. Just as they disappeared, a lone enemy rifleman bolted out of the mouth of the ravine and began tearing back toward the West Hill. McClure fired and missed. The man ducked behind a tree at the base of the hill. Mc-Clure could see his left arm and part of his ass sticking out from behind the scrawny sapling. He knelt, lifted the carbine to his shoulder — and felt a god-awful burning sensation in his back and under his right shoulder blade. He flopped like a fish and turned faceup.

McClure stared back at his own men, one of whom must have shot him in the back. *Jesus!* He was furious, searching the tree line for the asshole. Then he looked down and noticed a dark crimson circle about the size of a half-dollar on his fatigue jacket, just over his sternum. A through-and-through wound. He guessed the sniper had used an armor-piercing 7.62 round. He shook off his right glove and covered the puncture. With his bare palm he could feel the air rushing into and out of his chest with each breath.

Sergeant Harold Bean crawled out on the ledge. As he reached McClure he, too, keeled over, shot in the side. Oblivious of the sniper, the corpsman William McLean rushed onto the outcropping. McClure had raised himself to a half-sitting position, with his back to the small rock. Sergeant Bean was moaning on the ground next to him. Words came out of McClure's mouth in a gurgle: "Take care of Bean first." He didn't recognize his own voice.

The corpsman slipped a morphine syrette into McClure's jacket pocket and turned to bend over the sergeant. Then a strange thing happened.

McClure found himself looking down at himself. He was hovering perhaps ten feet over the outcropping. His gaze moved from his own inert body, to McLean working on Bean, to the Chinese moving in and out of the folds of the West Hill. He turned in the air, floating, and saw Lieutenant Elmo Peterson and Lieutenant Clark Wright several yards back in the tree line, ducking behind a large flat rock. Peterson was yelling something to the corpsman — McClure couldn't make out what. Wright, the company XO, was not saying anything. That suited McClure just fine. This was the same officer who had given his platoon a "blood and guts" speech, in the manner of General Patton, on the USS *Bradley* before the landing at Inchon. But now he wasn't making one move to assist the ballsy corpsman.

Just as suddenly as he had floated above this scene, McClure was back in his pain-racked body. At home in the Ozarks he'd wounded many a deer, and he now realized he had to move, immediately, before his

262

body stiffened up. He sat up and asked the corpsman for directions to the aid station. McLean turned from Sergeant Bean and pointed to the bottom of the hill. McClure noticed that he was warming a morphine syrette in his mouth.

McClure struggled to his feet and lunged back into the trees. Neither Peterson nor Wright made a move to help him. He would have spat at their feet as he passed them, if he had had any spit.

By 11:30 a.m., Lieutenant Colonel Lockwood's column was still pinned down near the old gold mines, barely more than a mile up the MSR from Hagaru-ri. Lockwood radioed to Colonel Alpha Bowser, the commander of the Marine contingent in the village, and requested reinforcements for his reinforcement company. Bowser directed the First Marine Division's Able Company, Third Battalion — the last of the last of the rear guard — to get ready. Before the company could go beyond the perimeter, however, the orders were canceled. Lockwood had managed to deliver a situation report to Colonel Litzenberg in Yudam-ni, and Litzenberg counterordered Lockwood's "cooks and bakers" unit to return to Hagaru-ri.

"We'll pick up Fox on our way south," Litzenberg had told Bowser before signing off. At least Litzenberg knew what was coming.

At about the same time, eight miles east across the reservoir, General Edward Almond, commander in chief of X Corps, choppered into the perimeter held by the army's battered task force. The elements from his Fifth and Seventh regiments as well as their supporting artillery units, close to three thousand soldiers in all, had taken nearly 35 percent casualties. When it was explained to Almond that parts of at least two Chinese divisions had hit them the previous night, and that even more Reds were swarming toward the Marines at Yudam-ni, Turkey Hill, and Fox Hill, Almond was skeptical.

"That's impossible," he said. "There aren't two Chinese divisions in the whole of North Korea. The enemy delaying you is nothing more than remnants fleeing north. We're still attacking, and we're going all the way to the Yalu. Don't let a bunch of goddamn Chinese laundrymen stop you."

Remnants fleeing north. Chinese laundrymen. Almond's battle commanders could only shake their heads at his dreadnaught pretensions.

As Almond's helicopter flew him south again, however, General MacArthur, seven hundred miles away in Tokyo, had been forced to officially swallow his premature declaration of victory. His situation report to the United Nations made that clear. "Enemy reactions developed in the course of our assault operations of the past four days disclose that a major segment of the Chinese continental forces in Army, Corps, and Divisional organization of an aggregate strength of 200,000 men is now arrayed against the United Nations forces in North Korea," he wrote. "Consequently, we face an entirely new war."

4

Warren McClure was lost and in pain when he nearly tripped over a wounded Chinese soldier. The man was half buried in the snow, and there were bullet holes all across his bare stomach. He seemed to be an officer. Now, he groped with his left arm and hand as if searching for a weapon. McClure could see none.

He half-circled the man, giving him a wide berth, and their eyes met. Something unsaid passed between them, a silent commiseration, an acknowledgment of the misfortunes of war. If he had had a weapon, McClure would have put the dying soldier out of his misery. But he didn't, and he left without looking back.

McClure stumbled through the trees before eventually finding the old command post tent at the bottom of the gully. He ripped back the flap, and the first person he saw was Lieutenant Joe Brady, the CO of the mortar section. Brady was the son of Irish immigrants and still carried the whiff of peat bog about him. He was sitting on an empty crate — he could not lie down because of grenade fragments in his back — and his left hand was bandaged. With his good right hand he reached into his field jacket and produced a fifth of White Horse scotch whisky. "Here," Brady said, "you look like you need a swig."

McClure took the bottle and swallowed a large portion. He teetered toward the back of the tent and found an open space on the floor. He collapsed onto his back and passed out.

It was just past noon, and Gray Davis was fed up with two particularly annoying snipers on the ridgeline of the West Hill. What bothered him most, he supposed, was how good they were. He and Luke Johnson had been ducking and diving all morning. Davis had always heard that the Belgians made the best damn guns in the world, even better than the Czechs, and he was itching to find out.

He loaded a full magazine into the automatic rifle he had recovered from the valley, took a deep breath, and stood up in his foxhole. He raked the ridgeline with the full clip. As he flopped back down beneath the lip of his hole, a light machine gunner farther up the west slope hollered down to offer his compliments. Davis had knocked one of the snipers off the crest.

At 1 p.m., Captain Barber ordered the corpsmen who were using the old mortarmen's tents at the bottom of the hill as an aid station to relocate. He had no doubt that there would be another attack after nightfall, and the wounded would be safer farther east, up and over the main central ridgeline. This would also put them out of harm's way with regard to the snipers on the West Hill and the rocky knoll.

A squad of Marines broke out the two eighteen-by-sixteen med tents that had never been erected and set them up in the trees behind the First Platoon's defensive line on the east slope. Fifteen minutes later corpsmen began carrying the most seriously wounded over the ridge on stretchers. The others limped and hobbled behind them. The tents were soon filled, and holes were dug in the snow beside them to accommodate the overflow. The more seriously wounded remained inside. The less seriously injured, swathed in sleeping bags, were rotated between the tents and the dugouts so that they would not freeze to death.

As the mortarmen's tent was being taken down, Warren McClure came to. He stared up at a gunmetal gray sky. He wondered for a moment where he was. Then he felt the stabbing pain in his chest. He and one other Marine — a man who seemed to be dying, although McClure could not see his injury — were the only two of the wounded who had not been evacuated to the new med tents. McClure listened as the other man asked to be left at the bottom of the hill with a sidearm.

A squad of Marines assisting the corpsmen, including the bazooka man Harry Burke, huddled to ponder this request. Then they wordlessly propped the man up against a tree facing the road. One of them handed him a forty-five-caliber pistol. The rest turned and lifted McClure. Then they put him back down, hard, at the sound of a plane.

■ ■ ■ ■

At 3 p.m., a Marine R4FD cargo plane, number 785, piloted by First Lieutenant Bobby Carter, swooped low over Fox Hill and waggled its wings. Around this time, Captain Barber decided to tell his XO, Clark Wright, that an hour earlier he'd heard from Litzenberg regarding Lieutenant Colonel Lockwood's reinforcement company. That company would not be coming. Under covering fire from their own reinforcements from the Third Battalion, First Marines, Lockwood had extracted his cooks and bakers and limped back to Hagaru-ri.

"We're on our own," Barber said, gazing up at the cargo plane. "Form up a recovery detail and let's see what they sent us."

On his dry run, Bobby Carter flew in over the rocky knoll, down the west valley, and banked left in front of the South Hill across the road. Now he was soaring directly over Fox Hill, following its main ridgeline, throttling back to eighty-five miles per hour perhaps three hundred feet above the treetops. The cargo doors on the left side of the aircraft slid open and bundles fell from them. The parachutes barely had time to open before the pallets smashed to the ground in the east valley about seventy-five yards in front of the First Platoon's perimeter.

Smith, the supply sergeant, was the first to reach them. Contrails from the plane disappeared in the southeast sky as he knelt over the parachutes, slashing at the tangled ropes. A bullet hit his right leg and he heard his tibia snap. Smith fell into a ditch.

The communications officer, Lieutenant Schmitt, grabbed a stretcher. A fire team from the First Platoon laid down covering fire and three more Marines joined Schmitt as he hustled out to the wounded man. Schmitt was rolling Smith onto the litter when the same sniper hit him in virtually the same place, shattering his shinbone. The three uninjured Marines were joined by two corpsmen. Together, dodging sniper fire, they dragged Smith and Schmitt back to the tree line. When they got to the med tent, Lieutenant Brady offered Smith and Schmitt slugs of White Horse scotch whiskey. They threw them back as corpsmen broke and shaved pine tree branches to form into splints.

The First Platoon's commanding officer, Lieutenant John Dunne, dispatched a four-man detail to smoke out the sniper. They found him easily, and as they buried him in a barrage of automatic weapons fire, a recovery team jumped from the tree line and began hauling the supplies back to the perimeter.

Boxes and bandoliers of thirty-caliber ammo, hand grenades, and 60-mm and 81-mm mortar rounds were handed out across the hill. Lieutenant McCarthy of the Third Platoon confiscated the several rolls of barbed wire to stretch across the mouth of the saddle, and ordered trip-wire grenades strung across the crest. The silk parachutes were cut into strips to be used as blankets for the wounded. Several hungry men noted that there were no C-rations in the air drop.

After the ammunition had been dragged in from the valley, eight unarmed Chinese soldiers jumped from the culvert where the MSR met the dry creek bed. Bob Ezell had been wrong; the Chinese were even smaller — or more supple — than he'd guessed. They took off in the direction of the woods that encircled the bottom of the South Hill like an apron. A burst from one of the First Platoon's light machine guns halted them. They fell to their knees, raised their hands above their heads, and were frog-marched back into the perimeter.

Forty minutes later the Americans were astonished to see a small helicopter approach the hill. Weeks earlier, as the Korean winter began, the Marine chopper fleet had been grounded when the oil in the gearboxes that controlled the rotors had frozen up. Since then the gearboxes had been drained and the standard lubricant had been replaced by thinner oil. Nonetheless it remained a dangerous adventure to take these little craft up into the windswept mountains. Apparently this particular chopper pilot, Captain George Farish, had been willing to take the risk.

Farish's little two-seater darted in like a mosquito over the east valley. When it reached treetop level over the First Platoon's position it hovered to drop fresh batteries for the SCR-300 radio and field phones. For an instant Farish appeared to be looking for a place to land. Several wounded men, including Warren McClure and Walt Hiskett, began to think of a medevac.

Their hope died when the helicopter took a sniper's bullet in its rotor transmission case and began leaking oil. Master Sergeant Charles Dana considered forcing the pilot down at gunpoint. Barber stopped him: "Do that and none will ever come back."

It was an academic point — Farish's

machine was mortally wounded. As he struggled to control his little chopper, he clipped several treetops with his rotor blades. Finally he gave a halfhearted salute and coaxed the damaged chopper toward the temporary airstrip at Hagaru-ri. (The Marines at Fox Hill would learn later that the chopper never made it; the transmission locked up and Farish crash-landed at the edge of the village. He walked away from the wreck unhurt.)

5

With sunset approaching a sense of grim urgency settled over Fox Hill. The temperature dropped to the minus twenties; the less seriously wounded drifted, unbidden, from the med tents back to their foxholes; and Marines across the hill prepared for what many suspected might be their last night alive.

Corporal Hiskett was heartsick. He had seen the corpsmen carry Private First Class Parker's body down from the two tall rocks. First Johnny Farley, he thought, and now Charlie Parker — his two best friends. He realized that no one was getting off the hill this day, and he resolved that his shoulder wound would still allow him to toss grenades. He stumbled from the med tent back to the Second Platoon lines. But the corpsman McLean saw him and talked him into returning to the aid station. It was not hard to persuade him. Hiskett was barely conscious.

Except for the Marines who had moved up from the road and the remnants of the badly hit Third Rifle Platoon — about twenty Marines in all who now fortified a new, smaller defensive line thirty yards below the crest of the hill — Fox Company's perimeter remained similar to the horseshoe shape it had taken the previous night. However, it now had gaps.

Lieutenant Peterson, ignoring his own shoulder wound, paced up and down behind the Second Platoon lines on the west slope with a grim message: "If we should be overrun tonight, don't — I repeat, don't — leave your foxholes." He knew that How Company's howitzer men had been given orders to shell the entire hill if Fox Company was overrun. "We're going to take some Chinese with us if we go," he told his men.

Individual men prepared for battle in their own ways. Up on the Third Platoon's front line, Ernest Gonzalez was hungry. While there was still light he snaked down through the trees, back to the position his fire team had originally occupied before being ordered to the hilltop. He found several of his squad's sleeping bags pierced with bullet holes. He also dug up two boxes of C-rations and popped a couple of frozen gumdrops into his mouth. Then nature called.

Gonzalez walked over to a stand of trees. The blowing snow had built up against their trunks, forming a small, three-sided embankment. One joke in the company was how you could get only half an inch of peter out of three inches of clothing in order to take a leak. But defecating was an entirely different story. The trick, everyone knew, was to move your bowels before your balls turned blue and broke off.

He squatted, encased in his tentlike parka, and dropped his dungarees, wool pants, long johns, and shorts. He did his business, cleaned up, and was buttoning up when a sniper's bullet snapped a pine branch over his head. Gonzalez's feet went out from under him and he plopped down on top of his deposit. He scrambled deeper into the trees, wondering how he would clean himself. But there was no need. His crap had frozen between the time he'd dropped it and the time it had taken to get his layers of pants on again. It hadn't even dented when he'd sat on it.

Gonzalez removed his helmet, found a

stick, and lifted the steel pot out from behind a tree — just like what he'd seen in war movies. Nothing happened. He swung the helmet to the other side of the tree. Still no sniper. Feeling safe, he skittered back toward the road. He snatched several enemy rifles and clips of ammo from the stack that had been piled up earlier and began scrounging among the dead Chinese in the shadow of the small hut. He discovered a camera with two rolls of film, and a Chinese backpack.

He was about to rip open the backpack when his eyes were drawn to a strangely discolored spot in the snow. It wasn't bright red with new blood; nor was it dirt. He kicked at it and then bent down to probe with his hand. *Jesus!* He jumped backward, realizing that it was a corpse, burned black by napalm. The Chinese must have held this hill before being burned out by the flyboys. *So that's who had dug the foxholes and trenches.*

Backing away, he turned and dragged his booty up the hill to share with his new foxhole buddy, Freddy Gonzales from San Pedro. *What would our aunts say if they could see us now?*

The two Marines went to work situating their six rifles, clips of ammo, and hand grenades within easy reach around the lip of the hole. Their gun pit fortified, they tore into the C-rations, but the food was frozen solid. They might as well have tried to eat concrete. The best they could manage was to melt the top quarter-inch layer of beef hash and beans over a small fire, drag their bayonets over that top layer, and scrape the tepid shavings into their mouths.

Next they rummaged through the captured backpack. It contained a small bowl of frozen rice, a pair of steel-spiked boots too small to fit either of them, a tin of special rifle oil — *whale oil?* — for use in subfreezing temperatures, and a foldout brochure with photographs of people they assumed were Chinese dignitaries. The only face they recognized was Mao's.

At the bottom of the backpack was a crinkled photograph of its owner. He was posing in front of a pagoda in what looked like a big city with his wife and two children. They were all wearing Western clothes and smiling. Ernest and Freddy glanced from the photo to each other. Neither said a word.

Up at the two tall rocks the First Platoon's resituated light machine gun emplacement was down to four men. Corporal Dytkiewicz and Private First Class Gleason, who manned the gun, knew by now what had happened to Corporal Ladner's team the last time the Chinese had attacked. They expected no subtlety from their opponents. The Chinese would charge down the saddle, straight on and straight up, until they died.

The only cover for the machine-gun nest was some thin brush, and Dytkiewicz and Gleason shot envious glances at Ezell and Triggs frantically chipping out a hole behind the larger, more forward rock a few yards away. As the sky glazed purple in the west, almost to the color of a mussel shell, more "dead" enemy soldiers jumped up from snow holes and dashed across the saddle. The four Marines snapped off shots at these blurry figures while sniper bullets from the rocky knoll and the rocky ridges ticked through the branches around them.

"We either get 'em now or get 'em when they come later," Ezell yelled to Dytkiewicz. The corporal replied with a long burst that raked the ridgelines of Toktong-san.

At 6:05 p.m., Ezell flinched at a crunching of snow behind him — but he lowered his weapon when he recognized a Marine uniform. "Here," the Marine said, handing over eight hand grenades to be divided among the four-man crew. "It's all we can spare."

He had taken only a few steps back down the hill when he stopped and turned. "Listen," he said, "when you pull the pin, don't forget to pull the spoons up, too. They're probably frozen to the skin of the grenades."

At 6:30, a light snow began to fall. Ezell, Triggs, Dytkiewicz, and Gleason settled into what was technically a fifty-fifty watch. Although they were all exhausted, no one really slept.

Sometime around 7 p.m., Warren McClure woke from a deep sleep. He saw that he was still lying in the northeast corner of a sixteen-by-eighteen tent, but something had changed. He was at such an angle that he felt he was about to slide down on top of the man below him. Then he remembered that the aid station had been moved and he was no longer on flat ground.

He looked around, wondering who had carried him here. Every square foot of the canvas tent floor was covered with wounded men. Most were suffering in silence, but many were in agonized positions. It was warm in the tent, the warmest McClure had felt in a long time, and he noticed pine branches burning in a portable kerosene stove near the tent's downhill flap.

Despite the heat McClure was in excruciating pain. Moving slowly, so as not to intensify what felt like the red-hot poker gouging into his chest, he began searching his pants and dungaree field jacket for his first-aid kit. In his right breast jacket pocket his fingers felt the morphine syrette that the corpsman McLean had left with him on the outcropping. He tore open the paper packaging and injected the tiny needle into his left wrist.

Someone — he couldn't tell who — pulled back the tent flap and announced that, according to scuttlebutt, a company of cooks and bakers was heading up the road from Hagaru-ri to relieve them. A smile creased McClure's face. *Imagine what they'll say back at battalion. A line company of Marine riflemen rescued by the kitchen staff?* Suddenly the pain was deadened and McClure nodded off into dreamless oblivion.

Dick Bonelli was certain this was a gag. He hadn't fired a machine gun since Pendleton and wasn't shy about letting Lieutenant McCarthy know it. The platoon commander had handed Sergeant Keirn's old light machine gun to one of the West Coast Marines, an Apache everyone called "Big

Indian." Then McCarthy had tapped Bonelli as his assistant gunner. Bonelli thought that being assigned a dead man's gun was a bad enough omen. But then the lieutenant had ordered them to set up their nest out in front of the Third Platoon's forward line at the top of the hill. *Like two sitting ducks.*

They had barely dug in when it began snowing hard. As the flakes built up on the gun barrel, the Big Indian started shaking. At first Bonelli thought it was from the cold. Then he realized something was not right, and he wondered if it had to do with the fact that the Big Indian had been the only member of Wayne Pickett's fire team to avoid capture during the first attack. He was pondering just how, in fact, this had occurred when the Apache bolted from the hole with nary a word. Not a good sign.

Bonelli kept an eye out for his return as he sorted through the machine gun belts. Half of them, each holding a hundred or so bullets, had "crimped," or bent beyond repair, in their ammo boxes. He stacked these defectives toward the back of the foxhole while laying all the good belts, maybe half a dozen, within easy reach.

When he finished this housekeeping there was still no sign of his gunner, so he left the hole himself and made his way back to

McCarthy's bunker command post. He found McCarthy and the Big Indian huddled around a single candle. The Apache had one lit cigarette in his mouth and another burning in his hand.

"What the hell's happening, Lieutenant?"

Bonelli was not one of Lieutenant McCarthy's favorite Marines. More than once McCarthy had to warn the wise-ass New Yorker to shape up or he'd be so deep in the brig they would have to shoot peas at him for chow. Now he just looked at Bonelli, exasperated.

"He can't make it," McCarthy said.

"Hell you mean he can't make it?"

McCarthy looked at Bonelli like he was three-quarters stupid. "I mean, he can't make it."

"Jesus Christ. The party's gonna start. Who's on the gun?"

"You got the gun," McCarthy said. "Get yourself an assistant. And when they come I'd better find you firing that gun or dead over it."

Bonelli took a last, disgusted look at the Big Indian, who would not return his gaze, and backed out of the dugout, fuming. The first foxhole he stumbled across was occupied by Private First Class Homer Penn of the Third Platoon — Penn from Pennsylvania, as everybody called him. Bonelli rapped him on the helmet. "You're coming with me," he said.

Penn from Pennsylvania cursed Bonelli during the entire trek up the hill. When they reached the machine-gun nest Penn eased himself into the foxhole as if there might be snakes inside.

At precisely 10 p.m., a loud series of beeps and electric feedback emanated from a loudspeaker set up under the lip of the west valley's deep ravine where it joined the saddle. A Chinese voice, speaking in perfectly enunciated English, explained that the Americans were surrounded and outnumbered, and their only rational course was to surrender. The man spoke patronizingly, as if he were addressing a classroom of particularly dull children.

A few Marines on the west slope caught an occasional glimpse of the Red behind the voice. He was tall and wore a full-length quilted coat with what appeared to be an officer's insignia on his shoulders and cap. They were maddening, these glimpses — too fleeting and coming from all about the shadowed ravine. It was as if the Chinese was aware of the Americans' desire to kill him and enjoyed playing this game of cat and mouse. He was too far away to reach with a grenade, and orders had been passed earlier among all Marines to save their little ammunition for a clear shot.

The enemy officer repeated his demand several times, and then the loudspeaker played Bing Crosby singing "White Christmas." When that ended, another song was played. It too was in English, but with a heavy accent. The chorus seemed to be, "Marines, tonight you die." When the music ended a huge bonfire erupted at the lee side of the rocky knoll, throwing into relief scores of moving, white-clad figures.

At 11 p.m., How Battery fired a white phosphorous shell from Hagaru-ri to register distance on the West Hill. The shell fell far short, and Gray Davis and Luke Johnson nearly jumped from their foxhole "all the way to Japan" when the round landed no more than ten yards in front of them. Unlike a howitzer shell, "Willie Peter" made no rustling whistle as it flew through the sky. The expanding shower of glowing, acrid-smelling, talclike orange particles filled the air around their hole. Both men were hit with chunks of the smoldering debris. Davis picked one up and studied it by the moonlight. The stuff was supposed to keep burning through anything it touched. *Too damn cold to burn,* he thought. *Good thing.*

Thirty minutes later, their range corrected, How Company began an intermittent howitzer bombardment of the West Hill, the rocky knoll, and the rocky ridge. Fox Company's 81-mm mortar unit joined in, concentrating its fire on the rocky knoll and what the Marines were now calling the "sniper ridges" of Toktong-san.

It was almost midnight, and the four men manning the First Platoon's light machine-gun emplacement by the two tall rocks could clearly see many Chinese moving into and out of the light of the glowing bonfire. To Bob Ezell they looked like Indians performing a slow-motion war dance.

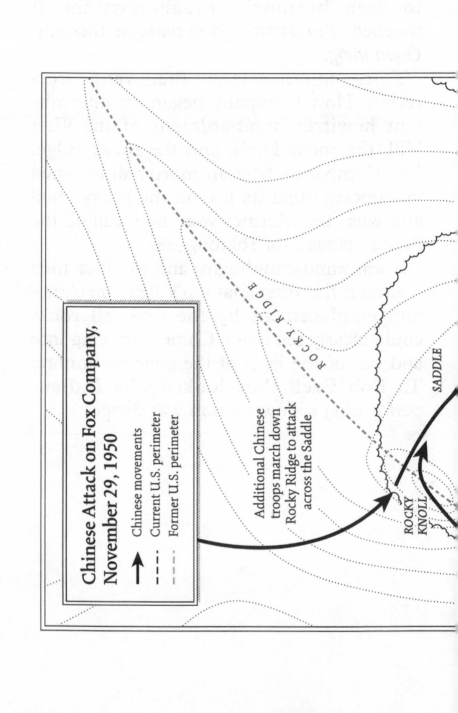

Chinese Attack on Fox Company, November 29, 1950

↑ Chinese movements
--- Current U.S. perimeter
--- Former U.S. perimeter

Additional Chinese troops march down Rocky Ridge to attack across the Saddle

ROCKY RIDGE

SADDLE

ROCKY KNOLL

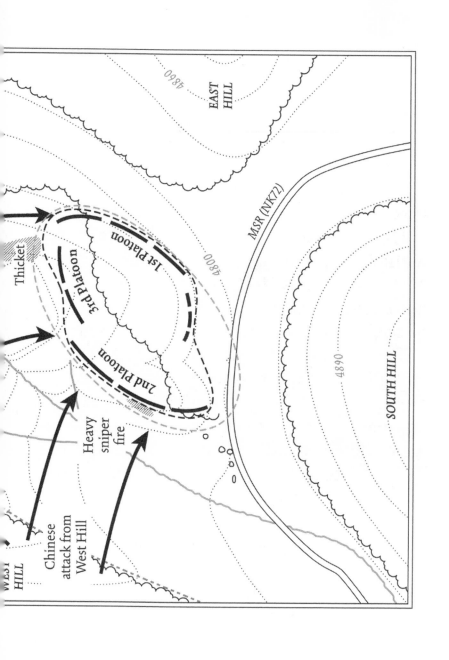

WEST HILL

Chinese attack from West Hill

Heavy sniper fire

Thicket

3rd Platoon

2nd Platoon

1st Platoon

MSR (NK72)

4800

4890

SOUTH HILL

EAST HILL

4860

DAY THREE

6

Fox Company was hit by friendly fire at 2:15 a.m. when two artillery shells fell within the perimeter almost simultaneously. No one could tell whether they were launched from the howitzers at Hagaru-ri or the company's own 81-mm mortars.

The first exploded in one of the wide gaps along the Second Platoon's lines on the west slope, knocking a corpsman, McLean, against a tree but otherwise causing no harm. The second landed nearly on top of a Third Platoon foxhole just below the hilltop, killing one Marine and wounding two others, including the squad leader — the former seminary student Corporal Ashdale. The company's forward air controller told Captain Barber that the below-zero temperature had probably compressed the gases in the shells' propelling charges. Nothing could have been done; it was just a cold-

288

weather accident.

As the friendly fire demonstrated, the weather was affecting more than just Barber's men. A few days before heading up to the pass the captain and his communications officer, Lieutenant Schmitt, had noticed that as the artillery recoil mechanisms in How Company's howitzers froze, the cannoneers were forced to push the tubes back into the batteries by hand. This prompted Barber to order Schmitt to set up a temporary firing range outside the village to test the company's weapons.

The M1 rifles had handled the subfreezing temperatures better than the carbines. The gases in the smaller cartridges of the carbines had compressed in the cold, and their clips had failed to feed ammunition into the chamber. Schmitt experimented with various options, including stretching the gun's operating slide spring to give more force to the forward motion of the bolt. The results were inconclusive. The BARs also proved balky as the temperature dropped lower. But both the heavy and the light machine guns test-fired adequately. Of course it was a hell of a lot colder up on Toktong Pass than it had been down at Hagaru-ri, as Jim Holt had discovered during last night's fighting when the water in the barrel jacket of his heavy machine gun froze solid.

Holt's gun crew had been forced to wait until sunrise, thaw the barrel, and substitute antifreeze. Corporal Jack Page did the same. The air-cooled light machine guns posed a different problem. The only way to prevent the carbon around the barrel tips from freezing up was to fire off a burst every hour or so. But cold, drowsy, lethargic men were likely to forget this task, and too often they were wary of giving away their emplacements. A couple of ingenious machine-gun crewmen hit on the idea of pissing on the barrels — if they were willing to expose themselves to enemy snipers.

The mortar crews also had difficulties. Their tubes' metal baseplates had to be relocated every few hours lest they freeze solid to the ground, and the baseplates were also beginning to show straining cracks from recoiling off the rock-hard hill. As for the grenade fuses, the men could only guess whether or not one would detonate after it was tossed.

The corpsmen were perhaps even more frustrated by the weather. Warming morphine syrettes in their mouths was the least of their problems. Plasma, frozen in its feeding tubes, was worthless, and their numb fingers fumbled to change dressings. Moreover, if a medic tried to cut off a man's clothing to get a closer look at his wounds, he was probably condemning the man to gangrene and a slow death by freezing. The corpsmen did, however, discover one unexpected boon — because of the low temperatures, bullet and shrapnel wounds were closing almost immediately, blood flow was congealing, and men were staying alive instead of bleeding to death before help could reach them.

There was one other advantage to fighting in such cold: the growing piles of corpses did not smell.

Five minutes after the friendly-fire incident, an enemy machine-gun crew wielding an ancient, Japanese-made Nambu opened up from the road, just to the east of the two huts. Marines saw the green tracers fly up the small gulley and into the rear of the reformed Third Platoon lines. Here was proof that enemy reinforcements had arrived: there had been no Chinese machine guns firing the previous night. As if to drive the point home two more machine guns immediately began raking the Third Platoon's forward positions from the rocky knoll and the rocky ridgeline leading to Toktong-san.

The Marines would soon learn that General Sung Shih-lun had ordered another Chinese battalion — five more companies — into the fight for Fox Hill.

Down near the MSR, Jack Page swung his barrel, aimed for the source of the tracers, and fired a burst from his heavy machine gun. Page and his crew had removed the red tracers from their own gun earlier in the day. Either he knocked out the Chinese gun or its crew cut and ran. In either case, there was no more machine-gun fire from the middle of the road. But now the Marines of the Second Platoon, up and down the west slope, reported that firing by rifles and automatic weapons from the West Hill was picking up, as if the company were being probed for weak spots. A wise-ass hollered something about Santa Ana and the Alamo. Nobody laughed. The wounded Lieutenant Elmo Peterson hobbled up and down behind the line, telling his men, "Hold fire 'til they come."

Up on the saddle, they were coming. The bursts from the machine guns on the knoll were followed by a rain of mortar shells — another new development. *When had they brought in mortar tubes?* Following the bombardment, the usual bugles, whistles, and cries of "Marine, you die!" echoed across the hill. To Bob Ezell, peering out from behind the two tall rocks, it looked as if the snow had come to life. In the moonlight, ghostly, white-clad soldiers, perhaps two hundred of them, were streaming across the land bridge. An illumination shell lit up the saddle, and the enemy's white quilted uniforms seemed to glisten. Ezell could hear one Chinese voice above all the others: "Son of a bitch Marine, we kill! Son of a bitch Marine, you die!"

Ezell watched, rapt, as O'Leary's 60-mm mortars tore up the point squads, breaking the Chinese ranks. But still they charged, even in disarray. The forward artillery observer Lieutenant Campbell called in a howitzer barrage from Hagaru-ri. As the boom of the heavy field pieces echoed off the rocky knoll and the rocky ridge, Ezell felt a sensation like an electric current pass through his body. The enemy machine guns quit. The infantry did not.

Clawing over the barbed-wire fence, they hit the Americans once more between the flanks of the Second and Third Platoons. Corporal Dytkiewicz's light machine-gun emplacement was the focus — he had failed to purge the tracers from his belts — and he was wounded immediately, his left shoulder torn up by submachine-gun fire. His hole mate, Private First Class Gleason, took the unconscious corporal on his back and made for the med tents. Up at the rocks Ezell and Jerry Triggs did not see Dytkiewicz and Gleason fall back, and soon they were virtually surrounded, much like Cafferata and Benson twenty-four hours earlier. They tossed their last four grenades, momentarily slowing the advance, and — their backs to one of the two tall rocks — shouldered their M1s.

Ezell emptied a clip on semiautomatic, but when he reloaded his rifle seized up — it would fire only one round at a time. The return lever was frozen and would catch on the next cartridge when he squeezed the trigger. With each shot he had to push the lever manually to force the round into the firing chamber. This was nearly impossible with frozen hands and bulky gloves.

Ezell and Triggs could only guess why Dytkiewicz's gun had gone silent. But the BARs and M1s of the forward firing teams of the Third Platoon, as well as Dick Bonelli's light machine gun, kept the Chinese off for a few seconds. The Chinese were so close that Ezell could hear them grunt and gag as they were hit. Lieutenant McCarthy's platoon, however, was stretched to the breaking point. It was only a matter of time.

Then something strange occurred. While Ezell and Triggs ducked to reload behind the forward rock, scores of Chinese rushed past on either side, paying no attention to them. For a moment there was an odd silence, broken only by the sound of canvas sneakers cracking the snow crust. Ezell heard rustling on the other side of the rock. He clicked his bayonet onto the barrel of his empty M1. Like all Marines, he had been instructed, during basic, in the classic Biddle bayonet offensive, but this technique was the last thing on his mind — he just wanted to stick someone. He leaped and lunged just as a hand grenade exploded between him and Triggs. Ezell was thrown through the air. He did not feel himself land.

For Ezell the next several moments were a kaleidoscopic chiaroscuro of moon, sky, snow, and stars, like a black-and-white movie broken only by the orange flashes flaming around him. He could not move, but he could see and hear the enemy swarm Triggs. There was much jabbering and whistle blowing and ragged *blats* of the bugles. There were grenade explosions, and now flares in the sky, and still the incessant blare of the damn bugles. He forced his eyes closed as a Chinese soldier, breathing hard, squatted down next to him, ripped off his gloves, and checked each wrist for a watch. A bugler — very close, Ezell thought — ceased blowing in the middle of a note. Ezell's mind drifted to the scene from *Gunga Din* in which Sam Jaffe is shot off the spire.

The Chinese moved on, leaving Ezell and Triggs for dead. Ezell tried to get to his feet. He could not.

7

The forward foxholes of the Third Platoon took the brunt of the attack.

From their two-man hole Ernest Gonzalez swept the hill to the left while Freddy Gonzales fired to the right. Ernest realized he did not need the waning moon to spot the advancing enemy — a nearly constant barrage of grenades and flares lit up the sky. He sighted in on a bugler standing up by the two tall rocks blowing a Chinese charge and shot him through the head.

At Pendleton, Ernest had turned out to be a crack shot, and from the first his M1 had felt like a natural extension of his body. The rifle rarely left his hands during his eleven-day passage from San Diego to Yokohama, Japan, despite the fact that he spent nearly the entire voyage in the head throwing up. Two things, he was certain, had saved him from dying on that troopship. The first was the expectation of firing this beautiful weapon in a real battle. The other was his daily readings from the Roman Catholic missal his mother had given him as a going-away gift. He could sure use the missal now, but the gun would have to do.

He was sighting in again when a potato masher exploded to his right. The concussion ripped his helmet and glasses off his head. He fell to his knees. Freddy turned. "Ernie, you all right?"

"I can't see."

Despite his wounds from the friendly fire, Corporal Ashdale manned the light machine gun in the center of the Third Platoon's line. He was overrun almost immediately and was nearly blinded by an exploding grenade. Still, he managed to wrestle with an enemy soldier who was trying to take the gun until another Chinese slammed the butt of a rifle into the back of his skull. Ashdale went out, and the two Chinese escaped with the machine gun.

One of Ashdale's assistant gunners staggered down the west slope toward the Second Platoon's right flank. He stumbled into a foxhole occupied by two privates first class: Don Childs and Norman Jackson, both firing at a frantic pace. They challenged him, and when he answered with the password they pulled him down into the hole. He was dazed, he was in his stocking feet, and his M1 had been shattered by a grenade. "Load," Childs said, and tossed him their spare rifles. Over the previous twenty-four hours they had each scrounged five Chinese Mausers.

All hell was breaking loose around Dick Bonelli and Homer Penn. Bonelli was just getting the hang of firing the light machine gun, and of sighting on the enemy's tracers, when an American voice from somewhere behind him shouted, "Let's go."

Penn made a move to stand. Bonelli clamped a hand on his shoulder. "Go? Go where, for Chrissake? No bus ride outta here."

Penn brushed Bonelli's hand away and bolted from the foxhole. He stumbled several feet and was shot in both shoulders. He fell, bleeding, into a hole occupied by Walt Klein and Private First Class Frank Valtierra. Together they picked him up and carried him down the hill.

Bonelli was still surrounded, and now alone.

Down at the command post Lieutenant

Campbell again radioed How Company's howitzer unit to ask them to "box" the crest of Fox Hill with incoming. There was a subsequent curtain of explosions. They fell so close to the Third Platoon's forward squads that any Marine still standing was blown off his feet by the concussive winds. They were too close for Dick Bonelli's liking. He dived for the bottom of his hole to wait out the bombardment.

At 2:30 a.m., while the battle raged on the heights, several Chinese platoons slipped down from the rocky ridge and made their way around the reverse slope of Fox Hill. They skirted the saddle and flanked the Marines around the bramble thicket on the northeast crest. Corporal Belmarez, on the First Platoon's line at the top of the eastern slope, never saw them coming. He was blown out of his foxhole, six feet straight into the air, by a concussion grenade.

Wounded in both legs, he crawled down the hill, leaving a bloody trail in the snow. When he couldn't go any farther he asked the Lord to save him.

Twenty yards below Belmarez, Private First Class Allen Thompson, a twenty-one-year-old reservist, swung his light machine gun toward the sound of the explosion. He aimed at the white figures darting down the hill and squeezed the trigger. The gun jammed; its head space where the firing pin connected was frozen solid. *Fuck.* Thompson was a rifleman by training who had been assigned to the machine gun after the First Platoon reached Fox Hill. He'd joked to his assistant gunner, Private First Class Roger Davis, that his entire knowledge of machine guns consisted of bullets going in one end and coming out the other. Still, he had test-fired the damn thing just two hours ago.

The Chinese came hard and fast. Thompson and Davis emptied their rifles and sidearms and dropped back to the cover of the trees. While Thompson reloaded, Davis was gutted by automatic weapons fire. *The last straw.* Thompson's emotions slipped their brake.

All alone, and impelled by God's own anger, he charged the nearest group of enemy soldiers, screaming at the top of his lungs, firing like a madman. He took out a squad. The Chinese were stunned. At the same time, Jack Page swung his heavy machine gun up the east slope and raked the charging enemy. At Page's burst more Marines from the First Platoon joined the fight. The Chinese fled in all directions.

Thompson fell to his knees in the snow, trembling and panting.

The surviving Chinese who had attacked down the east slope were now scattered on the hill, within the American lines. In his foxhole near the tree line the bazooka man Harry Burke heard pine boughs cracking to his right. He whirled and shot two men with his M1. In the next hole the cooks Phil Bavaro and John Bledsoe were about to charge up the hill when Bavaro saw movement down on the road. They each emptied a clip from their M1s. Up? Down? Which way to fight? "Best to stay here," Bavaro said.

It was a smart decision. Yet another platoon of Chinese had crept down from the South Hill three hundred yards across the road, had crossed the level ground, and were now forming up on the MSR. In the foxhole below Bavaro and Bledsoe, on the lower southeast corner of the hill, Corporal Robert Gaines jabbed Private First Class Rollin Hutchinson hard in the ribs with the butt of his M1: "See 'em?" Hutchinson nodded.

The two had laid out spare rifles, ammo, and grenades on the parapet of their hole. They had bayonets fixed. They watched in silence as a squad broke off from the platoon on the road and loped toward the larger hut.

Gaines and Hutchinson lit them up. One Chinese soldier with a Thompson submachine gun was particularly persistent. He darted from the hut to the trees and back again, spraying Gaines's and Hutchinson's position. Bullets flicked across the lip of their hole, knocking off the carefully stacked weapons. Gaines concentrated on following his muzzle flashes. From a corner of the hut the Thompson opened up again. Gaines stood and emptied a rifle clip at the flashes. The firing stopped.

Below them someone was crashing through the trees. They saw a crouching figure. "Don't shoot," a voice yelled in English. "I'm a Marine."

"What's the password?"

"Uh, uh . . . I don't know. Please. I'm a Marine. I swear to God."

Gaines looked at Hutchinson. They had both been brought up on World War II movies. Would the Hollywood technique come through? "Who won the World Series last month?" Gaines shouted.

"Yankees," the voice shot back instantly. "Four straight over the Phillies."

"Get your ass up here."

A platoon-size group of Chinese, perhaps forty men, were dispersed about the east slope. They crashed through the trees and penetrated deep into Fox's perimeter. Now they gathered in a small open vale just above the med tents, bunched up and milling around, chattering confusedly. Some of the wounded, including Warren McClure, heard the noises, the alien voices, and sat up and felt around for weapons. But there had been none to spare for the med tents, and the armed corpsmen were all out on the flanks.

Suddenly the flap of McClure's tent rose and he prepared for the worst. He wished he had his BAR. In crept Sergeant Robert Scully, the squad leader of the bazooka section, pressing a finger to his lips.

"They're all around us, right up the draw," Scully said in a hushed voice. "I don't know what to tell you, except to keep the fuck quiet." Scully hoisted his M1. "I'll be right outside," he said, and disappeared.

McClure looked around. Someone began saying the Lord's Prayer aloud, until someone else told him to keep quiet. After this not a whisper could be heard, although some men anxiously continued to mouth the words to prayers. Lieutenant Schmitt passed a whispered message: "If they stick their heads in here, stare them in the eye and show them you're Marines." McClure, still dopey from the morphine, decided that no matter what happened, he couldn't do a damned thing about it. He flopped back down to sleep.

In the adjacent tent, Corporal Walt Hiskett was fingering the rosary his mother had given him before her death. Hiskett was celebrated in the outfit for his huge, jutting, steely jaw, which had taken more than a few punches. He was a tough kid from a broken home, and he couldn't remember the last time he had prayed. In Chicago he had once had an elementary school teacher who made the entire class memorize the Twenty-third Psalm. And the janitor who had worked in his mother's apartment building gave a piece of candy to every kid who attended his weekly Bible studies. Hiskett liked the candy and recalled that the janitor had always closed the classes with the Lord's Prayer. Now he found it almost funny — almost — that the words of both the psalm and the prayer suddenly popped back into his head here in a med tent in North Korea.

Something suddenly became clear to Hiskett. He made a pledge: if he got off this hill alive he would serve God, forever, in any way he could. He closed his eyes and whispered softly, "The Lord is my shepherd; I shall not want. He maketh me to lie down in green pastures . . ."

Across the med tent, Hector Cafferata lay on a stretcher. Prayer was the last thing on his mind. He had never so much as taken an aspirin in his life, and the morphine coursing through his bloodstream was making him crazy. He thought he might actually go insane if he didn't get to use the Mauser machine pistol Kenny Benson had slipped past the corpsmen and given him — even if it did feel as if it weighed a hundred pounds when he tried to lift it.

He attempted to crawl, but despite the painkiller even the slightest movement left him in agony. He didn't know whether to laugh or cry. He had always been a strong kid, maybe the strongest in the outfit. Back in the States he had hated to fight because he just hated to hurt anyone. But not now.

Bullets and grenade fragments zipped through the canvas tent and ricocheted off the warming stoves. A corpsman dived through the flap and began wriggling, staying low to the ground. He told everyone to keep still and — Jesus Christ, of all things — to keep low.

"I'll be back," the corpsman said. "I'll try to bring some weapons."

Oh, you do that, Cafferata thought. Bring lots, and bring 'em fast. His animal instincts were aroused. He wanted to kill people.

■ ■ ■ ■

Privates first class Childs and Jackson, still occupying the hole on the west slope at the top of the Second Platoon's right flank, heard the enemy's chatter over their shoulders. They wheeled and saw thirty to forty Chinese soldiers behind them, between their position and the First Platoon, and pretty damn close to the med tents.

Jackson made a face. *What the hell they doing back there in the middle of the perimeter?* Childs could only shrug. Their loader, the Marine in his socks with the broken rifle, held two spare rifles at the ready. Without a word the two rose from their hole. Childs leveled his M1, Jackson his BAR. They nodded to each other. One, two, three, and they swept the little vale.

The Chinese who escaped Childs and Jackson ran east — and into a wall of bullets organized by Master Sergeant Dana, who had formed a squad of Marines from the headquarters unit just above the med tents. Dana, whose face was bleeding from grenade fragments, did not call a cease-fire until every last man was dead.

U.S. Marines returning from fighting Chinese forces at the Sudong Gorge, a battle that the commander of the Seventh Regiment viewed as "the beginning of World War III." *Courtesy of National Archives*

Captain William Barber, commanding officer of Fox Company, Second Battalion, Seventh Regiment. *Courtesy of Sharon Waldo*

Chinese soldiers captured by UN forces in November 1950. Notice their quilted uniforms. *Courtesy of National Archives*

The BAR man Warren McClure prior to shipping out to Korea. *Courtesy of Warren McClure*

Graydon Davis (right) before Fox Company marched up to Toktong Pass.
Courtesy of Michael Davis

Bob "Zeke" Ezell at
Camp Pendleton in the
spring of 1951, when
"Fox Hill" was a cold
memory. *Courtesy of
Bob Ezell*

Sergeant John Henry, the veteran machine-gunner attached to Fox Company. *Courtesy of John Henry*

Fortunately for Fox Company, Ken Benson had learned how to load a weapon with his eyes closed. *Courtesy of Ken Benson*

Wayne Pickett (right) and an unidentified fellow POW after their release from a Chinese prison camp. Pickett spent a total of 999 days as a POW. *Courtesy of Wayne Pickett*

This photo of bazooka man Harry Burke was taken during some R&R in Japan. *Courtesy of Harry Burke*

Lieutenant Robert McCarthy, who commanded the Third Platoon of Fox Company. *Courtesy of Robert McCarthy*

The photo taken by Ernest Gonzalez with a Chinese camera from his fighting hole on Fox Hill. *Courtesy of Ernest Gonzalez*

Lieutenant Elmo Peterson (left), commander of the Second Platoon, and one of his squad leaders, Sergeant Joseph Komoroski, on Fox Hill. *Courtesy of Bill McLean*

What the Navy Corpsman Bill McLean dubbed his "home on the hill." *Courtesy of Bill McLean*

There was plenty of sniper fire, but during the daylight hours the Marines of Fox Company did not have to face Chinese assaults. *Courtesy of Bill McLean*

As Chinese forces closed in on the Chosin Reservoir in early December 1950, First Division Marines broke camp to begin the "breakout" to Hagaru-ri. *Courtesy of National Archives*

Lieutenant Colonel Raymond G. Davis, one of three Medal of Honor recipients who was on Fox Hill. *Courtesy of National Archives*

Lieutenant Chew Een Lee, on October 11, 1950, at Inchon. He was the point man for the brutal overland trek of the Ridgerunners. *Courtesy of Chew Een Lee*

Exhausted Marines slept where they fell following the Battle of Fox Hill. *Courtesy of National Archives*

In subzero temperatures, Marines had to improvise ways to heat C-rations and brew coffee. *Courtesy of National Archives*

Between Fox Hill and Hagaru-ri, members of Baker Company, First Battalion, Seventh Regiment, took Chinese prisoners in the hills. *Courtesy of National Archives*

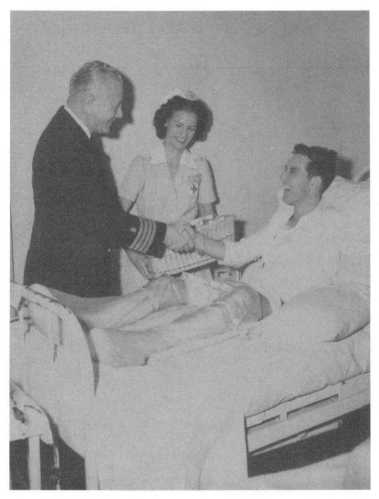

Private Dick Bonelli, still recovering from a near-fatal bullet wound and
frostbite, is greeted by Captain W. F. James in the hospital in Japan.
Courtesy of Dick Bonelli

The official Medal of Honor portrait of Private Hector Cafferata. *Courtesy of National Archives*

Bob Kirchner receives a Purple Heart from Captain James in December 1950 at the Yokosuka Naval Hospital. *Courtesy of Robert Kirchner*

Captain Bill Barber, with family members surrounding him, is awarded the Medal of Honor from President Harry Truman on August 20, 1952. *Courtesy of Sharon Waldo*

This photo of Walt Hiskett was taken in August 1965 when he served as the chaplain with Fox Company in Vietnam. *Courtesy of Walt Hiskett*

The reunion of the Fox 2/7 Association in Virginia in November 2006 to coincide with the opening of the National Museum of the U.S. Marine Corps. *Courtesy of Warren McClure*

Up and down the MSR, from Yudam-ni to Koto-ri, Chinese forces were attacking on all fronts. On the west side of the Chosin elements of the Fifth and Seventh Marine regiments were fending off repeated assaults, and Murray and Litzenberg were aware that more Reds were pouring into the area. On the east side of the reservoir, what remained of the Army units had buckled and were attempting to fight their way back to Hagaru-ri.

They had no idea that farther south the Fifty-eighth CCF Division was penetrating the perimeter surrounding Hagaru-ri. If the United Nations forces there were routed, no Americans trapped north of the village would find a safe haven.

In Tokyo General MacArthur did not yet have specifics; nor did he have any grasp of the desperate situation facing his X Corps. When he convened his top commanders, General Almond still seemed reluctant to accept the size and intensity of the Chinese opposition. Almond told MacArthur that he expected the Marines to continue their "attack" west and north, to carry out the plan to cut the enemy lines of communication, and to continue their march on to the Yalu River. According to one participant, "The meeting broke up after midnight on a note of confident resolution."

Lieutenant Bob McCarthy waited until the howitzer bombardment tailed off before heading for the crest of Fox Hill. Running west to east just below the hilltop he passed Dick Bonelli blazing away on the light machine gun and saw Freddy Gonzales and Ernest Gonzalez higher still, standing back-to-back in their foxhole and firing in opposite directions.

A little farther on, he reached Corporal "Ski" Golembieski, who occupied the foxhole on the Third Platoon's ultimate right flank. If McCarthy's calculations were correct, the left flank of Lieutenant Dunne's First Platoon should be about fifty yards down the east slope. He had no idea that the Chinese had already maneuvered around the bramble thicket and poured through the gap in the American lines. McCarthy ordered Golembieski down the hill to make contact with, and bring back, whatever men Lieutenant Dunne could spare.

Golembieski took off in a low crouch. After going about thirty yards he saw a group of soldiers huddled in a semicircle. In the moonlight he could make out the contours of their calf-length parkas, and he assumed they were Marines. He stood, walked a few paces, and was about to hail them when he heard one speaking Chinese. A burst of automatic weapons fire ripped through the loose folds of his field jacket. One bullet nicked off his cartridge belt, knocking him backward onto the snow. He rolled over into a prone position and fired. Several of the Chinese fell.

Golembieski's clip was almost empty when his M1 jammed. He lifted the rifle over his head, turned it backward, and tried to kick the bolt into place with his shoepac. It wouldn't budge. With enemy fire throwing up teardrops of snow all around him, he crawled back toward the northeast crest with the bad news for Lieutenant McCarthy.

For Dick Bonelli the spookiest aspect of night fighting was never knowing whether friend or foe was to his immediate left or right. There had been times during the first night, after Howard Koone went down, when he was certain he was the only Marine left standing on the hill; when the sun rose he had been surprised to see friendly faces in neighboring holes. Now, with the enemy again charging, he knew there were foxholes on either side of him that were supposed to be manned by Marines. But things changed fast in a firefight. Assaults started; holes were overrun; some people were killed or wounded; others, like Homer Penn, bugged out to regroup somewhere else. Worse, the contours of the hill made it difficult to communicate even with someone who was, in theory, only several yards away.

Earlier in the day Captain Barber had issued standing orders to the entire company: "Treat anything outside your foxhole as enemy." In other words, you were allowed to retreat as far as the back of your hole. Easier said than done, Bonelli thought. He could see no other Americans around him. White quilted uniforms flashed from all directions as the Chinese from the saddle meshed with the survivors from the bramble thicket. Bonelli's hole was an island.

He unlocked the light machine gun from its traverse bar and pointed it down the hill. He sprayed bullets as if he were watering a lawn. When it came to a "gook party," Dick Bonelli had a motto: *Too much ain't never enough.* And this was the party to end all parties. He scythed the lower slopes.

Lieutenant Elmo Peterson was wounded again, this time in the rib cage. But again he stayed on his feet and refused to leave his command. He ordered the upper flanks of his Second Platoon to turn in their holes and fire into the same confused mass.

Bullets cracked past Bonelli's head. Most, he deduced, were coming from his own lines. It was time to get out of there.

He hefted the machine gun and tripod and moved down the slope, four ammunition belts crisscrossing his chest like bandoliers. He swiveled back and forth, spraying pockets of the enemy as they came into view. Four here, reloading behind a rock; two there, trying to undo a jammed rifle.

Above him, the Chinese had momentarily bypassed the foxhole occupied by Ernest Gonzalez and Freddy Gonzales. They used the time to catch their breath and reload. Freddy was jamming bullets into his M1 when Ernest tapped him on the shoulder and pointed with his chin, down the slope. They both goggled at a frenzied Sergeant York zigzagging across the battlefield hauling forty pounds of weapons and a tripod. Bonelli was wrapped in so much ammo he looked like a mummy. *Crazy bastard.*

At 2:43 a.m., Captain Barber left his command post below the med tents and raced for the east slope. Just above the tree line he nearly tripped over the unconscious Eleazar Belmarez. The corporal's torn leggings were caked with frozen blood. Barber hollered for a corpsman. None appeared, but Private First Class William Garza heard the cry and bolted from his foxhole near the tree line. Barber left Garza with Belmarez and continued up the hill. Before he'd gone ten feet he spotted two Marines running toward him in their stocking feet, parkas flapping.

"Where you men going?"

"Getting the hell out of here."

Garza, confused and frightened himself, almost expected the CO to shoot them on the spot. Instead Barber merely held up a hand. "Hold on, you're not going anywhere," he said. "There's nowhere to go. We can talk about this, but now's not the time. I'll make a deal with you. Get back to your position and in the morning if you come up with a better plan than mine, I'll listen. But now's not the time."

The two men turned and trotted back up the hill. Garza was dumbstruck. Barber shrugged and took off after them.

When he reached the northeast corner of the hill where the flanks of the First Platoon and Third Platoon should have met, the area was pandemonium. Marines and Chinese ran in all directions, shooting, hollering, heaving grenades, cursing, fighting with knives and rifle butts and even hand to hand. One Marine was beating an enemy soldier to death with a helmet. The air was acrid, thick with smoke and the smell of blasted granite. There were, Barber realized, no more lines.

He saw Lieutenant McCarthy. They were both converging on a Marine lying on his back in the snow in the middle of the fire-fight, for some reason kicking his M1 with his shoepac. From out of this maelstrom Dick Bonelli abruptly appeared. He plopped down in a prone position between the two officers and set up his machine gun pointing down the east slope. The barrel glowed red-hot.

Barber pointed down the slope. "Are those Marines down there?"

"Gooks," Lieutenant McCarthy said. "They're shooting at us."

Barber nodded and Bonelli opened up, firing over the head of the soldier who was still lying on his back and kicking his rifle. They had no idea it was Stan Golembieski, still trying to un-jam his rifle. Out of the corner of his eye Bonelli saw a muzzle flash. He felt a rush of air past his ear as a bullet snapped by. It hit Lieutenant McCarthy in the thigh, ricocheted off the stock of the lieutenant's M1, and smashed into Captain Barber's pelvis.

They fell on either side of Bonelli. He saw a quarter-size red oval spread across Barber's upper left thigh, near his groin. Barber plugged the hole with his handkerchief. Bonelli again sprayed the Chinese. At the same time, Golembieski kick-started his rifle. Together they knocked down the entire group. Bonelli and Golembieski scanned the east slope for more targets; none appeared. They moved the machine gun around to face the crest, but the enemy on the hilltop also seemed to have been beaten back.

Bonelli felt a hand on his shoulder, swiveled, and came face-to-face with the platoon sergeant, John Audas. He was kneeling over McCarthy and Barber. McCarthy croaked to Audas to take over command of the Third Platoon. Audas hollered for a corpsman, but Barber waved him off. "We'll walk," he said. Using each other as a crutch, the two officers limped off toward the med tents.

On the way down the hill Barber was certain he heard a voice speaking English from somewhere in the west valley. "We're from the Eleventh Marines. Captain Barber, will you surrender?" He ignored it.

Bonelli watched the two officers recede, and his thoughts drifted to Barber's recent boast that there hadn't been a bullet made that could kill him. Then he remembered, farther back, the captain's coming-aboard speech in Koto-ri, the part about being a hell of a good infantry officer. *Damn right,* he thought.

■ ■ ■ ■

"WE WILL HOLD"

■ ■ ■ ■

DAY THREE
NOVEMBER 29, 1950,
3 A.M.–10 P.M.

1

The Chinese offensive was over. The corpsmen were still working on Captain Barber's wound in the med tent when he sent word that what was left of Lieutenant Peterson's Second Platoon was to take back the hilltop. Peterson, with two bullets in him, told Sergeant Audas to take one man from each foxhole on the west slope and organize a detail to clear out all of the enemy still remaining inside the company perimeter. They swept the hill from the road and prepared to counterattack toward the crest. Marines ran among the "dead" and wounded administering the coup de grâce. No more Chinese came down the saddle, but the steady enemy fire from the hilltop combined with sniping from the rocky knoll and rocky ridge to keep things lively.

Audas gave the order to charge. Private First Class Harrison Pomers jumped from the snow and emptied his eight-round clip as he tore up the hill. Fifty feet from the crest he saw an enemy rifleman aiming into the flank of Audas's detail. He ran at him with his bayonet. The man shot him. The bullet went through Pomers's neck and lodged in his spine. He felt as if a train had run him over. He couldn't hear a sound, and for the first time in days he felt warm. He lay on his back, staring up at the night sky, and said a prayer. *Dear God, forgive me all my sins and please take me quick. I have no fear. Thank you.*

Pomers was unconscious when the two corpsmen reached him. One dragged him into a gun pit while the other cupped a handful of snow and scrubbed the blood from his face and neck. When he was injected with a syrette of morphine, the pricking stab awakened him. He couldn't feel anything on his right side. His right leg and arm were useless. Private First Class Gerald Smith, who had been considered a new boot just a few days ago, watched the corpsmen carry Pomers down to the med tents. He pondered an irony: he was the only man left standing from the "last stand" fire team that had once consisted of the veterans Hector Cafferata, Kenny Benson, Pomers, and himself.

Smith was a gung-ho Marine, but this was not an inspiring thought.

Up between the two tall rocks Private First Class Bob Ezell had regained most of his senses, but not his mobility — his legs had been chewed up by the grenade. He tried to crawl but hadn't moved far when he heard Private First Class Gleason's voice down the slope.

"Get some mortar fire up by those rocks — there might be some Chinamen still up there."

Ezell hollered for all he was worth. "Jesus, no! There are Marines up here!"

Ezell turned to Triggs, who was unconscious — his chest heaved like a bellows. Ezell "kicked" off the crest with his elbows and tobogganed fifty yards down the slope on his stomach. He landed at the feet of the "Big Polack" — Sergeant Joe Komorowski, six-foot-three, 250 pounds — who picked him up as if he were a child and carried him to the aid station. Before Ezell passed out, he mumbled that Triggs was still alive up by the rocks. "No mortars," he said.

"Don't worry, we'll get him," Komorowski said.

Over the next several hours Ezell drifted into and out of consciousness. At one point he awoke outside a med tent and saw Triggs sprawled on the ground cover beside him.

Inside the tent, Walt Hiskett and others had stopped praying and were instead listening intently. Hour after hour, those still conscious waited for the flap to be thrown open by a squad of enemy soldiers. Would they shoot the unarmed wounded, most of whom were barely clinging to life? Hiskett guessed they would. But as it gradually grew quiet outside, his hopes rose. *If we could just get through 'til dawn.*

Then, a sign. One by one, from top to bottom, narrow streams of sunlight poured through the bullet holes in the canvas. Hiskett let out a deep breath. He needed no more confirmation that God had saved his life.

Amid the chaos of the firefight on the eastern slope, Private First Class Garza had managed to drag Corporal Belmarez close to the aid station. He had been rough, and the effort had caused the frozen scabs of coagulated blood on Belmarez's legs to crack open. His wounds were now leaking like water mains. It had still been dark when Garza had stopped and used his hands as makeshift tourniquets. He screamed for help and squeezed Belmarez's thighs and buttocks to keep the pressure on.

No one came. Garza spent the next four hours holding his friend's chopped and sliced legs and buttocks together to prevent him from bleeding out. Now, as dawn broke, two Marines appeared. Together they managed to deliver Belmarez to the med tents alive.

"Hell you think you were doing out there in the middle of a firefight?" one of them asked Garza.

"He's my friend," Garza said. In fact, Belmarez was the only man who knew that Garza had lied about his age on his enlistment form. Garza, the human tourniquet, had just turned sixteen.

Around 6 a.m., as the sun appeared over the mountains, the gunfire and explosions subsided, and Ernest Gonzalez and Freddy Gonzales could make out a muffled Chinese conversation a little way off and to the west of their hole. Ernest, who had cleared the blood, dirt, and broken shards of eyeglasses from his eyes, tossed a grenade. It didn't explode. He heard more talking. He pulled the pin on their last grenade, pried off the frozen spoon, and threw it again, high. This one detonated, and the conversation ceased.

The explosion, however, stirred up a

Chinese soldier who had been playing possum some yards to their east. He charged and leaped for their hole. Freddy shot him in the head, sending his cap, with its earflaps, skittering across the snow. The man had been carrying an American-made forty-five-caliber Grease Gun, but when Ernest slithered out to recover it he found it empty.

The two men hollered down the hill in the direction of Lieutenant McCarthy's old bunker command post, no more than seventy-five yards away. No one answered. Thinking themselves surrounded, they pooled their ammo for a last stand. They had between them no grenades, two bayonets, and five rounds. Again a Chinese bugler played taps from somewhere near the saddle. They sat in their hole listening to the mournful tune, awaiting the final rush that — inexplicably — never came.

The sky was clear and the frozen moisture in the air sparkled like diamonds refracting in the sky. Dappled shadows flickered across the folds of Fox Hill. Ernest Gonzalez and Freddy Gonzales locked eyes and together said an Act of Contrition. They slid over the downhill lip of their foxhole. They had monkey-run no more than a few steps before a machine gun from below tore up the snow in front of them. They turned and dived back into the hole.

"Gooks definitely got the hill," Ernest said. Freddy picked up a cartridge and nervously passed it from one hand to the other.

One hundred yards below them Dick Bonelli cursed. "Jesus Christ almighty, I didn't mean to do that. My hand is just kind of palsied out, stuck on the trigger from firing all night."

Sergeant Audas nodded.

"Think those were Marines I just shot at?" Bonelli said.

Captain William Barber had been at Iwo Jima, so he understood the cruel trade-off of men for territory. More than 6,800 Americans had been killed securing that tiny, eight-square-mile atoll. When Barber landed there on February 19, 1945, there had been 212 Marines in his company. When he was ordered to leave Iwo on March 26, he commanded ninety-two men. It was the way of warfare. He did not have to like it.

Sergeant Audas reported a new body count of about 150 Chinese dead at the top of the hill and another dozen or so down near the road. The company had lost five men, including the sniper's victim, Haney, whom the mail carrier Billy French had tried to rescue. Twenty-nine more Marines had been wounded, including Lieutenant Peterson for the second time.

After two nights of repulsing Chinese assaults, the 246 able-bodied Marines and corpsmen had been reduced to 159 "effectives," most of them frostbitten. Barber knew better than to show it, but doubt crossed his mind. He wondered if Fox Company had one more day — or night — of fight left in it.

After receiving Audas's casualty report Barber stumped across the hill to inspect his survivors. His cracked pelvis had been dressed with sulfa powder, bandaged, and splinted with two pine boughs. He used a large tree limb as a crutch. As difficult as it may be to believe in this more cynical age, the dramatic sight of their bloody, shambling CO making his way along the company perimeter, barking out orders while leaning on a goddamn tree branch, breathed a new spirit into the Marines of Fox.

It was another cold morning, with the temperature hovering in the minus-twenties. Near the lower northeast corner of the hill, Barber directed Lieutenant Dunne of the First Platoon to round up a four-man scout team. The captain wanted them to reconnoiter the East Hill, two hundred yards down the MSR. The Marines had yet to be attacked from that direction — which was the only direction from which no attack had come — and Barber needed a feel for the Chinese presence there. Two of the volunteers were the cooks Phil Bavaro and John Bledsoe. They'd do anything to get their blood flowing.

Bledsoe and Bavaro followed a blood trail that led east from the road. About fifty yards out they came upon two wounded Chinese huddled on the lee side of a snowbank, in an icy pool of their own congealing blood. The Chinese soldiers were terribly shot up, and the two cooks suspected they were the ones who had done it. The wounded men's quilted uniforms were pocked with bullet holes, and their hands were swollen to the size of catcher's mitts. Both had lost their caps, and their ears, lips, and noses were cobalt blue. One of the men's feet had burst from frostbite. Even in the frigid open air, the little depression smelled foul. Bavaro was reminded of a story he'd once read in *National Geographic* about how a mortally wounded lion draws a circle around itself with its own blood, waiting for a hyena to catch the scent.

Bavaro unhitched the canteen from his

belt and jerked his arm forward. The universal signal: *Want water?* Neither man changed his expression. Then Bledsoe waved his M1 in their faces. Their cracked lips parted and their watery eyes seemed to plead. Bledsoe mimicked the firing of the gun. Their mouths turned up again. Bledsoe shot them both.

The recon patrol crept as far as the base of the East Hill, where they saw several Chinese scampering up the slope. Upon their return Bavaro reported to Lieutenant Dunne that they had taken no enemy fire and had seen only a few enemy soldiers. Dunne passed the word up to Barber. The captain trained his binoculars on the East Hill. There was no sign of movement. He was perplexed. He knew that Lieutenant Colonel Lockwood had been pinned down trying to reinforce him from that direction. The Reds had to be there. Why hadn't they fired on his patrol?

Down near the road, Jack Page noticed Harry Burke sitting off by himself on a tree stump. Page, as a heavy machine gunner, and Burke as a bazooka man shared an awareness of being a part of the Marine rifle company team without being particularly *of* it. And in Burke's case, two of his best friends from Minneapolis — the ammo carrier for the machine-gun unit, Charlie Parker, and Corporal Johnny Farley — were now among the growing number of American dead. The "Minny Gang" was shrinking fast.

Page asked Burke to join him. He wanted to check out the site on the road from where the Japanese Nambu had opened up on them last night. The two crept out to just west of the large hut and found the machine gun set up in the middle of the MSR. There were no bodies or blood trails. The Chinese crew must have abandoned the gun when Page had given them a good burst. The Nambu was still in fine working order and they hefted it back into the perimeter.

In their hole on the east slope Corporal Gaines and Private First Class Hutchinson had again rearranged their parapet defenses, laying out their spare rifles, grenades, and extra clips. Gaines plucked the spade stuck into the lip of the foxhole and held it in front of his face like a Halloween mask. He grinned at Hutchinson, his eyes crinkling through two bullet holes. He guessed the holes had come from the persistent Thompson submachine gunner.

"Did the Yanks really sweep Philadelphia?" said Hutchinson.

"Beats me," said Gaines.

■ ■ ■ ■

By 7:30 a.m. the pale yellow sun vanished into a Rembrandt gloom. Storm clouds shrouded the surrounding peaks. It was the coldest morning since Fox Company had climbed Toktong Pass. Somebody said that somebody else knew somebody else with a thermometer — this was how news usually circulated at the front — and the mercury had quit falling at twenty-five below. Probably broken, the Marines figured. It felt colder than that.

Except for the warming stoves in the med tents, no fires had been lit yet, and men who were not out collecting weapons stood in their holes blowing into their gloves and stamping their feet. Gaines and Hutchinson were doing just that when slugs skittered across their parapet, upturning their neat rows of weapons and ammo yet again. They hit the dirt, and the curses were barely out of Gaines's mouth when he felt something, like a bee sting, pinching his leg. He reached down and pulled out a spent round that had penetrated his three layers of clothing but had barely broken the skin on his calf. He popped the bullet into his backpack as a souvenir.

The commotion at their hole attracted the attention of Gunnery Master Sergeant William Bunch, a tough veteran of World War II. He approached their position, ignoring their cries to stay low. As he placed his shoe-pac on the lip another burst swept the area and he was hit in the hand. Bunch let out a howl. He dived into the foxhole and the three Marines spent the next fifteen minutes scanning the south hill, three hundred yards away, for the sniper's position. But they could not spot him, and Bunch finally hopped out and headed back toward the med tents.

At 8 a.m., Marines along the hilltop saw two long columns of Chinese soldiers marching single file down the crown of Toktong-san's rocky ridge, toward the rear of the rocky knoll. *Jesus, another battalion.* When the enemy file moved to within five hundred yards of Fox Hill it disappeared from the skyline over the north side of the rocky ridge. Captain Barber ordered his two bazooka units to assemble on the middle of the hill, near the mortar emplacements just above the tree line.

When they arrived Barber stood on his crutch — the tree limb — and pointed to the rocky ridge. "Can you reach it?" he said.

331

Harry Burke was barely listening as Corporal Donald Thornton, the second gunner on the bazooka team, answered with an enthusiastic "Yes, sir." At twenty-one Burke was a seasoned bazooka handler, having been assigned to a rocket team shortly after he had enlisted in the reserves in 1948. He was from the tiny town of Clarkfield, Minnesota, and figured there had to be more to the world than crossing the South Dakota state line on Friday nights to drink beer and sing moony songs in cowboy bars. He wanted to travel, although North Korea was not exactly what he'd had in mind.

He had been driving home from a reservist camp in Virginia when news that the war had broken out came over the radio in his Studebaker convertible. Burke was elated. Given his experience, he had assumed he'd be ordered somewhere, most likely sunny California, as a bazooka instructor. Instead, almost three months to the day later, he landed at Inchon.

At weekend training camps in Minnesota, Burke had fired his bazooka in some frigid temperatures. But they had been nothing like this, and now he had his doubts. So far the fighting had been so close that there was no need — or time — for Burke to even load his tube. Now, as Thornton was assuring Captain Barber that their shaped-charge bazooka warheads could reach the ridges, Burke was reading the written warning etched on his tube: "Do Not Fire Below −20 Degrees Fahrenheit."

Barber said, "Let's send them a couple of rockets to let them know we're still fat and happy."

Burke and Thornton angled their tubes nearly vertical for maximum range. The assistant bazooka men loaded the rockets. "Fire," Barber said.

For some reason — Burke guessed it was the extreme cold — the propellant gases in the rockets not only ignited in the tubes but stayed lit as the rockets exited. They shot up spraying trails of flames and fell far short of the ridge. Thornton and Burke were knocked back flat on their asses. Thornton's eyebrows and whiskers were singed. Burke's thick eyebrows were actually aflame. A corpsman jumped to him, piled snow over his face to put out the stinging "brushfires," then slathered his brow with clots of semi-frozen Vaseline.

So much for that bright idea, Harry Burke thought as he lugged his tube back to his foxhole. At least he could use the worthless thing as a club the next time the Chinese attacked.

■ ■ ■ ■

Not long afterward, Colonel Litzenberg managed to make radio contact with Barber from Yudam-ni. Although this was only seven miles north of the Toktong Pass, the peaks surrounding the Chosin Reservoir were playing havoc with radio waves, and the Marines up north were having the same problems as Barber's communications crew with the batteries. It occurred to Litzenberg that, if not for the roadblocks the Chinese had thrown up across the MSR between Yudam-ni and Fox Hill, it would have been easier to keep in touch with Fox Company by runners.

But now that he'd finally gotten through to Fox, Litzenberg informed Barber that Hagaru-ri had been lightly reinforced by units from Koto-ri farther south. About three hundred men — a combined force of U.S. and British Royal Marines, as well as seventeen American tanks — had fought through to the Hagaru-ri perimeter, but the village was also nearly encircled by the Chinese. Though Colonel Alpha Bowser in Hagaru-ri now commanded perhaps three thousand fighters, he was in no position to reinforce Fox.

Bowser had also asked the CO of How Company, Captain Benjamin Read, to redeploy his howitzer unit back into the village, Litzenberg said. But Read argued that moving his big guns any farther south would take them beyond the range of Fox Hill. Read asked to remain outside the perimeter in an exposed position. Bowser reluctantly concurred. This brought a smile to Barber's face. *Good man, that Read.*

Now, still on the radio, Litzenberg hesitated for a moment. Barber sensed that he was pondering a hard decision. After an uncomfortable silence he came out with it. He offered Barber the option of leading Fox Company off the hill and fighting his way back down to Hagaru-ri. "Your call," he said.

Barber had discussed this alternative with his XO, Clark Wright, only moments before. Moving his wounded was a major consideration, but so was tactical strategy. "Well, hell, we're already here," he had finally told Wright. "If we're ever going to get the Seventh together in one piece anywhere, north or south, it's going to involve fighting for this damned hill anyway. It's probably better to keep it while we've got it."

Now he reiterated these thoughts to Litzenberg, who wondered if holding Fox

Hill and keeping Toktong Pass open were becoming a suicide mission. The colonel asked one more time if Fox Company would — if it could — fulfill its mission. The answer would become seared in the legacy of the U.S. Marine Corps: "We will hold, sir," Barber vowed. For both men, there was nothing more to say.

Barber put down the receiver and called his officers together to give them, as he laconically put it, "the latest dope from Division." The Chinese had invaded in force, he said. And not only were the Fifth, Seventh, and Eleventh taking heavy casualties at Yudam-ni, but Marines in Hagaru-ri and farther south in Koto-ri were also cut off. Scout planes had spotted eight enemy roadblocks between Koto-ri and Hagaru-ri. There was no need to reiterate their circumstances on Fox Hill. "Because of all this there's no possibility of relief for us," he said.

He leaned heavily on his crutch and took the measure of each man in the small circle around him, knowing that he had just told them their chances of surviving the next twenty-four hours were greatly reduced. They had a pass to keep open, and the lives of thousands of Marines depended on them. "We can expect heavy attacks tonight,"

Barber stated. "But we have nothing to worry about as long as we fight like Marines."

2

At Yudam-ni, Colonel Litzenberg spent the morning sussing out contingency plans for an evacuation. The eight thousand or so Marines ringing the reservoir had been hit hard the previous night by as many as fifty thousand Reds, and the men were bone-tired and battle-weary. The First Division's supply officers calculated that the Chosin garrison had roughly three days worth of food, fuel, and ammunition remaining — less if you factored in the Eleventh Regiment's dwindling artillery shells.

The safety of these Marines was topmost in Litzenberg's mind, but he could not keep the fate of Fox Company from creeping into his thoughts. Sooner than later (he hoped) General MacArthur and General Almond would have to admit that their grand push to the Yalu River had been effectively crushed by the Chinese offensive, and Litzenberg was certain that the order to abandon Yudam-ni would arrive at any moment. He was just as certain that the enemy knew the key to the entire division's survival was Fox Hill.

Litzenberg suspected that the events of the last two days had provoked the Chinese military leaders to revise their strategy. Now, they didn't want merely to drive the Americans out of North Korea. They wanted to annihilate them, so they would never come back.

It had been hours since Litzenberg had gotten through to Captain Barber, but he was confident that nothing had dramatically altered the picture Barber had painted for him earlier. With the Marine Corsairs and Aussie Mustangs patrolling the skies, the Chinese would not dare attack in daylight. Tonight, however, was a different story. They would throw everything they had at Fox to sweep it off that pass.

And if they succeeded? What if Barber and his men were not even alive tomorrow morning? Litzenberg thought the odds were grim and grimmer, and he conferred with his counterpart, Colonel Murray of the Fifth Regiment, about precisely such a possibility. If the Chinese broke through and commanded Toktong Pass, they decided, their regiments would be surrounded and probably wiped out. Their only chance would be to destroy their own vehicles and artillery and fight their way south on foot, ridgeline to ridgeline, avoiding the road.

Toktong was too strong a chokepoint for the transport of rolling stock. If it fell into enemy hands the Americans trying to blast past the roadblocks on the MSR would be cut to pieces from the overhanging ridges. The two colonels assumed that an overland retreat would result in at least 50 percent casualties. Neither cared to dwell on the likelihood of losing more than four thousand Marines.

There was one other hope. Litzenberg put it to Murray. What if they used the cover of night to dispatch a stripped-down rifle battalion overland toward the pass before the remaining Marines trapped at Yudam-ni left and set off down the meandering MSR for Hagaru-ri? This rump battalion could serve two purposes. First, if Barber was still holding out, he would certainly need the reinforcements. Second, if Fox had been wiped out, the flanking maneuver might result in a big enough surprise attack to recapture the heights from any occupying Chinese.

Murray liked this "backdoor" scheme, and Litzenberg sent a runner to find Lieutenant Colonel Ray Davis, the man he wanted to lead the march. Davis, the commanding officer of the Seventh Regiment's First Battalion, had already proved his mettle three days earlier by rescuing his own "Hard Luck

Charlie" Company from Turkey Hill, and earlier in the war he had captured the Fusen Reservoir with only three Jeeploads of Marines and a dozen shotguns.

Litzenberg was relieved that Davis was still in the vicinity. Turkey Hill was two miles south of Yudam-ni, and when Davis had set off to save Charlie Company the colonel had left it to Davis's discretion whether to return to the reservoir with his survivors or continue the five miles south to link up with Barber on Fox Hill. Davis had taken too many casualties on Turkey Hill to continue a southern assault, however. Now Litzenberg was going to send him back again, in the same direction, and this time the route would be much harsher.

Bob Ezell woke up in the east med tent and tried to rub his legs. But his hands, which had turned pearly-white, were numb and swollen to the size and texture of small footballs.

"Here, gimme." It was Private Bernard "Goldy" Goldstein, lying next to him. Ezell extended the two *things* attached to his wrists. Goldstein's left hand had been shredded by a grenade, but with his good right hand he began massaging Ezell's hands to bring back some circulation.

Gradually the blood returned, and though they remained grotesquely swollen, Ezell finally got some feeling back. He ran his hands over his legs, bandaged from hip to ankle. He thought of his baseball career. Over.

"Corpsman said the cold saved your life," Goldstein said. "Kept you from bleeding out."

Ezell didn't know what to think. Would he have been better off dying up by those rocks, better off to have gone down fighting? Was that better than being bayoneted, helpless in an aid station, when the Chinese finally overran the outfit? Was it better than never playing ball again?

His self-pity evaporated when the tent flap opened and he watched two corpsmen carrying in Private First Class Cecil Bendy, an assistant mortarman who had just been shot in the head by a sniper. No, no, Ezell wouldn't have been better off dying. It was good here. It was warm. He would walk again. He'd make it off this hill. He might even play baseball — just not the outfield.

The corpsmen lowered Bendy into an empty space where Private First Class Alvin Haney had recently died. Haney's body was the latest to be added to the growing pile of American dead just west of, and downhill from, the aid station. The frozen corpses, wrapped in ponchos and covered by half tents, were stacked three feet high by fifteen feet long.

When he watched them carry Haney out, Warren McClure remembered a conversation he'd had with Haney a week earlier, over chow in Hagaru-ri. Haney had told McClure that his goal in Korea was to win the Medal of Honor, "for the Corps."

Now a corpsman stepped carefully among the prone bodies in the tent handing out morphine syrettes. McClure, though still in excruciating pain, declined. He was afraid any more medication would put him under so deep that he would stop breathing. Next, boxes of C-rations were passed around, but again McClure begged off. He knew his lung was punctured, but what else had the bullet torn up in there? He was afraid that a piece of food clogged in his innards might pose difficulties for the docs who would open him up when he got back to a real field hospital. *When they got him back. Ha!*

Both med tents, erected on slopes, were truly uncomfortable. It was only with painful squirming, and by digging in the heels of his shoepacs, that McClure was able to keep from sliding down on top of the man beneath him. He was fucking miserable. Yet, like Ezell, each time he began feeling too sorry for himself, he needed only to look to his right. There a young Marine whose name he did not even know was paralyzed with a bullet in his spine. The kid, who appeared to be no more than sixteen, was conscious, and to pass the time McClure spoke to him, comforted him. Once he'd tried to sit up to wipe the kid's brow. But he couldn't stand the pain. It bugged the hell out of him.

Just past 9:30 a.m., McClure's fire team leader, Private First Class Robert Schmidt, entered the tent to check on his condition. The scare from last night was fresh in McClure's memory and he begged Schmidt to bring him a weapon, any weapon: a carbine, maybe a forty-five-caliber pistol. He thought it likely that the same frightening scene would play out again tonight. Schmidt was sympathetic but told McClure there was nothing he could do. The riflemen on the line needed every weapon they had. As he turned to go, however, Schmidt slid his K-bar from its sheath and buried it in the ground next to McClure. "Best I can do," he said. They smiled at each other, and Schmidt left the tent.

McClure wobbled the knife from the dirt with his good left hand, turned on his right side, and with all his strength buried the thick blade up to its hilt. He counted his luck that the earth beneath the tent had softened from the warming stoves. He hooked his right armpit around the knife's handle as a brace against sliding. Better. His heels relaxed. But even this small exertion exhausted him, and he was asleep before the company XO, Lieutenant Clark Wright, entered to explain Fox Company's dire situation to the wounded. Just as well. By now McClure hated the guy.

The sun had crested the eastern peaks when Lieutenant Peterson's mopping-up detail stumbled across Ernest Gonzalez and Freddy Gonzales crouched in their hole. They had already been added to the KIA list posted below, and the Marines who found them, huddling in a corner of their foxhole, stared popeyed at the two "ghosts."

Ernest and Freddy, equally astonished that Fox still held the hill, goggled back. Near the site where Ernest had tossed his grenade at the chattering Chinese a Marine stepped over an enemy officer lying across a field phone. There was a German-made Mauser machine pistol next to the dead man, and the Marine presented it to Ernest as a gift. Ernest checked; it had no bullets.

Before he left to find some grub, Ernest pulled out the camera he had scrounged at the bottom of the hill the previous evening and took a picture from their foxhole.

On his way down the hill Ernest ran into Kenny Benson, who had trudged back up at dawn after medics had swabbed his eyes. Now Benson decided to join Gonzalez and pay a visit to Cafferata. The two parted ways at the aid station, and after Benson filled a tin cup with hot coffee he raised the flap of Hector's med tent. Hours earlier every stretcher had been occupied. Half a dozen empty spaces now dotted the ground — men who had died from their wounds, including his fire team leader, Corporal James Iverson. The last time Benson saw Iverson, he had been lying unconscious beside Cafferata.

Hector was wearing a pair of boots taken from a dead corpsman. They were too small, so someone had chopped the toes off. Benson sat down next to him and offered him a sip of coffee. Hector was sweating like a wheel of cheese.

"Bense, my feet are terrible. If I gotta spend much more time here I'm gonna shoot 'em off." Pain was etched on his face, and Benson heard something in his voice he would never have expected — fear. As he rubbed the warmth back into his buddy's feet Benson recognized a familiar NCO lying wounded across the tent.

"Hey, Hec," he said. "Remember Sergeant D.J.?"

How could Cafferata forget? Just hours before ascending Toktong Pass, Sergeant D.J. had ordered Hector to break his arm. It had all started when the distraught noncom received a Dear John letter from his wife — hence the nickname D.J. As Cafferata's fire team had gotten warm around barrel fires in Hagaru-ri, Sergeant D.J. approached Cafferata and informed him that he was going home.

"Sure, Sarge," Cafferata had said. "I'll call you a cab."

"No, Moose, I'm serious. I want you to knock me out and break my arm."

Cafferata was stunned. Was this a joke on the new boot? One look in the man's eyes and Cafferata realized he was serious.

"Jesus, Sarge, I can't hit you. How about if I just squeeze you unconscious?"

That is what Cafferata had proceeded to do. After the sergeant passed out, Benson laid his arm across a snowbank while Cafferata clubbed it with the stock of his rifle. The sergeant came to and howled in agony.

"Cafferata, you clumsy son of a bitch, it

didn't break!"

In truth, the bewildered Cafferata had held back on his swing, as he did when the sergeant insisted he try it again. The same thing happened. The sergeant was debating whether to have Cafferata shoot him in the leg when an officer approached and the entire idea was abandoned.

Now, as Cafferata lay in the god-awful med tent, his face scrunched up and he shot a quizzical look at Benson. He seemed to forget, for the moment, his aching feet. "What about him?" he said.

Benson rolled his eyes. "He's two stretchers over. And get this. Took a bullet in the leg."

Both men grinned. The memory had just the effect on Cafferata's spirits that Benson had hoped for.

3

At 10 a.m., Captain Barber learned that Hagaru-ri had been hit hard the previous night. The fighting had been touch and go for several hours, but despite waves of attacks by a full Chinese division the supply depot, airstrip, and field hospital remained in the Marines' hands. Barber was also told to expect a supply plane within the hour.

He recalled yesterday's drop in the east

valley and the two Marines taken out by snipers. Today, he decided, he would chance the drop on the open space below the crest of the hill. It was vulnerable to sharpshooters on the rocky knoll but had the advantage of being closer to the tree line. He ordered a detail to tear strips from the parachutes and form them into a large circle just below the crest of the hill. The middle of the circle was marked with an "X" using the company's air panels.

At 10:30, the R4FD Marine cargo plane, Lieutenant Bobby Carter again flying number 785, appeared over the southern horizon. He came in low on the deck, took scattered small arms fire from the rocky knoll and rocky ridge, and after a test run jettisoned his first bundles. Each parachute landed inside the circle. On Carter's second pass, unknown to the Marines on the hill, enemy machine gun fire tore through the aircraft's flimsy skin. Its radio operator was wounded in both legs. The plane's crew chief, Master Sergeant John Hart, applied tourniquets to the operator's bleeding legs while Carter made two more runs over the target. Despite the activity just outside his cockpit he hit it every time.

The drop included cartons of hand grenades, M1 clips, belts of thirty-caliber machine-gun ammunition, and 60-mm and 81-mm mortar rounds. Fox Company was once again loaded for bear — but still hungry, for no C-rations were to be found. To some men this didn't matter. Dick Bonelli, for instance, had settled into a daily routine that did not include eating. He had lugged the light machine gun back up the hill and set the weapon in a depression with rocks on three sides. He may have been living in a hole in the ground, like an animal, but he refused to eat like one. Instead he spent the daylight hours collecting spare weapons and ammo before visiting the med tents to grab a cup of coffee and talk.

Pulling back the tent flap shortly after the airdrop, a big smile on his face, he shouted, "All of you goldbricks, it's survival of the fittest, so get off your asses and join the party." He proceeded to regale the wounded with yarns about the tittie bars of New York City, outrunning MPs during a drunken shore leave in Lisbon, buying phony identification cards in order to drink in the taverns ringing Camp Pendleton, or having been court-martialed for stealing a rickshaw in Kobe.

Bonelli's clowning was effective. Years later, wounded men who'd been dazed by morphine at the time and had trouble recalling events on Fox Hill easily remembered Bonelli's bad jokes and lousy stories. After Bonelli left, Hector Cafferata fingered an M1 he had scavenged and turned to the Marine lying next to him. "Don't know who that guy is," he said, "but he's damn lucky we need every man we got."

As on the previous day, the supply drop was followed by the approach of a two-seater chopper that flitted and darted to avoid the enemy fire. Its pilot, Lieutenant Floyd Englehardt, was bold enough to land in the open on top of the hill and push out his supply of radio and field phone batteries. But before he could even think about evacuating any of the wounded, slugs punctured the little chopper's windshield and fuselage. Englehardt got out of there fast.

At 11:30 a.m., a tremendous explosion rocked the area near the Third Platoon's command post. No one was killed, but Private First Class Edward Gonzales — one of the Texas Gonzaleses — was buried alive under a huge mound of snow and dirt. He was unconscious when corpsmen dug him out and carried him to the med tent.

No one could tell if the detonation had been caused by a faulty mortar or howitzer round — both the company's own 81-mms

and the Hagaru-ri battery had been intermittently shelling the rocky knoll and rocky
ridge throughout the morning — or if
perhaps a satchel charge dropped by one of
the infiltrating Chinese during the previous
night's firefight had somehow been ignited
by the subzero temperatures. At any rate,
Captain Barber ordered Sergeant George
Reitz to man up a detail to clear the perimeter of all unexploded ordnance. Reitz
found volunteers hard to come by.

As Reitz and his squad grid-searched the
hill they discovered no unexploded satchel
charges, but they did run across plenty of
dud American hand grenades — at least,
Reitz prayed they were duds. They littered
the battlefield, especially near the eastern
crest, their pins pulled, some still with
spoons and some without, their fuses like
damp firecrackers. It seemed as if half the
grenades tossed by the Americans had failed
to explode, owing to a combination of the
cold and old age. The grenades had been
manufactured at least a decade earlier; they
were Army surplus from before World War
II.

Each time the men on Reitz's team saw
one, they would call the sergeant over. The
American grenades had seven-second fuses,
and it was impossible to tell how far a fuse

had burned down, if at all, before fizzling out. Reitz would approach the explosive on his hands and knees, bring his empty right hand back, and then swing his hand forward, clutching the grenade and heaving it a hundred feet or so over the slope in one continuous swoop. None exploded, but that did not stop Reitz's Marines from backing away and ducking for cover on every throw.

Sergeant Reitz wondered why Barber had chosen him for this assignment. In the Corps a company commander was expected to know each of his charges personally, from the grizzled gunnies to the raw boots. He acted not only as their military leader, but also as a combination psychological counselor, financial adviser, umpire, religious confessor, and surrogate father figure.

Reitz, like Bob Ezell, had been a semipro baseball player in the States. Was that why he'd been chosen to toss the grenades? Reitz couldn't imagine that Barber knew much about his background. The captain had only just joined the outfit. Or, Reitz wondered, was he that good?

Throughout the day the Second Platoon Marines on the west slope continued to dig in as sniper fire from the West Hill across the valley pinged around them. Poke your head up, draw a shot. By 1 p.m., however, Private First Class Gray Davis decided he was going to die anyway — of starvation — if he didn't get something to eat. Somebody had to have some extra C-rations.

He hopped from the hole he still shared with Luke Johnson, ducked the slugs that flew over his head, zigzagged back to the tree line at top speed, and crouched behind a thick sapling to catch his breath. *Jesus.* He wondered what happened to you when you got scared half to death twice. As he disappeared into the pines, he heard Johnson yell, "Bring some ammo, too."

He worked his way up the gulley toward the med tents beneath pewter skies on iron ground, using the trees that grew horizontally out of the hill like the rungs of a ladder. Midway to the aid station, his hands bleeding from the rough, cold bark, Davis stopped to chat with a couple of buddies from the Third Platoon. They were shocked to see him because his name had appeared on the KIA list near the command post. "Hell you talking about?" he said, and double-timed it up the slope.

Near the med tents he found the list and saw the name of Roger Davis, Allen Thompson's assistant machine gunner from the First Platoon. This gave him pause. Weighed down with food and ammo, Gray Davis returned to his hole. Luke Johnson noticed that he seemed preoccupied.

In fact, Davis didn't say a word for the next hour. He was brooding not only over Roger Davis's death but over all his comrades who had died to hold this god-awful hunk of rock. He and Claude Peoples, another Florida kid and one of the two black guys in the outfit, had enlisted together. He remembered back during the dicey summer campaign, on the retreat to Pusan, when Gunny Kalinowski, his face covered with soot and dust like everyone else's, remarked, "Now we all look the same."

Every head had swiveled toward Peoples. Claude was a stoic guy who rarely smiled, a sort of sphinx without a riddle, Davis thought, but he had grinned then, as if at some personal joke. Now Claude was dead — as was his former platoon leader, Sergeant Peach, who seemed to know it was coming.

On the LST sailing to Wonsan, Sergeant Earl Peach had pulled Davis aside and said, very calmly, that he wasn't coming back. Peach was a veteran of World War II "from the great state of Kansas" (as he always put it), and his wife had died of an illness several years before. He had told Davis that lately she was appearing to him in his dreams every night, telling him that they would be together soon. He would sit up in his bunk and reach out for her, slamming his head into the upper bunk every time. Then at Sudong, Peachy had tried to save a wounded Marine and had his head cut in half by machine-gun fire. He had been awarded the Navy Cross posthumously. There were too many dead, Gray Davis thought.

Just after Sudong a new boot had been assigned to the outfit, an overweight kid who obviously couldn't take the punishment. He'd just been transferred out of the rifle company and into the motor pool when they had taken incoming from a Russian T-34 tank. Davis watched the fat kid dive under a truck just as a shell hit the front end. He came out without a scratch, but when anyone tried to talk to him all he could do was mewl and blubber. They gave him a Section Eight. *Yeah, he was crazy,* Davis thought now, *crazy like a goddamn fox.*

As suddenly as it had come over him, Davis's pensive mood was broken by the arrival of Lieutenant Peterson, who was distributing Chinese-issue white blankets taken from the packs of the enemy dead.

Peterson had multiple wounds to his shoulder and sternum, and his uniform was bloody and in tatters. The heavy Australian rifle he carried completed the bizarre picture.

"Where'd you get the cannon, El-Tee?" Johnson said.

"Dead gook," Peterson said. "Just wanted to let you know that we'll be kind of thin on this line tonight. Lotta wounded. Lotta empty holes."

Then Peterson produced a pint of whiskey from inside his field jacket, passed it to both men, and jerked his chin toward the Chinese on the West Hill. "What they doin' out there?"

Davis and Johnson exchanged brief glances. *Hell you think they're doing?*

"They're firing at us, sir, and I believe you better get down in the hole," Johnson said. He and Davis prided themselves on having the deepest foxhole on the west slope.

Peterson ignored their warning and gingerly assumed a sitting position on the lip of the foxhole, his legs dangling inside.

Davis said, "Lieutenant, what do you think happens if the tables are turned? You know, a couple, three Marine battalions attacking a company of Chinese holding this hill?"

Peterson smiled but did not deign to answer such a silly question. Instead he pulled out a pair of 6×30 Zeiss binoculars and scanned the surroundings left to right — over the West Hill, up the rocky knoll, and beyond to the rocky ridge.

"Machine gunner up there," he said, pointing to a position about four hundred yards away atop the rocky ridge. "Looks like he's sighting in on us."

Davis and Johnson threw the white blankets over their shoulders and scrunched farther down into the hole. Peterson didn't seem bothered. It was if he were eyeballing girls on the beach. "Yup, definitely sighting in on us."

Machine-gun bullets beat the ground and the scrub around the foxhole. They tore through the trees behind the three Marines, cracking branches large and small. The gunner must have emptied an entire canister.

"Over now," Peterson said, "he's done." He placed his binoculars back in their leather case and began the painful act of standing up. Davis and Johnson watched him limp a bit up the hill before he stopped. Over his shoulder Elmo Peterson said, "Your question? Tables turned? Over in half an hour."

He continued up the slope and sat down

on the lip of the next foxhole.

At 3 p.m., two U.S. Air Force C-82 Flying Boxcars soared over the southern horizon. They flew much higher than the Marine cargo plane and made one run apiece, both missing the "X" of air panels near the crest with their drops. The supplies landed in a column that ran several hundred yards down the center of the west valley. Most of the parachutes failed to open, and the Marines watched cases of hand grenades smash apart and scatter in all directions. They cursed the Air Force pilots, who had neither the balls nor the aim of their Marine counterparts.

"They're supplying the enemy," Captain Barber said as he watched the Boxcars disappear. But he knew someone was going to have to go out and get that ammunition. Lieutenant Peterson stepped up.

Barber said he didn't expect Peterson's detail to recover every single crate. "Concentrate on blankets, stretchers, medical supplies, and C-rations," he said. "Ammo after that."

This recovery run would be much more hazardous than that of the previous day, when the Marines merely had to worry about a few snipers on the far South Hill.

Peterson sent the men in his detail out one by one, unarmed except for knives. As each approached a multicolored parachute, mortar and machine-gun covering fire from all over Fox Hill blasted the enemy lines.

Despite the fusillade, the Chinese opened up from the ridgeline and folds of the West Hill, from the rocky knoll and the rocky ridge, and from a small patch of woods that wrapped around the base of the West Hill near the MSR. One of the men providing covering fire was Gray Davis, who had been assigned a light machine gun. Davis had protested that he hadn't fired a machine gun since boot camp. Good enough, Peterson said.

Now, hunched over in the emplacement, spraying the West Hill and the little woods for all he was worth, Davis felt as if he were back in the stands at a Florida State game. Marines ran through the broken field like tailbacks. Directly in front of him Lieutenant Joseph Brady — the mortar unit commander, who still had grenade fragments in his back and hands and who indeed had been a star halfback at Dartmouth — dashed toward a box of 81-mm rounds, cradled a shell under each arm like two footballs, and scatted back across the valley as if the bullets pocking the packed snow at his feet were tacklers.

Several men got back safely, dropped off their haul, and went looking for Davis. They were not happy. They felt that his covering fire had strayed a bit too close to their scalps. "Then cover your own ass next time," he told them.

Up at the command post, tabulating the haul, Captain Barber was incredulous and then enraged. Peterson reported that his detail had managed to bring in stretchers and blankets as well as ammunition: belted slugs for the thirty-caliber machine guns, several mortar shells, and boxes of forty-five-caliber bullets that could be used in the captured Thompson submachine guns. There were also a few C-rations, although not nearly enough.

But when his men — under fire, Peterson emphasized — had crow-barred open crates searching for medical supplies or, most important, more food, they had found helmet liners, unusable fifty-caliber rounds and howitzer shells, barbed wire, and forty-seven-year-old Springfield rifles and their stripper-clipped, World War I–era ammo. Inexplicably, they had also discovered five-gallon cans of fresh water that had frozen to ice.

Ice. Just what we need up here.

When Barber regained his composure he decided it was too dangerous to send another detail out to the supply drop while it was still daylight. He had been lucky. Despite the Chinese barrage, none of his men had been hit. He couldn't afford to press that good fortune. Plus, there was more urgent business to tend to.

He called together the officers and platoon leaders who were still standing and told them he'd managed to get through to Division headquarters. Up on the east side of the Chosin, he said, the Army battalions were getting their heads handed to them, and the Fifth, Seventh, and Eleventh Marine regiments at Yudam-ni had been surrounded for almost twenty-four hours. Interrogations of Chinese prisoners revealed that three enemy divisions — more than 30,000 soldiers — to the north, northwest, and southwest had closed on the shrinking American perimeters along the fourteen-mile stretch from Hagaru-ri to the reservoir, with more on the way. For all intents and purposes, he said, the American push toward the Yalu was over.

Barber told his men that he was proud of them, that Fox had held out longer than the Chinese had expected. He added that though he didn't have it officially, he was certain that a combined "pullback" of what was left of the eight thousand Marines up near the Chosin was imminent, and that holding Toktong Pass would make the difference between a successful breakout and a massacre of Americans.

The men around Barber fell silent. Each knew what this meant — for himself, for Fox Company, for their friends and comrades up north, for General MacArthur, and for the United States. It was all on them now.

Barber broke the silence. "Pass the word. Tell every man to conserve whatever C-rations he has left. It's all the food we're likely to have for a while. And I want booby traps and trip flares placed all around the perimeter."

Although the Chinese high command was perplexed that its strategy of isolating individual American units and chewing them up with superior firepower was proceeding more slowly than expected — both Charlie Company and Fox Company, after all, should have been eliminated by now — General Sung Shih-lun assured the leaders in Peking that the final outcome was certain. And, at almost the same time that Barber was meeting with his officers on Fox Hill,

General MacArthur was following up his report to the United Nations with a communiqué to the Joint Chiefs of Staff in Washington.

He began with the same wording he had sent to the UN — "We face an entirely new war" — but added a separate coda. "It is quite evident that our present state of forces is not sufficient to meet the undeclared war by the Chinese," he wrote. "This command . . . is now faced with conditions beyond its control and its strength."

It was not a coincidence that, during a press conference the next day, President Truman refused to rule out the use of atomic weapons in North Korea. In fact, hours earlier the U.S. Air Force's Strategic Air Command (SAC) had been ordered to prepare to dispatch several bomber groups to Asia carrying "atomic capabilities."

As it became more and more evident that the United States' forces in North Korea were facing a rout, Marine battle commanders were anxious to recast this national humiliation as similar to the British "spirit" exhibited at Dunkirk in the early days of World War II. It worked. After covering news conferences in Washington, D.C., American journalists echoed the Marines' "gung ho" proclamations in their copy —

missing the irony that *gung ho* was actually a Chinese phrase (loosely translated as "to work together"). In one case, sympathetic war correspondents, visiting the rear areas, asked the commander of the First Division, General Oliver P. Smith, about the Chosin withdrawal. They subsequently converted his rambling response into a stirring battle cry. "Retreat, hell," he was quoted as saying. "We're just attacking in another direction."

Smith's brio was not lost on Litzenberg, who now issued the following directive at Yudam-ni: "In our order for the march south there will be no intermediate objectives. The *attack* will start at 0800 on 1 December. Objective: Hagaru-ri."

4

As their third night on the hill approached, the weary Marines of Fox Company began placing bets on what time the Chinese would come. They also wondered how the enemy, clad in their thin canvas sneakers, managed to keep their feet from falling off in the subfreezing temperatures — no campfires were visible on the surrounding hills — and whether frostbite would slow them down as the hours passed. Though the sun had intermittently broken through the clouds, the day had been the coldest so far on Toktong Pass. Evening shadows were settling over the hill at 5:30 p.m. when Kenny Benson moved up behind Bob Kirchner's position. He had recovered his BAR and was also carrying an old Japanese Nambu automatic rifle (the version with a banana clip extending from the top). "Lieutenant Peterson says to fill an empty hole," he said.

Kirchner nodded to a gun pit about ten feet away. There was a dead Chinese soldier lying in it.

"I ain't touching that," Benson said.

"Oh fer Christ's sake." Kirchner crab-walked to the hole, lugged the corpse out, and laid it along the rim facing the West Hill. "The next one's yours," he said. "Make your own cover."

Farther down the slope Gray Davis and Luke Johnson had been joined in their foxhole by Private First Class Clifford Gamble. The three Second Platoon Marines chewed the fat for a while — there was not much else to chew — until a glint of reflected sunlight far to the northwest caught Gamble's eye. He rapped on his friends' helmets and pointed in the direction of a mountain pass about six hundred yards away, on the far side of the West Hill. Three companies of Chinese troops — each company five men across and twenty-five rows deep — were parade-marching down the MSR.

Jesus, it's like watching a movie, Davis thought. The three Marines followed the columns until they disappeared into the piney woods that wrapped around the southwest base of the West Hill. There seemed to be an endless supply of Red reinforcements.

At the same moment Lieutenant Peterson was making his first evening rounds. He too saw the enemy columns disappear into the fir trees. When Peterson reached Davis and Johnson's foxhole they all watched a fourth column, and then a fifth, follow the first three into the trees. That made a battalion. Peterson took out his field phone, unfolded his topographic map, and relayed the information and the coordinates of the woods to Lieutenant Campbell up at Barber's command post. Campbell in turn radioed How Company's howitzer battery at Hagaru-ri.

Within five minutes a registering round burst over the woods. Peterson cradled his field phone. "On target," he told Campbell. "Fire for effect."

A minute later multiple salvos of proximity-fused antipersonnel rounds exploded over the small forest. Marines on the west slope watched in wonder as rounds burst fifty feet above the trees. Thousands of pieces of shrapnel rained iron on the Chinese. The variably timed airbursts exploded in groups of six, at thirty-second intervals. The artillerymen walked the entire grid pattern from one coordinate square to the next. The shelling lasted twenty minutes. When it was over the Marines could see no movement in the trees.

Fish bait, Gray Davis thought. He was still a Florida boy, after all. A few moments later, just to satisfy his curiosity, he loaded a tracer into the barrel of his M1 and fired it toward the trees. The muzzle blast gave him spots before his eyes, and he had no idea in which direction the bullet went. Luke Johnson, who had repeatedly warned his foxhole buddy that firing a tracer from a rifle was a stupid idea, looked on with a satisfied smirk.

As night fell, Colonel Homer Litzenberg sat on the cot in his small tent command post at the southern end of Yudam-ni. He and Colonel Murray had just adjourned a meeting with all of their battalion commanders, at which assignments were handed out for what was unofficially being called the "breakout" from the Chosin Reservoir. As the officers filed out Litzenberg asked Lieutenant Colonel Ray Davis to remain behind.

"With our trucks and artillery, the enemy assumes we're road-bound," he said.

Davis nodded. He was standing over Litzenberg, who was unfurling an old Japanese map.

Litzenberg said, "We have a good chance of catching him by surprise with an overland move."

Davis's head moved almost imperceptibly.

"I want you to work up a plan to do just that and bring it back as soon as you can. We've got to get going on this."

Davis glanced up from the map and nodded again.

Ray Davis may not have been a man of many words, but Litzenberg considered him far and away his most ferocious battalion commander. He needed such a warrior right now. Contradictory orders were flying into Yudam-ni — the Chosin garrison had actually been instructed by the Army's General Almond to break west eighty miles to attack the flank of the Chinese who were destroying the hapless Eighth Army *after* Litzenberg received orders from the Marines' General Smith to attack southward toward Hagaru-ri — but Litzenberg had plans of his own. The foremost involved this steely, hawk-nosed Georgian who, one fellow officer noted, would look as natural in bib overalls as in dress blues.

Davis was tall and laconic, a graduate of Georgia Tech who carried himself with an unassuming countenance that concealed a combat readiness not found in every officer, or even in every Marine officer. Davis liked to tell friends, "Above all, I see myself as a man of action." He was among the rare military men who relied on neither gruffness nor bluff to inspire their charges, but instead on his poise at the center of any fray. This was an attribute that early on caught the attention of the notoriously belligerent Marine Colonel Lewis B. "Chesty" Puller, who had trained Davis at basic school.

Davis's war experience went back to World War II, in which he had led Marine units against the Japanese across Guadalcanal, New Guinea, and New Britain. His skill as a leader increased with his rank, and as a major in late 1944 he had commanded a Marine battalion at Peleliu, one of the most vicious of coral island campaigns. He had been shot during the first minutes of the landings at Peleliu, but he refused to abandon his command. When a Japanese banzai charge shattered his outfit's defensive lines, he personally led the counterattack despite his leg wound. For this act of bravery he was awarded the Navy Cross. In the summer of 1950, remembering the kid from basic who had shown such leadership qualities, Puller handed Davis his first frontline rifle battalion and told him to report to Colonel Litzenberg in California and prepare for Korea.

Davis had been serving as the inspector-instructor of a reserve battalion in Chicago when Puller tapped him. He accompanied his men by train to Camp Pendleton and was dismayed when, upon arrival, his unit was abruptly disbanded and randomly assigned to various other battalions. Davis resented how his "family" had been broken apart in that predawn episode.

After a few days in California, however, mostly he went about the business, in military parlance, of standing up Litzenberg's First Rifle Battalion. This included not only stopping his Jeep near every work detail or idle group of Marines to shanghai "volunteers," but also "borrowing" wayward trucks in order to scrounge supplies from the train depot in Barstow. Soon his trucks were also filled with disparate Marines ready and willing to fight in Korea — wherever the hell that was.

At Pendleton, Litzenberg had tacitly approved of Davis's unorthodox recruiting methods, and now, at the Chosin Reservoir, the colonel had a stack of "after action" reports detailing how Davis, not content with studying an ongoing battle from a battalion commander's standard position in the rear, invariably "stayed on the low ground" at the front of his column whenever his unit engaged in a gunfight. Litzenberg also had firsthand testimony regarding Davis's fearlessness during the rescue at Turkey Hill. He wondered if there would be anyone left on Fox Hill for Davis to rescue.

Davis listened intently as Litzenberg spoke about the chances of relieving Captain Barber and Fox. He told Davis he had not been able to make contact with Barber since earlier that morning, and he was certain the company would be attacked again tonight. He warned that Fox's chances were so slim that if Davis did make it to Toktong Pass via the backdoor route, he might very well be walking into an American graveyard. Litzenberg added that if he managed to reach Barber by radio, "I just might have to tell him to bug out before you even get there."

Davis said nothing.

■ ■ ■ ■

At 6:30 p.m., Captain Barber ordered his XO, Clark Wright, to form up another supply recovery detail while the 81-mm mortars and the howitzers at Hagaru-ri bombarded the Chinese. Wright's unarmed Marines ran full speed out into the valley carrying empty stretchers, filled them with ammunition, and returned without drawing fire.

The men were glad of the exercise — some had reached the point where being taken out by a sniper was preferable to hunching down in a foxhole waiting to slowly freeze to death — but Barber found the lack of enemy activity strange. He decided to press his luck and sent Wright and his men out for another run. Still no fire. Barber had no idea what it meant, but he was not a man to spit in fortune's eye. This was, however, enough for the night; the enemy could have whatever remaining scattered grenades they could find. His "effectives" might be hungry and cold but they would not lack weaponry and ammunition.

As a result of the airdrops and the captured weapons, each American foxhole now resembled an international gun show. At least that was Dick Bonelli's thought as he eyed the armaments lining the parapet of the hole near his light machine gun emplacement up on the east crest. Walt Klein and Frank Valtierra had covered the rim with two Thompson submachine guns, an 8-mm Mauser rifle, a forty-five-caliber American-made Grease Gun, a German-made machine pistol with a sack of ammo, and a 1903 Springfield rifle complete with stripper-clipped ammunition rounds. Their M1s were crisscrossed across a box of grenades.

"Startin' a war?" Bonelli yelled.

Klein hollered back, "You remember what the El-Tee told us."

Once, out on a recon patrol near Hagaru-ri, Klein and Lieutenant McCarthy had stumbled upon a field covered with mounds of human feces. Somewhere along the march the lieutenant had picked up an old Chinese-made Mauser rifle. He took Klein aside, pointed to the frozen feces, and explained that in his opinion they were up against a hell of a lot more Reds than Division allowed. Then, brandishing the Mauser, he advised Klein never to pass up an opportunity to add an extra gun to his gear.

Now Klein cupped his hands to his mouth and yelled to Bonelli, "You know, about how you can never have enough firepower?"

Bonelli had no idea what he was talking about.

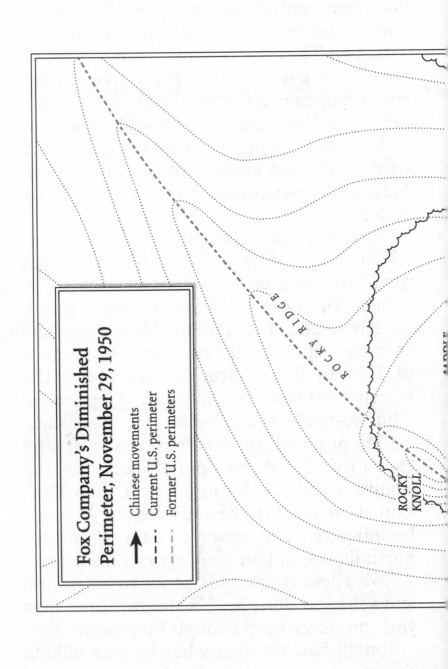

Fox Company's Diminished
Perimeter, November 29, 1950

Chinese movements
Current U.S. perimeter
Former U.S. perimeters

ROCKY RIDGE

ROCKY
KNOLL

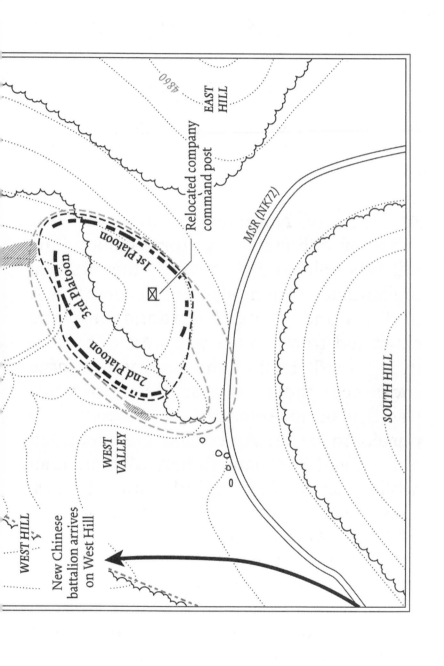

WEST HILL

New Chinese battalion arrives on West Hill

3rd Platoon

2nd Platoon

1st Platoon

Relocated company command post

4860

EAST HILL

WEST VALLEY

MSR (NK72)

SOUTH HILL

DAY FOUR

5

At 2 a.m. on November 30 the moon was suddenly obliterated by storm clouds. The hill was cold and dark when the whining loudspeaker system again screeched across its folds and pleats. The sound this time emanated from somewhere west of the cut in the road, behind the pile of five large rocks near the southwest base. The voice was that of an American, or someone purported to be an American. He identified himself as Lieutenant Robert Messman, an artillery officer from the Eleventh Marines. Messman announced that he had been captured two days earlier by the CCF near the Chosin, and he asked Fox Company to lay down its weapons and surrender.

"Just walk off the hill," the voice repeated over and again. Unlike the Chinese officer's conversational tone the previous night, this American voice sounded like someone reading from a script. "If you give yourselves up you will be treated fairly, in accordance with the Geneva Conventions, given food, and taken to shelter."

The idea that one of their own had turned traitor was too much for Fox Company. But because of the large rock pile no one could get a shot at the son of a bitch. Even after the 81-mm mortar crew sent up an illumination round, the American captive — if he was indeed an American — remained hidden. Up on the west slope Fidel Gomez fired off a short burst from a captured Thompson in the general direction of the five rocks, but that was mostly for show. It was, however, a good show — Marines all over the hill stood and cheered. "Messman" was not heard from again.

Five minutes later about a dozen men closest to the road on the left flank of the Second Platoon, including Gray Davis and Luke Johnson, watched as a squad of Chinese soldiers crept down the MSR. They settled in behind the pile of five rocks and began moving through the brush toward the American line. Hours earlier the Marines had squirmed several yards back from their holes and camouflaged themselves beneath the captured white blankets. They were so well concealed they appeared to be nothing more than lumps on the snow-covered hill. Lying prone and still, they allowed the Chinese to reach their old foxholes before they opened up. They cut every man down.

Farther up the west slope Bob Kirchner and Kenny Benson had fallen in with some more Second Platoon Marines who had gathered the sleeping bags of the American dead, stuffed them with snow and pine boughs, and placed them out in front of their foxholes. Then, on Lieutenant Peterson's orders, five American corpses were dragged from the "dead pile" and arranged in a sitting position in a semicircle near the sleeping bags, as if keeping watch. Soon enough Kirchner, Benson, and their squad saw the silhouettes of another Chinese squad creeping out of the deep ravine that bisected the west valley.

The enemy divided into two units. One attacked the decoy sleeping bags, running them through with bayonets several times. The other slipped behind the sitting corpses. It took several moments for the Chinese to realize something was not right. They stood, whispered to each other in nervous voices, and fell on the dead men with knives and bayonets. When their weapons failed to penetrate the frozen corpses, they understood the ruse. They instinctively swiveled toward the American lines. The Marines opened up with their rifles and BARs.

Standing near the command post tent, a sergeant named Robicheau — a last-minute addition to John Henry's heavy weapons unit on loan to Fox — listened to the firing on the west slope. *They were coming again.* But for some reason, call it a hunch, instead of looking toward the saddle, Robicheau made his way down the hill until he reached the bottom of the stand of fir trees.

He unpacked his night-vision binoculars and scanned the level ground across the MSR. In front of the woods at the base of the south hill, about 250 yards away, he saw three infantry companies massing into attack formation. More than five hundred men jogged in place and pumped their arms and knees while their political commissars urged them into a frenzy for "Mother China." To Robicheau they resembled nothing so much as a high school band preparing for a halftime show.

Out in front, like majorettes, were the grenadiers and sappers, their sacks of potato mashers slung over their shoulders, their satchel charges in hand. Next came the riflemen, with bayonets fixed, shouldering their Mausers like a horn section. Finally came the drummers, their booming automatic weapons, mostly Thompson submachine guns and Russian burp guns, pointed and at the ready.

By the time Robicheau raced back up the hill to inform Captain Barber, the Chinese were already on the move. Their jogging in place turned into a brisk trot. They performed a right flank maneuver and lanced across the snow-covered field. Their five lines stretched about seventy-five yards, with ten paces between each two lines. Then the trot became a cattle stampede. By the time they reached the road, the full frontal attack extended from just east of the larger hut to the west end of the cut bank on the MSR. This night they blew no bugles or whistles, and they held their fire in the minute or so it took them to cross the level ground between the South Hill and Fox Hill.

Barber watched them come. He assumed the advancing troops were the remnants of the five companies that had been torn up by howitzer shrapnel in the woods skirting the West Hill. He studied his defensive perimeter. From his vantage point looking down the hill, slightly to his left, were his heavy machine gunners and, to their left, the lowest foxholes of the First Platoon Marines, perhaps forty yards back from the road. To his right were the men from the Second Platoon who had ambushed the enemy squad from beneath their white blankets. They were now back in their holes and had again pulled their blankets over them. Though Peterson and his men were closer to the road by twenty yards than the men on the east slope, they were a bit more protected by the steep cut on the west end.

As usual, Jack Page's heavy machine gun was the first to let loose. He slapped the hatch shut, double-primed the gun, and squeezed off two long bursts followed by a shorter burst. He toppled the first row of Chinese, who were just stepping onto the road. Jim Holt on the other heavy gun followed Page's cue, as did the two light machine gunners on either slope of the hill. Then every Marine rifle and BAR in between opened up.

It was a slaughter.

The bodies of the first two rows of attackers lay fanned out across the MSR in the same formations in which they had charged. As the third, fourth, and fifth files became entangled in the corpses, many Chinese turned and ran. But the 60-mm mortarmen lifted a brace of illumination rounds — 220,000 candlepower of light turning night into day — while the 81-mm mortars tore

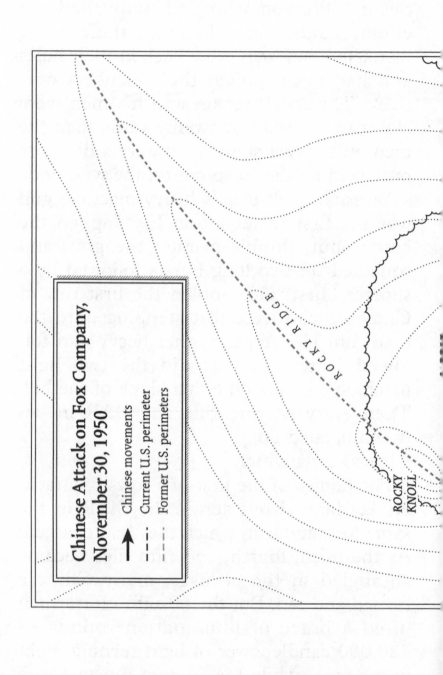

Chinese Attack on Fox Company,
November 30, 1950

Chinese movements
Current U.S. perimeter
Former U.S. perimeters

ROCKY RIDGE

ROCKY
KNOLL

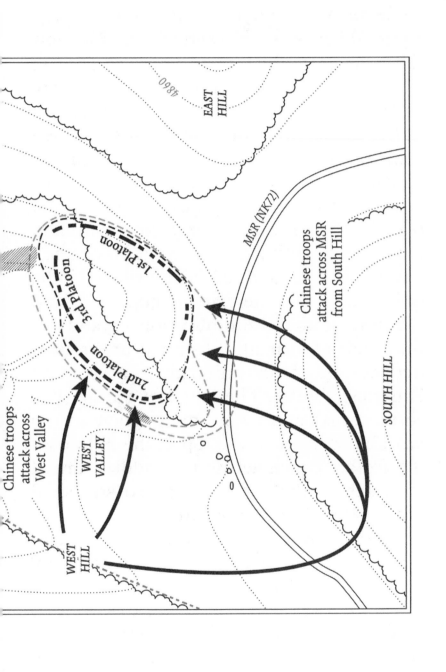

EAST HILL

4860

MSR (NK72)

Chinese troops attack across MSR from South Hill

SOUTH HILL

1st Platoon

3rd Platoon

2nd Platoon

Chinese troops attack across West Valley

WEST VALLEY

WEST HILL

into the rear of the Chinese ranks.

Those who had fled turned to charge again. They were mowed down. The few Chinese left alive tried to take shelter beneath the wall of the cut. They were showered with rolling hand grenades. Finally, at Lieutenant Campbell's radioed request, the 105-mm howitzer unit in Hagaru-ri provided the death stroke. Salvo after salvo of proximity-fused rounds burst over the South Hill behind the devastated companies, cutting off any route of escape.

Abruptly the field fell nearly silent — the only sound the intermittent pop of a dead Chinese soldier's ammunition exploding, the result of a small fire started in the padded cotton of his uniform by a scalding American bullet. The smell of sulfur (like rotten eggs) and ozone hung heavy in the air. The Marines at the top of the hill, bracing for an attack across the saddle, turned to watch as the last tear-shaped star shell arced 250 feet before fluttering quietly beneath its parachute to the bloody snowfield. To some the landscape was eerily reminiscent of the final scene of a movie from a decade earlier starring Errol Flynn — Custer and his 202 dead troopers strewn across the Montana grasslands of the Little Bighorn. Now, there were four hundred bodies, and they were not blue-clad American cavalrymen but white-clad Communist Chinese regulars.

It was 2:41 a.m. The battle had lasted ten minutes. One Marine, Private First Class John Senzig, had been killed. Another, grazed by a bullet, refused medical attention. The attack across the saddle never came. It was a fitting birthday present for Captain Barber, who had not mentioned to anyone that he had turned thirty-one at midnight.

6

At daybreak there was a palpable sense of relief across the hill. Small groups of men huddled over fires — joshing, laughing, teasing one another. Some brewed coffee and shared their last C-rations. On each corner of Fox Hill the Americans had similar thoughts. *Why didn't they come across the saddle last night? Have they had enough?*

The men were disabused of the latter notion an hour later, when Captain Barber visited the two med tents with a stark request: any wounded man with the strength to walk and squeeze off a round should return to his position on the line. *If you could squeeze, you fought.* Barber instructed

385

his platoon leaders to pair wounded Marines with uninjured men — or at least men as uninjured as they could find.

Sensing the unease in the med tents, he softened the harsh dictum with a pledge. "Here it is, men. Things are pretty bad. But I've seen them worse. One more thing — we're not pulling off this hill unless we all go together. Nobody stays unless we all stay. I led you onto this hill and I'm leading you off. That's it."

Among the gaunt Marines who tried to answer the captain's call was Private First Class Harrison Pomers. The entire right side of his body burned with pain, but Pomers rolled to his left and attempted to stand. A corpsman rushed to his side.

"Think you're goin'?"

"To fight," Pomers said. "I can still use my left hand."

Now that he had parachute silk to re-bandage him, the corpsman took a chance and slit open Pomer's shirt and long johns. "You've got a hole as big as a fist in your back," he said. "Your spinal column is exposed."

Pomers rolled back over. "I could use some more morphine. My right hand is killing me."

The medic was already applying pressure

to Pomers's right hand. "We're out," he said.

"Squeeze it harder," Pomers said.

"If I squeeze any harder I'll break your fingers."

"It's useless anyway, doc. Go ahead and break them."

Hector Cafferata turned to Pomers from a nearby stretcher and tried to lighten the mood. "Boy," he said, "is my mother gonna be pissed off if I get myself killed here."

"Ha," someone else said, "more like is *your* mother gonna be pissed if *I* get myself killed here."

From across the room Howard Koone yelled, "Don't nobody worry about that. We're all going to be home for Christmas, remember?"

Around 7 a.m., the Marines stationed on the lower east slopes were flabbergasted to see two enemy officers sauntering dreamily up the MSR. They were dressed more appropriately for a Gilbert and Sullivan performance than for a war zone, in flowing parade-ground capes lined with scarlet silk, bright red fedoras, and black knee-length boots polished so brilliantly they reflected the sun. The two Chinese stepped over and around the frozen corpses of their countrymen as if they were so many piles of debris.

When they ambled to within twenty-five yards of the larger hut, Corporal Page yelled, "Halt." At the sound of an American voice they swiveled and instinctively reached for their sidearms. Page's heavy machine gun cut them in half.

The blast of Page's Browning invigorated the enemy sharpshooters; suddenly the Americans were awash in incoming fire from the West Hill, the rocky knoll, and the rocky ridge. It was as if the Chinese on the heights were trying to atone for their failure to attack during the previous night's massacre. A bullet knocked a mug of hot cocoa right out of John Henry's hand, and when Harry Burke, his face still singed and smudged with dirt and Vaseline ointment, raised his head to see if Henry was all right he nearly had it blown off. *The hell with this.*

He ducked back into his foxhole and removed his gloves in order to light a cigarette. He placed them on top of a log on the lip of the depression. Both gloves were immediately blasted back into the hole, one landing in his lap, the other on his helmet.

Reports of snipers streamed into Captain Barber's command post. On the crest a slug spun Private First Class Gleason's helmet 180 degrees as he hunched behind Corporal

Dytkiewicz's old light machine gun. The bullet left an entry hole and an exit hole in the side of his steel pot without giving him a scratch. Farther down the west slope a bullet blew the cigarette from between the platoon sergeant Richard Danford's fingers. Danford was humbled, if uninjured. Not far away, automatic weapons fire felled a small tree in front of the foxhole occupied by privates first class Childs and Jackson. They both ducked as it crashed across their pit.

The tree, snapping at its base, sounded quite a bit like the report of an M1, and before Childs and Jackson knew it an NCO whom they did not recognize was standing over them chewing their asses for wasting ammunition. Childs cursed under his breath as the sergeant stalked off, turned back toward the enemy lines, and came face-to-face with a Chinese soldier not twenty yards away sighting down the barrel of a Thompson submachine gun. Childs ducked at the same moment the man fired. A bullet creased his helmet at dead center, knocking him unconscious. Jackson tended to Childs while the wounded Lieutenant Brady rushed from his foxhole and heaved a grenade at the Chinese soldier, who was slithering back into the ravine that cut through the west valley. He could not tell if he got the man.

This was enough for Captain Barber. He instructed Lieutenant Campbell to request another howitzer strike, again with anti-personnel rounds, on the West Hill, the rocky knoll, and the rocky ridge.

Men along the west slope heard the price-less shells before seeing them. They whistled overhead and culminated in a string of large black puffs of smoke detonating about fifty feet above each target. One Marine likened the Chinese across the valley and the saddle to "ants scrambling away from an ant hill that's been kicked over." The Americans could hear clearly the cries of the dying and wounded and watched as those still able ran for cover on the reverse side of the West Hill or clawed their way over and in back of the knoll and the ridge.

When How Company ceased firing eight minutes later, only a few diehard snipers remained. Even this annoyance was too much for Barber. His men were wounded, tired, cold, and hungry. He lifted the radio receiver and prayed to get through to the air base. Connection. He requested an air strike on the same three positions.

At 9:30 a.m., three F4U Marine Corsair fighter-bombers appeared high above Fox Hill. The Marines recognized them as the "Checkerboard" squadron by the black-

and-white squares painted on their engine cowlings. The lead fighter broke off and flew an observation run over the rocky knoll and rocky ridge. All sniper fire ceased — the Chinese had learned a lesson from the Australian Mustangs — while across the valley Americans stood up in their holes.

Barber carried no radio that allowed him to talk to the pilots directly on their frequency, but he managed to communicate the targets to them through a cumbersome series of relayed messages to the air base. Within seconds the Checkerboards broke their vector. The first plane strafed and rocketed the rocky ridge just north of the rocky knoll. The second loosed a five-hundred-pound bomb. The third dropped a canister of napalm behind the knoll.

The Corsairs pulled up, turned, and swooped down for a second run, and then a third. The knoll and the entire ridgeline were aflame. To the Marines the scene resembled an exaggerated version of the bonfire the Chinese had lit during their second night on the hill.

After the third bombing run several Marines noticed a high-winged Navy trainer observation plane circling a valley about six hundred yards beyond the West Hill. The depression between the mountains was the terminus of the same lower pass through which Private First Class Gamble had spotted the Chinese battalion marching the previous evening. The Corsairs broke off their attack on the knoll and the ridgeline and screamed west. The men of Fox Company could not see what — or who — was in that valley, but they could certainly make an educated guess as the planes fired their last rockets and strafed the area with their "death rattlers." When the Corsairs turned for home they overflew Fox Hill and waggled their wings. A roar rose up to meet them.

Meanwhile, down by the road, John Henry decided to use the Corsair runs as cover to take out two or three persistent snipers who had been pouring bullets into Jack Page's heavy machine-gun emplacement for the last hour. They were the same sharpshooters who had spilled his cocoa, and he was angry.

Henry didn't anger easily. Even when his father had taken him out behind their home in Chattanooga eight years earlier and whupped his ass with a strap for making his mother cry, he had taken the beating stoically. He figured he probably deserved it. Henry had been a seventeen-year-old freshman at Michigan State at the time, 1942, and his father expected him to graduate, follow in his footsteps, and become an electrical engineer. Instead Henry had left Michigan, had come home to Tennessee, and had signed up for the Corps. When he brought the enlistment papers home for his mother to sign, however, she wept so hard, right there in the driveway, that his father had to "rectify" the situation. Or so he thought. A week later, back up at school, Henry passed the test for Army aviation cadets and was enrolled in the Army Air Corps' pilot training program. This time his parents didn't try to stop him. Despite the fact that he had piloted or copiloted five flight tests in the States, he was shipped out to the Pacific as a turret gunner. He joked to friends that the average life span in his line of work was approximately minus-three seconds. He had managed, however, to make it through the war unscathed.

The Marines remained in Henry's blood, and he and his brother had both enlisted when war broke out in Korea. Given his experience and sagacity, he rose fast through the enlisted ranks, and when his heavy weapons unit reached Hagaru-ri he expected to be assigned to an outfit up on the Chosin. Instead he was attached to Captain Barber's Fox Company, and he'd be lying if he said he wasn't disappointed by having to babysit at some backwater bottleneck.

But John Henry was a big enough man to admit when he was wrong, and he had certainly been wrong about Toktong Pass. Among the peaks rising on all sides of him, one in particular, far off to the west — a high, wide plateau surrounded by perpendicular cliffs — reminded him a little of Lookout Mountain back home. He wondered what his mother would think if she could see him scrounging up volunteers to go kill snipers in the frozen mountains of North Korea.

Now, with the Corsairs still circling, Henry and two of his ammunition carriers crawled across the MSR as the fighter-bombers kept the enemy at bay. The three Marines set up a classic V ambush and waited. Sure enough, when the Corsairs disappeared over the horizon Henry and his men saw three heads pop up from behind a snowbank midway to the South Hill. They cut loose with BARs and killed all three.

Private First Class Warren McClure had slept for twenty-four hours. It must have been a healing sleep because when he awoke at 10 a.m. he found he could not only sit up but stand without too much pain — for a moment, anyway. He sat down again. His throbbing right hand and right arm were useless; he could live with that. He was alive.

C-rations were being passed around the med tents, and though he was still wary of "chunking up" his innards, his hunger drove him to palm two cans of peaches from one of the boxes. With difficulty he used his left hand to open one tin with a can opener. He shared the peaches with the paralyzed Marine lying next to him, spooning them into the kid's mouth. His next order of business, he decided, would be to recover his gear.

On the northeast corner of the hill Private First Class Lee D. Wilson of the First Platoon was cold and thirsty. There were fewer boulders to crouch behind here, and the icy gale funneling through the pass swept the area with particular ferocity. Wilson thought about making a small fire to melt snow, but the snow around his hole was a grimy mixture of blood, human excrement, and fouled earth. At any rate, he assumed that the cleared perimeter was safe enough to traverse to the spring near the road. He laid his M1 across his foxhole, stuffed a grenade in a pocket of his field jacket, and took off down the slope, along and behind the American firing line. Midway down the hill, as he neared one of his platoon's light machine-gun emplacements, a squad of Chinese snipers in the woods at the base of the South Hill opened up. Wilson ate dirt.

At a lull in the sniping he rolled over and crawled into the machine-gun nest. The crew told him that the sharpshooters had been firing at anyone near their emplacement all morning in an attempt to draw return fire and expose the gun. Wilson was a veteran of World War II whose steel nerves were held in awe by the new boots. And right now he was livid. *Jesus Christ, and nobody thought to warn me when I came strolling down the hill?* The laughter from the machine-gun unit pissed him off even more. He asked what the fuck was more important, the life of a Marine or a hidden machine-gun emplacement. The machine gunners' silence was an answer he did not care for one bit.

Wilson crawled from the nest and zigzagged back up to his hole at the top of the hill. He grabbed his M1 and a Thompson submachine gun he had liberated from a dead Chinese and inched his way on his belly down the east slope. He slithered about midway to the East Hill, made a hard right turn, and reached the MSR. He dashed across the road and threw himself into a snowbank. With pantherish grace he darted from one snow mound to another until he reached the tree line at the bottom of the South Hill. He slipped from tree to tree. He was perhaps twenty yards to the right of the snipers. He stood and emptied his M1 at them. To make sure, he also emptied the Thompson.

Lee D. Wilson walked back across the level ground and crossed the MSR as if he were ambling to chow. He stopped at the spring, filled his canteen, and resumed his walk up the east slope. When he passed the light machine-gun emplacement he stopped and stared without saying a word.

7

Captain Barber wore a scowl as he limped in a circle in front of the command post. It was 2 p.m. and he had been promised an airdrop three hours earlier. His men, he knew, might make it through another night without food. But they badly needed ammunition. He had sent out a detail to scavenge among the dead Chinese in the road, but the men had not recovered nearly enough. If the enemy came down the saddle again tonight the Marines would have to beat them back with snowballs.

Half an hour later another helicopter braved the hilltop to deliver fresh batteries for the company's radio and field phones. Like its predecessors the chopper was sniped at so heavily there was no possibility of evacuating any of the wounded. When Barber loaded the new batteries into the SCR-300 and radioed about the supply drop, he was told that a cargo plane was on its way. By 5:30 p.m., another three hours later, it had yet to arrive.

At the same time, on the northeast crest of the hill, Walt Klein and Frank Valtierra were engaged in a spirited gunfight with a Chinese rifleman positioned on top of the rocky knoll. In the exchange both sides barely missed each other several times. From his machine-gun nest twenty paces away, Dick Bonelli peered over a rock and watched this ruckus in disgust and annoyance. *Can't anybody around here shoot straight?*

Since he had settled into what he called his rock "fort," not a single officer or NCO had come around to check on his machine-gun emplacement. He hadn't even been assigned an assistant. He liked it that way. It left him to his thoughts. The sky had partially cleared, and from his position on the hill he could look down through the clouds blowing in and see the fading sunlight glinting off the ice of the Chosin Reservoir.

Down through the clouds! He had never been on an airplane in his life, and he figured this was as close as he would ever get. He gazed toward Toktong-san in the silvery half-light and realized for the first time that the big, bald mountain didn't so much rise from the reservoir as rear from it, like some great startled bear. He muttered to himself, "I'm nineteen years old and I wouldn't give you two cents for my life right now."

He said a prayer and went back to squaring away his ammunition belts.

A thick cloud cover settled over Toktong Pass, making this the darkest night yet. Captain Barber ordered what was left of his trip flares set out across the saddle and hoped for the best. There was nothing much else to hope for. His company was down to surviving, more or less, on guts and nerve. And though he had no doubt that the men still had both, neither would amount to much against a fourth night of attacks. If he knew this, he was certain, the Chinese knew it as well. But he was mistaken.

The Battle for Toktong-san, as well as the

stiff resistance shown by the Marines up and down the MSR, had forced General Sung Shih-lun and his staff to reappraise their strategy. The Chinese Communist offensive had fared well on the east side of the reservoir against the U.S. Army troops, but not as well in the west. They had underestimated the grit of the U.S. Marines, not least the stubborn stand by Fox Company. It had gone on too long, and Toktong Pass was still open.

Sung decided to change tactics. He would continue his probes into Yudam-ni from the west, but at the same time further concentrate additional forces to destroy the U.S. Army units on the east, and sweep down overland into Hagaru-ri behind what was left of the survivors, avoiding the pass. Once Hagaru-ri was in Chinese hands, he could pick off, at his leisure, whatever Marine units remained at Yudam-ni. As for the small contingent at Toktong Pass, if his snipers didn't finish them, they would be dead from the cold, or starvation, or both, before long.

On Fox Hill, the morning's sensation of relief had given way to anxiety. Captain Barber, still hobbling on his improvised crutch, made rounds just after nightfall in an attempt to tighten the lines anywhere possible. It was futile. There was too much ground to defend, and there were not enough men to defend it. The best he could do was to direct the Second Platoon Marines closest to the road on the southwest corner to pull back from their holes in the brush near the pile of five rocks and position themselves within the stand of fir trees. *Fat lot of good that would do without more ammo. Where the hell was the supply plane?*

Barber had just completed his perimeter inspection when he heard the low rumble of an Air Force C-119 approaching from the south. He ordered a detail of men up to the crest, where they surrounded the drop zone, turned on their flashlights, and pointed them to the sky.

The pilot's first observation pass appeared textbook-perfect. But — perhaps because of the gunfire that erupted from the rocky knoll and the rocky ridge — on his second pass he seemed to want no part of the hilltop. He dropped the supplies in the valley about three hundred yards southeast of the hill. *Chickenshit Air Force.*

It was a long walk in the dark, but at least Fox Hill itself provided cover from the snipers to the west. Clark Wright's recovery detail reached the supplies without trouble. As the Marines tore open the bundles, searching for C-rations, a feather-light snow began to fall. Again, no food had been dropped. By the time Wright's grumbling men returned with stretchers loaded with ammunition, the snow showed no sign of letting up, and the new snow cover was already an inch deep.

The Marines did not mind this. The snow clouds seemed to trap at least some of the day's heat — they guessed it was no colder than ten-below. The new snow on the ground also hid the contorted faces of the Chinese dead.

At 6 p.m., Gray Davis, still sharing a hole with Luke Johnson down on the southwest corner facing the West Hill, shook the snow from his M1 and test-fired it. He aimed at a brazen squad of Chinese assembling in the drizzle of flakes behind the pile of five rocks, not thirty yards away. He did not hit any of them. Damn mountains, playing tricks with his eyes again. The Chinese popped up from behind the rocks and began marching, single file, directly in front of him. Davis wondered if these drones were given drugs by their officers before a fight, or perhaps were even brainwashed. This was just too easy.

The BAR man in the next foxhole opened

up first, dropping two or three men. Davis stood, sighted, squeezed — click. Misfire. He racked the bolt and squeezed the trigger again. Click. *Jesus!* He threw down his gun and yanked the pins and spoons on two hand grenades. They exploded in the middle of the clustered enemy. Five Chinese turned tail and ran. Another six to eight lay dead in the snow. He picked up a carbine and began firing at the retreating men. He was certain he hit a couple but none of them fell. Damn carbines.

After the brief firefight Davis peered into the chamber of his M1. A wedge of ice blocked the bullets from entering the chamber from the clip, and the blot face had just enough snow on it to prevent the firing pin from hitting the primer. He cleaned it out. Loose snow, he figured, must have fallen in there from the recoil when he had test-fired the rifle. *Damned if you do and damned if you don't.*

By the time Captain Barber made his final inspection of the perimeter at 10 p.m., four to five inches of new snow had accumulated on the hill.

■ ■ ■ ■

THE RIDGERUNNERS

■ ■ ■ ■

DAY FIVE
DECEMBER 1, 1950

1

In all his years as a Marine, Sergeant Clyde Pitts had never seen anything like it. Eleven minutes earlier, at precisely 1 a.m., Captain Barber had gotten through to Hagaru-ri and requested a shelling of the four new enemy machine guns that were stitching Fox Hill from the rocky knoll. The moon had long since disappeared behind the snow clouds; the Chinese had wised up and removed their tracers; and though the Americans could vaguely make out the emplacements, no one could get a clear shot at them. Barber instructed Lieutenant Campbell to maintain radio contact with How Company's artillery battery in order to synchronize their howitzer salvo with a brace of star shells from his own 81-mm mortars. He had then ordered Sergeant Pitts to carry a field phone to the crest of the hill and register the barrage.

When Pitts reached the hilltop he waved to Barber at the command post, who in turn nodded to Campbell. Captain Benjamin Read's scratchy voice came over the radio from Hagaru-ri. "Four guns at your command."

"Fire," Campbell said.

"Four rounds on the way." The distant crack of the field guns echoing off the mountains was sharp enough to cut falling silk.

Barber turned to the mortarman Private First Class O'Leary. "Fire."

Two illumination rounds lit up the knoll. Seconds later Pitts watched, with awe verging on disbelief, as four 105-mm shells landed directly on the machine-gun nests. Bodies and gun barrels — including one that appeared to be from a British-made Lewis gun, with its drum mounted horizontally above the breech — soared through the night sky. Pitts was nearly speechless when he phoned the information to Lieutenant Campbell. Campbell also had doubts about the pinpoint accuracy of the artillery gunners.

Barber grabbed the phone. "Are you positive?"

"I'm watchin' it with my own eyes, Cap'n." For once Barber understood Pitts's syrupy drawl. "Wonderful, lovely, beautiful."

"All four of them?"

"I swear to God. All four. Bam. Gone."

Barber passed the receiver back to Campbell, who rather breathlessly congratulated Read on a fine piece of shooting. "Cease fire," he said. "Target destroyed. Mission accomplished."

But even Read seemed stunned. He asked for a reconfirmation. "Say again after 'Cease fire.'" Lobbing four shells directly on target from seven miles away on the first volley didn't happen often.

"You got them all," Campbell said. "Thanks again."

An hour later, near the southeast corner of the hill, Phil Bavaro and John Bledsoe heard scratching in the thick new snow piling up below their foxhole. Bledsoe peered over the lip. He could barely make out a white-clad figure ten yards down the slope. The man was fidgeting with something on the ground. Before Bledsoe could reach his M1, the soldier glanced up at him, dashed back across the road, and dived behind a snow-bank strewn with Chinese corpses. Bledsoe pulled Bavaro to the bottom of the hole seconds before the satchel charge detonated.

No one was injured.

The explosion, however, appeared to be a signal. Now the Chinese who were hiding in the trees skirting the South Hill began walking rifle and submachine-gun fire up and down the east slope. The Americans guessed it was another attempt to flush out their heavy machine-gun emplacements. No one took the bait — until Bavaro and Bledsoe saw Captain Barber stumping on his tree branch through the screen of blowing snow and bullets. He stopped at their hole.

"Fire off a couple of rounds," he said, motioning toward the trees about two hundred yards away. "Let's see where *their* machine guns are."

The two cooks were not happy with the order. An M1's orange muzzle flash, particularly against the background of a heavy snowfall, would be like a bull's-eye hoisted over their position. Barber must have realized this, for to assuage their fear he remained upright behind their hole. They opened up. Nothing. The Chinese, Bavaro thought, must have swallowed smart pills. Not only did the enemy machine guns remain silent; all fire from the woods ceased.

Barber limped away. The cooks couldn't tell if he was satisfied or angry. As Barber's figure receded into the trees, they went about setting up grenade booby traps below their hole. This was as close as Fox Company came to a firefight in the early morning hours of the fourth night on the hill.

"Incidents," however, occurred — as incidents have a tendency to do on a battlefield. In the thinning darkness moments before dawn the bazooka section squad leader Sergeant Scully observed a sniper burrowing among the frozen enemy corpses one hundred yards across the road. Scully aimed and squeezed his trigger but his M1 jammed. He yelled to Bavaro in the next foxhole, pointing out the skulking figure. Bavaro fired and killed the man.

"Nice shot for a cook," said Scully.

"Got my expert marksman's patch long before I knew what a ladle was," Bavaro said. Remarks like Scully's really pissed him off.

Phil Bavaro considered himself as much of a warrior as any other Marine in Fox Company. He was from Newark, New Jersey, and he had enlisted in 1946 and completed the cooks and bakers course at Camp Lejeune in North Carolina that year. But then he had injured his back in — of all things — a kitchen accident; he received an honorable medical discharge in 1947. Still, he was determined to fight in the next war

— any war — with the Corps. His older brother Frank had landed in Normandy on D-Day, and Phil was damned well not going to let Frank hog all the family glory. So he had reenlisted after his injury healed and had been assigned to a Marine rifle company.

His battalion had been completing training maneuvers at Camp Lejeune when the North Koreans crossed the 38th Parallel, and he was disappointed upon his debarkation in San Diego to be issued a tropical uniform, mosquito netting, and antimalaria pills. The landings at Inchon were just taking place, but according to scuttlebutt his outfit was heading for French Indochina, where the French were getting their asses handed to them by the Vietminh. So when the coast of Japan hove into view from the deck of the USS *General Walker,* a 20,000-ton troop transport, Bavaro and his rifle company whooped with delight. They were going to Korea.

Since arriving at Wonsan nineteen days earlier, Bavaro had been miserable. There were not enough experienced cooks in-country, and some pencil pusher had obviously gone through his personnel file because he'd immediately been handed a skillet and a coffee grinder to tote with his

412

rifle and grenades. Also, he learned that he was replacing a Fox Company cook who had been killed by a land mine — a bad omen. It was not long before Bavaro learned that cooks and bakers operated differently out in the field. They were expected not only to prepare meals for the company but to fill in as stretcher bearers, runners, foxhole diggers, ammunition carriers, and riflemen. Bavaro could live with that, even if he was rusty.

At Sudong, he had stood watch with a light machine gun for four consecutive nights, anxious every moment about figures he could barely see moving in the shadows. Were they civilian refugees? Most likely. But the thought never left his mind that they could be an enemy force about to overrun the outfit. One starless night at Koto-ri, when the first severe, icy cold had struck Fox, he had forgone the trench latrine to defecate in what he thought was a spare helmet — only to discover the next morning that the helmet was his platoon sergeant's steel pot. And in Hagaru-ri he had nearly burned down the field kitchen with a stove fire.

OK, so maybe he wasn't the Marine on the recruiting posters. And maybe he wasn't even very handy in the kitchen. But he could sure as hell handle an M1. *Nice shot for a cook? Fuck that!*

At 6 a.m., the machine gunner Jack Page again saw two Chinese officers ambling up the MSR as if they were looking for a picnic spot. *What is with these Chinamen?* They stopped at the shot-up hulk that had once been Private First Class French's mail Jeep, climbed in, and stood on the backseat.

Page and his assistant gunner grabbed their M1s, counted silently to three, and blasted the Chinese off the vehicle with a single shot apiece. They then crawled down to the road and appropriated the sacks of grenades the two men had carried, as well as several maps and other papers from inside their uniforms. On the way back Page detoured past the frozen bodies of yesterday's two sightseers to grab a red fedora as a souvenir. His assistant gunner was disappointed to find the other red hat pocked with bullet holes.

An hour later, at 7 a.m., Captain Barber was informed of yet another battalion of Chinese marching down the rocky ridge from behind Toktong-san, headed for the rocky knoll. This was, by Barber's reckoning, the third enemy battalion — fifteen companies — committed to sweeping him

414

off Fox Hill. It struck him that Litzenberg and Murray must be on the move from the Chosin — the Reds seemed to want Tok-tong Pass in the worst way. Four days earlier enemy scouts, and no doubt their officers, had surely watched Fox Company climb this hill. They must have assumed the un-dermanned American outfit could be swat-ted away in a night.

Now Barber wondered. Hadn't they read the military manual, specifically the chapter explaining that even the best-laid battle plans never survive the first contact with the enemy?

Bill Barber may have been in the dark about the precarious state of the American out-posts stranded at the Chosin Reservoir, but the world was not. The Marines at Yudam-ni, Hagaru-ri, and Fox Hill had already taken nearly 1,200 casualties — and another five hundred were reported from the Army task force east of the reservoir. Headlines around the world used words like "Trapped" and "Surrounded." The headline in the *New York Times* was typical — "U.S. Marines Encircled Near Reservoir in North-east Beat Off Attacks by Chinese."

Switchboards at Marine bases across the United States lit up with calls from anxious wives and parents. The head of the Central Intelligence Agency, General Walter Bedell Smith, who had been Dwight D. Eisenhower's chief of staff during World War II, declared that only international diplomacy could now prevent MacArthur's right pincer column from being swallowed by the Chinese.

Moreover, in just twenty-four hours the questions from the press had become, uncharacteristically, more pointed. The "gung ho" image and the comparison to Dunkirk were not being accepted. In Washington a Marine spokesman, thronged by reporters, was forced to admit for the first time that X Corps' situation was "serious, but not hopeless." In Korea, however, the Marine First Division was conceding nothing. The pugnacious Colonel "Chesty" Puller, commanding two battalions twenty-six miles south of the Chosin at Koto-ri, asserted, "We've been looking for the enemy for some time now. We finally found him. We're surrounded. That simplifies things."

When President Truman refused to rule out the use of atomic bombs against China, other nations were appalled, as was the United Nations General Assembly. The British prime minister, Clement Attlee, promised to fly to Washington to dissuade

Truman from starting another world war. It would be the first of four such trips by a rattled Attlee.

On the ground near the Chosin, the possible onset of World War III was not the most pressing problem. General Almond had abandoned the irrational plan to use the Marines to relieve the Eighth Army in the west, and colonels Litzenberg and Murray had received General Smith's Joint Operation Order No. 1 to evacuate Yudam-ni. Both officers realized that fighting their way down to Hagaru-ri was the key to the survival of the entire First Division.

Gone were the days of Tootsie Rolls and shoe polish at the Hagaru-ri PX. The village was now an island in a sea of Chinese. Yet though the enemy might have entrapped American positions as far south as Puller's bivouac in Koto-ri, at Hagaru-ri there were supply and ammunition dumps as well as the integral airstrip, now close enough to completion to receive cargo planes. Inside the Hagaru-ri perimeter, the Fifth and Seventh regiments could regroup and re-equip. Inside Hagaru-ri, the Marines could fly their wounded to safety and take under their wing the beaten Army "doggies" ensnared on the other side of the reservoir. Inside Hagaru-ri, they could reestablish contact with the outside world, catch their breath, and continue the long breakout to the waiting Navy evacuation ships seventy-eight miles to the south off the port of Hungnam.

According to Colonel Alpha Bowser at Hagaru-ri, two prayers were appropriate on this day: "First, that the Fifth and Seventh Marines would reach Hagaru-ri quickly with their fighting ability intact. Second, that we would hold on to Hagaru-ri as they fought their way toward us."

He might have added a third: that Barber's company would still exist when Litzenberg and Murray reached Fox Hill.

2

At just past 7 a.m., Lieutenant Campbell stood on the west slope watching the latest Chinese battalion file down the ridge. He was struck by what could be considered a crazy idea. He turned his gaze down the hill and saw the company's two heavy machine-gun emplacements dug in forty yards below him. Campbell's training as a forward artillery spotter had included studies of all long-firing weapons, and he knew well the range of a Browning thirty-caliber water-cooled machine gun. Perhaps, just maybe . . .

He yelled to the gunners Page and Holt

418

— and did a double take when a red fedora worn on top of a parka popped up from one of their holes. He pointed to the enemy column five hundred to six hundred yards away. "You think you can elevate your barrels, fire up through the treetops, and over the crest of that ridge?"

"Aye-aye, sir."

The machine gunners grabbed spare belts of ammunition still laced with red tracers, positioned their guns, and lit off a couple of short bursts. The tracers arced to the top of the rocky ridge and over it. The gunners went through several belts as the Chinese on the ridge fell dead or wounded or dived for cover.

Near the command post Captain Barber reached for his field phone and called Campbell: "Good job, son."

Son? To the lieutenant this seemed odd. Barber was only a few years older than he was.

Meanwhile, the blasts from the machine guns had awakened Warren McClure from another morphine dream. He sat up and then stood, tentatively. His legs felt wobbly, but he forced himself to walk to the entrance of the med tent. Someone offered him a dented tin mug filled with steaming coffee. This seemed to fortify him — enough, he thought, to let him traverse the one hundred yards to the west slope and get back to his old foxhole to fetch his gear. If he ran across a weapon on the trip, all the better. His left hand was still strong enough to hold a grenade or a sidearm, maybe even a carbine.

His spirit willing but his flesh weak, Mc-Clure had to give up after ten yards. He could walk a little, downhill, and even a bit on level ground. But trudging up the high ground in the direction of his old hole proved too much. He could hear the blood sloshing around in his right lung cavity when he moved, and the bullet hole in his chest began to seep a watery pink substance — a putrid combination of blood and pus. He sat, out of breath, among several wounded Marines who were smoking cigarettes around a campfire near the med tent.

These men, though too badly wounded to fight, had been out gathering firewood. One was his old friend Private First Class Amos Fixico, with whom McClure had landed at Inchon. A bloody bandage covered both of Fixico's eyes, and he complained of a searing headache. Despite this obvious disadvantage, he was still able to carry wood in one hand and hold onto the flap of a fellow Marine's parka with the other.

The sight of the wounded Fixico stirred

up memories in McClure. One was Fixico's almost comical intolerance for alcohol. As the butt of hillbilly jokes, McClure had never put much stock in stereotypes, so he rejected the notion about Indians and firewater. But it was true that Fixico, a Ute, needed no more than a sniff of whiskey to make him want to kill every white man he'd ever met. Once, in Japan, McClure had actually needed to tie the drunken Fixico to his bunk. Now, he was glad Fixico had not been carried to the same tent as Lieutenant Brady, who had the bottle of White Horse scotch.

As he and Fixico talked, McClure said that he had at first believed one of his own squadmates had shot him in the back during the first night's firefight, and Fixico told him about Sergeant Keirn's light machine-gun nest being overrun, and his own adventures in the woods with Dick Bonelli and the wounded Corporal Koone.

The more Warren McClure discussed their circumstances the more frustrated and angry he became — at himself, at his useless right arm, at his shot-up lung, at the Chinese, at MacArthur, at the goddamn Korean War. He stood up and wheezed his way back to his stretcher in the med tent. His fury dissipated at the sight of the paralyzed Marine. He opened another can of peaches and began spoon-feeding the wounded boy.

Harry Burke crouched behind the smaller hut among a dozen exhausted, thirsty Marines. It was 8:15 a.m. The spring at the bottom of the hill was exactly thirty-five paces away — across open terrain. A couple of the men had already made the dash to fill their canteens cups, drawing the attention of a sniper in the woods at the base of the South Hill. To call this enemy soldier a sharpshooter would be to overstate the case. In fact, he was a lousy shot, and as more Marines took their turn at the spring he had barely nicked a couple in the legs. Still.

Now it was Burke's turn, and he ran for all he was worth. When he reached the spring he danced from side to side, a moving target, as the fresh water splashed into his canteen. A few rifle slugs cracked the ice around him, but that was as close as they came. His canteen full, Burke took off. But instead of heading back for the cover of the small hut, he made a beeline to the larger hut, which was closer to the spring and closer to the road. He doubted that anyone had ventured very near this shack since he had returned for his sleeping bag the first morning and taken a souvenir whistle and some pamphlets from a dead Chinese officer.

With the sniper's bullets at his feet, Burke dived behind the hut and nearly banged heads with a wounded Red sitting with his back to the wall. The kid, another conscript barely into his teens, was conscious, if evidently dying. His head was encrusted with a thin layer of ice, and blood-red icicles hung from his bullet-pocked uniform. The only signs of life were small white puffs of condensation escaping his mouth. Burke couldn't believe the boy wasn't dead yet.

During basic training, before shipping out to Korea, Burke had made friends with a couple of old China hands, and he'd picked up a little of the lingo. Now he tried to communicate, but the boy was unresponsive. *Too far gone,* Burke thought. He unholstered his sidearm, paused, and slid the pistol back into its leather harness. *What's the point?*

Picking his way back up to his foxhole, Burke passed Sergeant Kipp and Corporal Gaines coming down the hill. They asked if he had seen anything, or anybody, inside the large hut. Burke said he hadn't looked in. Kipp and Gaines continued on down, and a moment later Burke heard rifle reports from inside. Kipp and Gaines had run across several wounded Chinese. Burke didn't wait around to ask if they had shot the dying kid.

About forty-five minutes later, at just past 9 a.m., Staff Sergeant John Henry saw two North Korean officers in full field uniforms walking up the MSR from the east. This was a rare occurrence. Henry couldn't remember the last time he'd seen hostile North Koreans. Even more unusual was the fact that the machine gunner Jack Page wasn't around to shoot them; the aroma of brewing coffee had lured him up to the med tents. When the North Koreans turned the corner of the road near the southeast base of the hill, Henry and one of his ammunition carriers were waiting for them behind a growth of tall brush.

Henry had no compunction about shooting oblivious enemy combatants, even two soldiers bughouse enough to mistakenly wander into an active battlefield. But these officers might be of value. At the very least, unlike the Chinese prisoners, they would be able to communicate with the civilian Korean interpreter, Mr. Chung. Perhaps they could serve as intermediaries, linguistic bridges, between Mr. Chung and the Chinese captives. *Might know where all the rest of the gooks are. Might help us figure out a way to get off this goddamn hill.*

These notions raced through John Henry's mind as the ammunition carrier, his face unclouded by thought, shot one man dead. Henry was so startled by the rifle report next to his ear that he instinctively squeezed the trigger on his Thompson. The second officer fell to the ground, his chest caved in.

Seven miles to the north, not far from the western bank of the Chosin Reservoir, a collection of some 350 Marines — the tattered remnants of the First Battalion's Abel, Baker, and Charlie rifle companies — shuffled into uneven rows. As they tried to keep warm, Lieutenant Colonel Ray Davis emerged from his command post tent with his officers and strode to and fro before them.

Davis was freshly shaved, but his face was creased with deep lines of strain and exhaustion. Most of his men were baffled. All around them fellow leathernecks from the Fifth, Seventh, and Eleventh regiments were making frantic final preparations to quit the Chosin — in General Oliver Smith's euphemistic words, to "attack in another direction." But Davis's men, the survivors of his First Rifle Battalion, did not seem to be a part of this evacuation plan. They wondered why.

The "breakout" strategy was not complicated. Units from Colonel Murray's Fifth Regiment would lead the attack out of Yudam-ni, fighting for and seizing the high ground on both sides of the MSR, while Colonel Litzenberg's Seventh Regiment disengaged the main column from the village — a thorny undertaking. It wasn't just a matter of marching south. There were scores of vehicles, wounded, and dead involved. The three Chinese divisions surrounding them would not simply sit back and wave good-bye. Therefore, a rear guard from the Fifth Regiment, with assistance from several guns of the Eleventh Regiment, would be asked to hold off the enemy troops who were sure to flow into the abandoned hamlet. But with luck — a lot of luck — most of the Marines in the rear guard would be at Hagaru-ri for chow by the following day.

Davis's men knew nothing of this as their commander paced in front of them. Finally he halted, swiveled toward them, and stood still. Enlisted men in battle usually receive small-bore intelligence, faulty or incomplete. But on this occasion Davis believed his Marines had the right to know what they would be soon up against. After several uncomfortable minutes he swept his arm to encompass the controlled chaos of more than two Marine regiments breaking camp and turning themselves around to head the fourteen miles south.

"They are going down the road," he said. "We are not. Fellow Marines are in trouble, and we are going to rescue them. Nothing is going to stand in our way."

The First Battalion, he continued, would march southeast down the MSR, leading Litzenberg's main column for just a little over two miles to Hill 1419 — Turkey Hill. This information drew a sardonic laugh. Davis allowed it to die down. At Turkey Hill, he said, they would jump off the road under cover of darkness to begin an overland trek to Toktong Pass while Litzenberg's main column continued down the MSR.

"Surprise will be our essential weapon," Davis told the men. "Marines don't usually attack at night, so the Chinese won't be expecting us."

He had already explained to his officers that their tiny detachment would break off the road in single file, traverse the hill, and set off cross-country in a northeast direction for the back door to the pass. The distance was four and a half miles as the crow flies, and their slog would take them over three mountain ridges before they reached the fourth, final, and highest one — the rocky ridgeline snaking down from Toktong-san. On the other side of it lay Fox Hill. Davis knew that, taking ascents and descents into consideration, the march would be more than nine miles — if they managed to stay on course.

He did not mention this to his enlisted men. He did tell them that elements of the howitzer battery at Yudam-ni had agreed to guide at least the early leg of their night march with intermittent star shells. "They're staying here so we can get there," he said.

He reemphasized that once they punched through the Chinese line at Turkey Hill, which was about a hundred yards off the east side of the road, the success of their mission would depend on stealth and speed. No cook fires would be lit to heat meals, and each man was to carry only one full canteen. He also suggested that his men discard everything in their C-rations except the canned fruit, crackers, and chocolate. The entire battalion, he said, was to jettison all superfluous equipment and lug only essential weapons, extra ammunition, and sleeping bags (for all the good the sleeping bags would do; most men still carried

428

summer-weight bags issued months ago). Crews for the heavy and light machine guns were doubled, and each rifleman was handed an 81-mm mortar shell to lug in his mummy bag. A squad had already been assigned to haul two 81-mm mortar tubes, six heavy machine guns, and spare ammo on litters and stretchers.

As Davis went among his Marines for a final culling of the sick and wounded, Baker Company's mortar officer Lieutenant Joe Owen sidled up to his company commander, First Lieutenant Joseph Kurcaba. Kurcaba was the son of Polish immigrants who had settled in Brooklyn, New York; Owen's wife, in upstate New York, was also of Polish descent. The two officers had been together under Davis since Pendleton, when he had stood up the First Battalion, and over the next months they had bonded, trading friendly banter in the few Polish words and phrases Owen had picked up from his in-laws. Though at six-foot-five Owen towered over the stocky Kurcaba, he had come to consider Kurcaba his big brother, and some Marines referred to them as the Warsaw version of Mutt and Jeff. This morning, however, their conversation included no jokes about kielbasa or potato *wódka.*

Owen was not worried so much about finding and reaching Fox Hill as he was about getting past Turkey Hill. He and Kurcaba had both been there, under precarious circumstances, and they remembered the tangle of deep gullies and thick woods on its steep, slippery slopes. If the Chinese still maintained a stronghold on Turkey Hill, as Owen was certain they did, this little side trip would be getting off to a dodgy start.

Kurcaba shrugged. He had fought through World War II and had seen worse. There was nothing to be done, he told Owen, except to put one foot in front of the other.

When Davis finished his inspection, he formed up the Marines he had tapped for the march. As if he had read Owen's mind, he knew they felt this was a suicide mission. He needed to give them some little hope. "With any luck," he said, "by the time we relieve Fox Company and get the hill squared away, we should be in a position to meet up with the main column on the MSR."

If Davis felt any apprehension about relying on outdated topographic maps to guide him around sheer slopes and unexpected cliffs — or about leading hungry, spent men miles across uncharted enemy-held terrain, or about further splitting the undermanned

Marine breakout forces abandoning the Chosin Reservoir — he did not betray it.

After the assembly broke up, Kurcaba sought out his Second Platoon leader, First Lieutenant Chew-Een Lee. "Battalion wants you as the lead platoon," he said.

Kurcaba had enlisted in 1935, and he figured that in his fifteen years as a Marine he'd seen everything the Corps had to throw at him. But he was taken aback when Lee — a slight Chinese-American officer — smiled. This was rare. Lee had a chip on his shoulder and was known throughout the Seventh Regiment as a blister of a man. His arrogance, however, was matched by his competence as a leader and fighter.

For his part, Lee knew that by *battalion,* Kurcaba meant *Davis.* He thought, *Well, of course he does. Who else would he want?* Still, the directive rankled — not in itself but because of how it had been delivered. It should have been Lieutenant Kurcaba, not "battalion," who ordered him to take the point. That was the Marine Corps way; orders were passed down through the hierarchy, by the book. And if Chew-Een Lee went by anything, he went by the book.

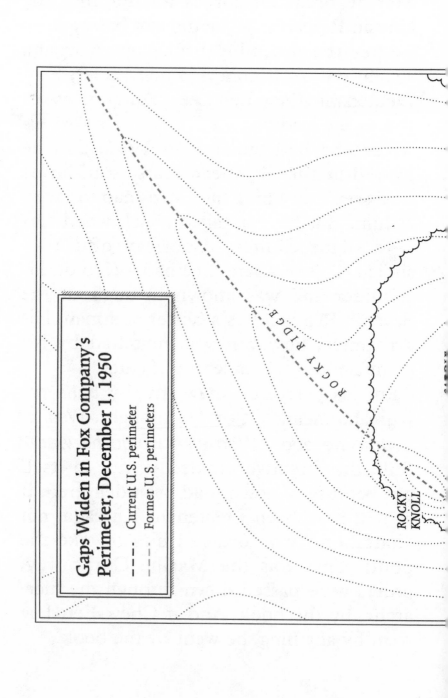

Gaps Widen in Fox Company's
Perimeter, December 1, 1950

- - - Current U.S. perimeter
- - - Former U.S. perimeters

ROCKY RIDGE

ROCKY
KNOLL

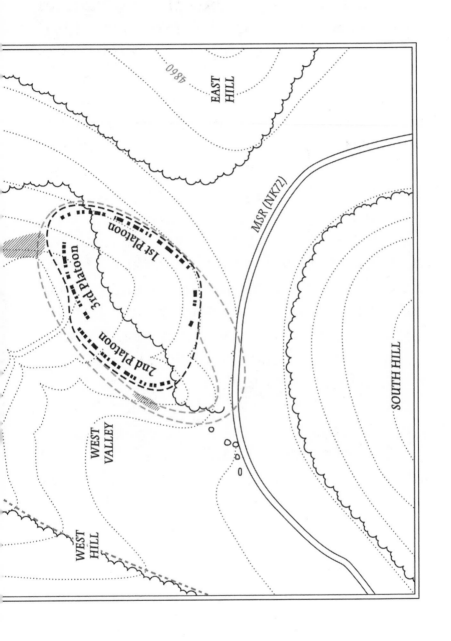

EAST HILL

4860

MSR (NK72)

1st Platoon

2nd Platoon

3rd Platoon

SOUTH HILL

WEST VALLEY

WEST HILL

On their fourth day on Fox Hill the Marines watched as the Corsairs returned, eight fighter-bombers riding the air currents above the mountains like great green metallic hawks. The Marines could make out the letters L and D on the tails, for the Love Dog Squadron. There was a competition brewing, a game of one-upmanship. The Love Dogs were trying to top yesterday's performance by the Checkerboards.

They flew in so low that men near the crest ducked. They strafed both sides of the same ridge that the machine gunners Page and Holt had blasted two hours before. They regrouped and swooped again, scraping off bombs, rockets, and napalm canisters in a perfectly straight line from the rocky knoll and up the rocky ridges to the base of Toktong-san.

They were re-forming for a third run when Captain Barber called them off by way of their air controller. Two Flying Boxcars had appeared over the southern horizon, and Barber requested that the Corsair squadron flight leader keep his pilots in the area as the cargo planes made their drop. While the fighter-bombers flew low in the sky, no Chinese sniper would dare show his face. The Boxcars vectored leisurely over the "X" in the center of the parachute circle and delivered nearly all their bundles on target. A few overshot the mark, landing in the east valley just beyond the First Platoon's perimeter.

Barber asked the Corsairs to machine-gun the East Hill and South Hill while a small detail moved to recover the wayward pallets. The pilots complied, and after every crate had been dragged behind the lines the aircraft took one more run at the rocky knoll and the rocky ridges, discharging their last bullets and bombs. Then they waggled their wings and were gone, accompanied by another exuberant cheer from the Americans on the hill.

Listening to the roar from his men, Barber sensed a change in their mood. It was 12:30 p.m. and the blizzard had lightened to a few scattered flakes, but the temperature was dropping about one degree every hour. He called together his officers and platoon leaders; it was time, he said, to take the fight to the enemy. "Let's see how many the Love Dogs left standing," he said.

Barber knew that — more than by the miserable weather, more than by their hunger, more than by their untenable tactical situation — his men had been sapped by four straight days of defensive fighting.

They were Marines, and they had been trained to attack. If he could get them out of their foxholes and on their feet, if he could make them see they were taking the fight to the Chinese, their morale would return.

He was not wrong. When his officers returned from spreading the word, they reported that this was the best news Fox Company had heard in five days.

The captain organized a patrol in force — a four-man fire team from the First Platoon headed by the squad leader Sergeant Daniel Slapinskas, augmented by eight mortarmen from one of the 81-mm crews. The thirteen-man recon detail would cross the saddle and poke around in the nooks and crannies at the base of the rocky knoll in search of any surviving, or regrouping, Chinese. Dick Kline's second 81-mm unit would cover them with suppressing fire from the hilltop. As word of this "offensive" spread, Fox Hill throbbed with energy.

It took Kline and his men ten minutes to lug their 81-mm tubes up to a slight depression near the crest of the hill. They began laying down covering fire soon after, walking shells at twenty-yard intervals the three hundred yards across the saddle to the bottom of the rocky knoll. Gouts of dark earth flecked with chunks of hard-packed white snow erupted like geysers. Into this maelstrom raced Slapinskas's patrol, the Marines leapfrogging over each other in a classic advance-and-cover maneuver.

The point fire team — corporals Charles North and Dan Montville and privates first class John Scott and Lee D. Wilson — met no resistance as they moved out fifty yards in front of the main body. Scott and Montville assumed covering positions just short of the rocky knoll while North and Wilson skirted the huge ledge. The four Marines were somewhat shocked. From Fox Hill you couldn't really tell how high this stone outcropping rose. Up close it looked about the size of the Capitol in Washington, D.C. North and Wilson cautiously worked their way around to its back.

The ground on either side and behind the knoll was crisscrossed with trenches, most leading back up to the rocky ridge. North and Wilson crept into one of these dugouts on their hands and knees. They had nearly circumvented the outcropping when they saw numerous dead soldiers in a half-dug ditch, most likely a work detail that had been deepening the trough. Then they heard snoring. Wilson nearly jumped out of his skin. These men weren't dead; they were asleep. *How the hell had they slept through that Corsair bombardment?*

The Marines leveled their M1s and emptied the clips, killing many of the Chinese and scattering the rest. As the survivors fled haphazardly, Scott and Montville picked them off. A Chinese officer jumped from behind a rock and tried to rally the panicked troops. Scott noticed, just before shooting him, that he was wearing a blue baseball cap.

The knoll was large, and its south side sloped gently to the saddle. Wilson and North climbed to the top, reloaded, and fired into another enemy platoon that was rushing down the ridgeline. With North and Wilson still on the knoll, Scott approached the half-dug trench. Someone threw a potato masher. Scott leaped backward, and as he fell his rifle clanked on a rock. He was uninjured, but when he aimed his M1 it would not fire on automatic. He settled for one round at a time. Then he saw a squad break off from the platoon engaged by North and Wilson and begin moving toward him. Individual rifle rounds were not going to stop them.

He looked around. When the enemy work crew fled, they had abandoned their gear. Scott picked up a sack of hand grenades.

438

He reached in — there were nearly a dozen — and started heaving them at the twenty or so Chinese soldiers closing on his position.

In a moment Scott was out of grenades and armed with only a rifle firing one bullet at a time. He turned to Montville, about twenty yards behind him. He was about to yell when a concussion grenade landed at Montville's feet, knocked him backward to the ground, and shattered *his* M1.

Now Scott did holler, "Fall back — I'll cover you." But Montville, still cradling his broken rifle in his arms, appeared stunned.

"Fall back!" Scott shouted again, this time with heat in his voice. Montville snapped to. He lurched off the saddle and into the west valley, ran a few yards, and instinctively took up a covering position, despite his useless rifle. Scott leaped past him down into the valley, eyeing Montville's smashed M1 as he raced by. The two retreated in this manner until they neared the Second Platoon's lines on the west slope.

Montville, still somewhat in shock, had to be tackled by Gray Davis as he stumbled back through the perimeter. He had nearly walked into the field of booby-trap grenades that Davis and Luke Johnson had strung through the low tree branches. Scott stuck closer to the edge of the saddle. He had almost made the tree line when a bullet tore through his shoulder. He crawled the rest of the way.

Across the saddle, North and Wilson were pinned down on the rocky knoll. Sergeant Slapinskas led the rest of his detail to cover their escape. Chinese soldiers streamed out of foxholes, caves, and rock crevices behind the knoll. More were surging down the rocky ridge. North and Wilson backed their way down the knoll, jumped the final fifteen feet, and landed amid Slapinskas's men. The entire patrol began zigzagging back across the saddle, counting on covering fire from Kline's 81-mms and the forward foxholes of the Third Platoon. Again plumes of dirt, snow, and smoke erupted across the land bridge, this time behind the retreating patrol.

A mortarman was shot in the gut and went down. Two Marines running past grabbed him under each arm and dragged him away. A Navy corpsman raced to meet them. He, too, was hit. Two Marines from the Third Platoon ran out to retrieve him. Directing covering fire, the XO, Clark Wright, stood up in his hole and was shot twice in the side.

When Slapinskas's detail finally reached

the safety of the perimeter, two Marines carried Captain Barber up the hill on a stretcher. His wound had worsened, and his improvised crutch would no longer suffice. The bullet he'd taken had glanced off his thighbone and lodged in his hip. The shattered bone was causing an infection to creep down his entire leg, and there was no penicillin for it. Even crawling in and out of his sleeping bag had become torturous, and after forty-eight hours of bearing the pain he had relented and allowed a corpsman to dose him with a morphine syrette. Before he'd taken it, however, he summoned his XO and first sergeant to his tent and told them to keep an eye on him.

"I want you to analyze every decision I make, everything I say. If you find me befuddled or irrational, I want you to tell me. And if you think I can't understand . . ." Barber paused to let his instructions sink in. "Do whatever you think is necessary."

But the captain showed no signs of incoherence as Sergeant Slapinskas delivered his recon report. One Marine was dead, four more were wounded, and at least a company of Chinese were still holding the rocky knoll. Slapinskas thought about the plastering the rocky knoll had taken from the Marine fighter-bombers. "The Corsair jockeys will not be happy," he said.

Barber gazed across the saddle. No Chinese were following. He could already sense that the adrenaline was ebbing in his tired troops. He decided that if his men were not going to have to fight, he was not going to let their minds go slack. "OK, let's get this hill cleaned up," he said. He wanted trash buried, the remaining C-rations counted, and every spare weapon stacked near the command post. The rest of the afternoon passed uneventfully.

On the banks of the Chosin it was late morning by the time Lieutenant Colonel Davis ordered his relief column to mount up. Factoring in the wind chill, he estimated that the temperature was close to minus-twenty-five and falling. When the Marines reached the hills the gale would make it feel more like minus-fifty. Each of his weary men carried nearly fifty pounds of equipment; the battalion groaned under all this weight.

Davis tramped in among the men, reminding them that although they were surrounded by the enemy, this was not a retreat. He pointed toward the barren heights. "Fox Company is just over those ridges," he said. "They're surrounded and need our help. They held the road open for us, and now it's our turn to return the favor."

Semper fidelis.

As the column inched forward, Lieutenant Peter Arioli of the Navy appeared out of the snowy mist and introduced himself to Davis. Arioli, a regimental surgeon, had heard that Davis's medic had been wounded and volunteered to join the rescue mission. The battalion commander extended a hand. "Glad to have you with us," he said.

Lieutenant Chew-Een Lee looked at the new doc with a jaundiced eye. Arioli was too thin and seemed *soft,* as if he had never raised a callus in his life. Lee thought, *Good intentions, but he'll never make it.*

Although no Marine was daft enough to mention it, much less josh him about it, Chew-Een Lee realized he looked like a court jester: he was wearing bright pink supply-drop air panels, which he had draped over his shoulders like a cape. He didn't care how he looked. The idea was that his men would be able to find him in a tight spot. As usual, he would be out front. This was typical of Chew-Een Lee's military career. He didn't like following, and he didn't like followers.

Lee, who was twenty-four, had joined the

Marine Corps six years earlier. One reason was to obliterate the stereotype of Chinese-Americans as just laundrymen and waiters. His height had been recorded (perhaps overgenerously) as five feet six, and he weighed only about 130 pounds, so he was one of the smallest men in the First Division. But he was also a hard man, and a hard taskmaster.

During the fourteen-day voyage from San Diego to Japan, other platoon leaders had scoffed when Lee "held school" for his enlisted men day and night on the deck of the troopship. Even Lee had suspected he was drilling his men so hard that half would have gone over the hill had they been on land. But he had a point to make, and he believed he had made it. If Red China entered the war, as Lee privately believed it would, he would be leading men with no experience and virtually no training against a numerically superior and ideologically committed force. The result of his harsh regimen on the troopship, Lee was certain, was that his raw Marines were now more terrified of him than they ever could be of the enemy.

A month earlier Baker Company had caught the brunt of the first fight against the Chinese in the Sudong Gorge. An enemy squad, perhaps twenty men, had held one of the smaller hills overlooking the gorge, and Lee single-handedly charged them and wiped them out, an act for which he was awarded the Navy Cross. As he was on his way down to the road, a sniper's bullet had shattered his right elbow, and he was evacuated against his wishes to a temporary Army hospital in Hamhung.

He was about to be flown to Japan when he and another wounded Marine went AWOL, stole a Jeep from the motor pool, and began making their way north, back to their units. When the Jeep ran out of gas, Lee — who was surely wanted by the MPs for stealing a vehicle, and whose arm was still bound in a cast and sling — walked the final ten miles back to the First Battalion. As he passed through American positions he was aware that even though he didn't carry a weapon, he might be shot for looking so "gooky."

Lieutenant Kurcaba had nearly fallen over when he saw Lee limp into Baker Company's bivouac to resume his command. (Lee did not tell Kurcaba or anyone else that in escaping from the hospital he had also been fleeing probable charges for assaulting a soldier. In sick bay, Lee had encountered a man suffering from battle fatigue. When Lee demanded to see a physical wound, the soldier merely shrank away. Enraged at what he considered cowardice, Lee slapped him.)

Lee had worn the sling and the cast on his arm ever since — through Hagaru-ri and up the MSR to the Chosin — always taking the point on patrols, never once complaining as he hefted his carbine in his good left hand and used his hip to balance the rifle when he fired. His knee was also badly injured — it wouldn't lock and kept buckling — and he had a cold that was getting worse by the day. He told no one. But now, as the First Battalion began its overland march, he discarded the sling, which was reduced to a bloody rag. He thought that the sling could be seen as a sign of weakness, and he could not abide that. Inside the cast his elbow still felt as if a sledgehammer had smashed it, but he would will himself to overcome the pain. His father would have been proud of him.

In California members of the Lee family were known throughout the Sacramento Valley's Chinese-American community as the "golden ones." Sometime after World War I — no one was sure of the exact year — Lee's father had emigrated from Guangzhou (Canton), the provincial capital of Guangdon Province. The elder Lee, whose

Chinese name meant "Brilliant Scholar," had a knack for languages and picked up English quickly. He fast rose from farmworker to owner of a small farm to labor contractor, allocating fruit and vegetable pickers to the valley's white farmers.

After establishing himself in his adoptive country, Lee's father returned to Guangdon for an arranged marriage with a beautiful woman named Gold Jade. The two returned to the United States, and in the first five years of their marriage they had five of their seven children — four boys and three girls. Chew-Een was the eldest son.

The Lee farmstead failed early in the Great Depression, and the senior Lee moved his family to Sacramento itself, where he started a grocery business that evolved into a wholesale produce company supplying local restaurants and hotels. A point of pride for the Lees was that they came from the same Central Mountain district of Guangdon as the Chinese revolutionary and political leader Dr. Sun Yat-sen, often regarded as the father of modern China. Although not wealthy, the Lees considered themselves a sort of local aristocracy ruling over the Chinese migrant version of Okies. Throughout the 1930s, during the Sino-Japanese War, Lee's father was an influential political activist and fund-raiser for Sun Yat-sen's government.

Chew-Een Lee attended an elementary school in Sacramento consisting primarily of immigrant children — predominantly Chinese- and Japanese-Americans, with a few Mexicans, blacks, and whites. He was aware of Americans' attitudes toward the Chinese — these attitudes had led to the Chinese Exclusion Act of 1886, then still in effect — but he rarely encountered overt racial prejudice. He did have some fights with Japanese boys whose girlfriends swooned over his strong, handsome facial features, particularly his high cheekbones. And once, during a family outing, the Lees' car overheated in a white suburb of Sacramento, and young Lee watched as a white man humiliated his father by spraying him with a garden hose after being asked for water to refill the car's radiator. From that day on, Lee recalled, his father had drilled into the four boys a determination never to wash anybody's shirts.

Lee was a good student and an avid reader of history. His dream was to become a pilot in the U.S. Army Air Corps during World War II, so he joined his high school's ROTC program. But when he was drafted in 1944, Army doctors told him that he lacked the depth perception necessary to fly a plane. Although he put himself through a rigorous program of eye exercises, he still could not pass the flight test by the time he was shipped to an Army depot in San Francisco later that year. He had never heard of the Marines Corps, but while he was in the depot awaiting an assignment, a recruiting officer wearing a uniform with red-bordered chevrons asked for volunteers. Lee liked the uniform, and he also heard the Army draftees saying that the leathernecks were "the first in combat and the first to die." This suited Lee fine and he immediately signed up for the Marines. He thought the highest honor he could achieve was to be killed in a just war.

At first the Marine recruiting officer eyed Lee's scrawny frame with skepticism. "Are you sure you can carry a pack?" he said.

Lee may have been small but he was all sinew, and to prove it he hefted two rucksacks off the floor, threw them over his shoulders, and marched back and forth across the depot. He became a Marine that day.

At boot camp he listed his three service goals in order of preference: the Para-Marines, the Tank Corps, and scout-sniper school. To his dismay he was instead assigned to a six-month Japanese-language school. He was the only regular Marine of Asian descent among the mostly reservist Caucasian scholars in his class, and when he was promoted to buck sergeant — the first regular Asian-American NCO in the Corps' history — he took his three stripes seriously. He prided himself on being the most ornery NCO the Marines had ever produced, and his attitude offended subordinates as well as fellow officers. Lee had no friends.

At the language academy he realized, to his chagrin, that he would miss the fighting in World War II. But he was cheered to recall from his studies of history that, on average, the United States had engaged in combat somewhere in the world, in declared or undeclared wars, every five years. He enrolled in officer candidate school and, as the youngest in his class, began smoking a pipe in the hope that this habit might compensate for his youth, and for his small physical stature.

His fellow Marines continued to be leery of him. Superior officers often tried to counsel him about the chip on his shoulder. He ignored them. Openly and vociferously, he challenged even captains and colonels whose lax standards did not rise to what he considered the right level for the Marine Corps.

Following his postwar deployments to China and Guam to debrief Japanese prisoners, he had been summoned back to Camp Pendleton, where in early 1950 Colonel Homer Litzenberg had been ordered to reconstitute the Seventh Regiment. Lee, now a lieutenant — this rank was another milestone for a regular Asian-American in the Corps — was the first platoon leader selected for the First Battalion's Baker Company. Lee had reservations about Litzenberg and was offended when Litzenberg's eyes teared up during his briefing to the assembled regiment prior to shipping out for Japan: such emotion seemed more appropriate for a grandfather than for a soldier. But Lee's wary respect for the battalion commander Lieutenant Colonel Davis grew as he studied Davis in action. Davis's ability in battle was like his bearing, Lee thought; it radiated confidence.

After the landings at Inchon Lee ran into a younger brother, Chew-Mon "Buck" Lee, in Seoul, the South Korean capital. Chew-Mon Lee was a lieutenant in the Army's Second Infantry Division and had just returned to the front lines from Japan, having been wounded during the North Korean invasion two and a half months earlier. (Another brother, Chew-Fan Lee, the second oldest, was a pacifist, but he served with the Army Medical Service as a pharmacist and would be awarded the Bronze Star after the Chosin campaign.) Lee complained to Chew-Mon that in Japan, before Inchon, Division authorities had tried to make him a staff officer, a move he resisted bitterly.

"They are fools; they see slanted eyes and immediately want to make you an interpreter or some other such nonsense," he told Chew-Mon. "I'm no language officer, and I'm nobody's interpreter. I'm a regular Marine rifle platoon leader. I will lead troops in battle, and if I have to fight American staff officers in order to fight communists, you know I will do it."

During their brief reunion Chew-Mon gave his brother two new Army-issue banana clips that held thirty carbine rounds, twice as many as the Marines' clips carried. Chew-Een then noticed his brother's Army-issue web suspenders. It dawned on him that they would be superb for carrying hand grenades. He asked Chew-Mon for them. He was the *dai-go,* the respected older brother. Chew-Mon complied.

At heart Lee was a fatalist, and his primary goal in life was to honor his family by dying in combat — and give them the added benefit of his $10,000 National Service Life Insurance policy. When he'd enlisted he had not expected to survive World War II, and he considered not being given a chance to fight a blot on his honor. Now the Korean War had given him a second opportunity to fulfill his destiny — to die for his family, his country, his principles. He fully, and happily, expected precisely that to occur on the march to Toktong Pass.

4

When the time came for Lieutenant Colonel Davis's First Battalion to jump off the road south of Yudam-ni, their route was immediately stymied by the Chinese occupying Turkey Hill.

Since Davis's rescue of Charlie Company four nights earlier, numerous enemy machine-gun nests, flanked by mini-mortar emplacements and infantrymen in force, had dug in deep along the hill's four finger ridges. Even repeated air strikes had not been able to root them out. The Third Battalion's How Company (a Seventh Regiment rifle company, not to be confused with the artillery company of the same designation in Hagaru-ri) had been ordered by Colonel Litzenberg to clear the hill prior to

Davis's advance. But How's numbers had been seriously depleted by three days of nearly continuous battle west of Yudam-ni. How was outnumbered two to one, and the men were in no shape to take on an enemy in such strength. This became evident when their initial thrust into the Chinese machine guns was repulsed. Twelve more Marines of How Company were killed and another twenty-seven wounded.

Marine Corps officers prided themselves on their synchronized maneuvers. The Seventh Regiment's disengagement from Yudam-ni while elements from the Fifth Regiment covered them from the surrounding heights was a striking example of a well-conceived battle plan. But Turkey Hill was different. There, Davis's First Battalion was now placed in the position of reinforcing How Company — in essence, Davis led his men into a firefight in order to secure their own line of departure. But there was no way to avoid this. A bloody struggle ensued across the flanks of Turkey Hill, with Able Company joining the few remaining Marines of How Company and slithering into the worst of the enemy fire.

The fight lasted throughout the afternoon; it was dusk before the Americans cleared the Chinese from the summit in hand-to-hand fighting. Davis fretted as he surveyed the battlefield. Too many men had been wounded, and there had been a dreadful loss of ammunition that the column would surely need later. As he reorganized his rifle companies he called for his radioman. He had to speak to Litzenberg. He needed more ammo, and he needed more men.

At 6:30 p.m. on Fox Hill, Captain Barber conducted his perimeter inspection from a stretcher. It was his one concession to his pain. He was amused to find the company cooks Bavaro and Bledsoe — after five days — still scratching their foxhole out of the frozen earth. The foxhole was now chest-high, the deepest by far on the hill, although not quite as wide as Bavaro and Bledsoe would have liked. They flashed the captain a thumbs-up sign as he was carried past, and then flipped a coin for the first watch. Bledsoe won and settled uncomfortably into the bottom of the pit, his body nearly crushing Bavaro's legs and feet. He hadn't slept for two days and he went out like a light.

By 7:30 p.m., Bavaro's frozen feet were excruciatingly painful. He decided he couldn't take it anymore. He tried to wake Bledsoe, first with whispered words, then by shaking him, and finally by yelling into his ear — a dangerous act with the snipers so close around the South Hill. Bledsoe did not stir.

Following the second battle for Turkey Hill, Lieutenant Colonel Davis helped carry his wounded Marines down to the MSR, where they were loaded onto six-by-sixes. He radioed to Colonel Litzenberg and asked to press on immediately. The plan had always been to travel by night, and he knew that if he didn't start his column moving now, the tired, sweaty men might freeze to death where they stood.

Litzenberg agreed, and added that in order to make up for his losses on Turkey Hill, Davis was free to augment his battalion with the approximately fifty-five Marines remaining from How Company. This gave Davis just over four hundred men. At one-sixth its original size, How was, in effect and in fact, no longer a Marine rifle company. When the news of Litzenberg's decision spread through the dilapidated outfit, one of the enlisted men — noting that the company had been more than halved in just the past week — mused that How's "fire-and-maneuver tactics now lacked the maneuver part."

Davis instructed his platoon leaders to

light as many cooking fires as possible all over Turkey Hill, in the hope of fooling the Chinese watching from the heights. *Maybe they'll think we're bedding down for the night.* Then he ordered his battalion to their feet.

Baker Company, with Chew-Een Lee's platoon on point, took the lead. Able and Charlie followed, with How as the rear guard. The column stretched half a mile, and Davis stationed two sergeants on the shoulder of the road at the jump-off mark. The Marines were ordered to secure their gear against any clinking or rattling, and as each man climbed over the snowbank, the NCOs made him jog in place to test for sound.

A blizzard whipped through the mountains above him as Davis radioed to Yudam-ni for the final time. On his pre-arranged signal, the artillery units remaining in the village to cover the main column's movement south opened up on the surrounding heights. Davis hoped that this would keep the enemy's heads down as his column sneaked off. Lee's point squad began breaking trail at 9 p.m. Davis went up to the lieutenant and pointed to a particularly bright star just rising on the horizon. It appeared to be blinking on and off amid the swirling clouds. "That's our guide for as long as we can see it," he said.

The BAR man Richard Gilling, a nineteen-year-old private first class from How Company, was one of the last men to peel off the MSR. If there was a Marine in his depleted unit who felt cheered by the order to march on Toktong Pass, it was Dick Gilling. Gilling, who came from northern New Jersey, had enlisted in 1949 and had been at reservist summer camps and weekend meetings with Kenny Benson and Hector Cafferata. Unlike Cafferata, Gilling liked drinking and playing cards. Now, he missed that camaraderie.

When Gilling was posted to How, it was already a company of experienced regulars: it had been formed at Pendleton before the war broke out. As a greenhorn, he had felt ostracized ever since reaching Wonsan. Even his assistant BAR man resented being subordinate to a reservist who hadn't been through boot camp. This bothered Gilling.

When he and Hector had been split up a month earlier, they had vowed that if something should happen to either of them, the survivor would look after the other's family. That pledge was on Gilling's mind as he reached the shoulder of the MSR, climbed over the snowbank, and jogged in place for the sergeants. He paused for a moment to say good-bye to a buddy, another reservist, who had been wounded on Turkey Hill. As he bent over the stretcher to shake his friend's hand, he also handed the man his own last two boxes of C-rations. When Gilling left with the others, the wounded Marine turned to a man on an adjacent litter.

"There go the Ridgerunners," he said. "Wonder if we'll ever see them again." The name stuck — and it would earn a permanent place in Marine Corps lore.

Within moments there was no trace of Davis's battalion. The Ridgerunners were alone, in the dark, marching deep into enemy territory.

5

The moment Lieutenant Chew-Een Lee and his three-man scout team started down the reverse slope of Turkey Hill, their guiding star vanished behind a mountain. "Clouds would have covered it soon anyway," Lee said to a scout.

The climb to the first ridgeline was brutal. Lee's point detail formed up as a small arrowhead with Lee on the point — his scouts were so close he could touch them. As they trudged through knee-deep, and sometimes waist-deep, snow, Lee sometimes had to jab his drowsy scouts with the butt of his

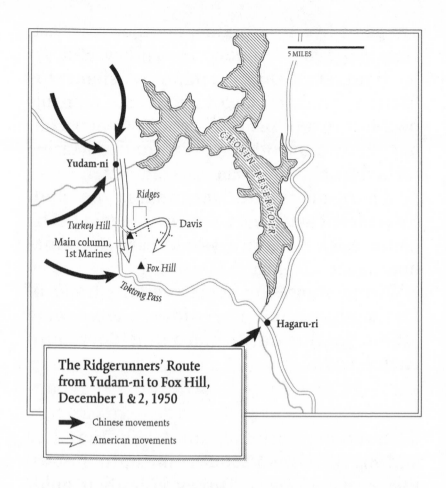

5 MILES

CHOSIN RESERVOIR

Yudam-ni

Ridges

Turkey Hill — Davis

Main column, 1st Marines

▲ Fox Hill

Toktong Pass

Hagaru-ri

The Ridgerunners' Route
from Yudam-ni to Fox Hill,
December 1 & 2, 1950

➡ Chinese movements
⇨ American movements

carbine in order to keep them alert. The remainder of Baker Company, led by Lieutenant Kurcaba, followed in single file; behind them, a path as slick and icy as a toboggan run developed.

A number of Marines — drained from nearly twenty-four hours with no sleep, and coming off the firefight at Turkey Hill — faltered and fell. The wind whipped their faces as they crawled up the slope on their hands and knees, grunting, grumbling, and moaning softly. The occasional report from a Chinese sniper carried like the sound of a howitzer shell through the brittle night air. After the snow clouds moved in, blotting out the moon and stars, it became so dark each Marine had to grab hold of the parka of the one in front of him. There were deep defiles and crevasses in several places so that the column had to take a detour, and twice Lee had to dogleg around insurmountable granite walls rising from the snow.

He sensed he was drifting off course. He checked his maps, but that was a waste of time. The scale on the old Japanese charts was 1 to 50,000 — a real world of mountains, ridges, valleys, and steep gorges ludicrously compressed to the size of a pinkie nail. The contour lines would have been barely legible in the bright sunlight, much less in the pitch blackness on a snowy night. *It's like shadow boxing in a black box,* Lee thought.

He plodded forward, but he hadn't moved more than a mile before he concluded that he was lost. He pulled out his compass but it spun wildly. Was that because of the cold? Belatedly he realized that the men in the battalion trailing him were carrying enough metal to throw the compass off.

With the column stalled, Davis ran up to the point. Lee explained the problem. Davis decided to risk asking for white phosphorous shells to guide them — the element of surprise meant nothing if they didn't know where they were going. He radioed to the artillery command in Yudam-ni and asked for several rounds of Willie Peter; then he returned to the center of the line. But the shells were blown off course by mountain winds so fierce that they made breathing difficult. Lee began drifting farther to the right, down the slope, the path of least resistance.

A moment later he picked up a whiff of garlic, followed by the sound of Chinese voices not twenty-five yards away. Lee spoke some pidgin Mandarin that he had picked up as a boy but was not at all familiar with China's ten other major dialects, or with its hundreds of regional accents. Still, he understood this:

"Ching du ma?" *Do you hear something?*
"Tara da?" *We attack?*

He had come dangerously close to an enemy mortar emplacement overlooking the MSR. He realized that the Chinese could not see him in the snow and darkness, and he sensed that they were as cold and miserable as he was. From his postwar deployment in China, Lee knew that CCF regulars, especially the NCOs and officers, had little respect for the American Army. The Marines, on the other hand, they considered "highly competent criminals." Lee instinctively felt that these Chinese mortarmen wanted no part of a firefight tonight and would be content to pretend that the column of soldiers passing so close by were actually their own. The way their fur caps popped up and down from their gun pits suggested that the men were searching but not wanting to see — they reminded Lee of prairie dogs. He took a hard left and passed them by.

Near the center of the line, Lieutenant Colonel Davis grew increasingly frustrated with the sluggish pace. Each of Lee's halts had an accordion effect on the column. Davis also worried that Lee's scouts were swerving too far off course, heading back toward the road and toward the known enemy positions that had been targeted for an artillery barrage from Yudam-ni during the breakout.

He tried and failed to contact Lieutenant Kurcaba, who was following close behind Chew-Een Lee. The batteries in Kurcaba's radio had died. Davis tried to pass word along the column up to Baker's point. That did not work, either. The Marines were muffled up to the ears with ragged towels and tightly wrapped parka hoods, so they could scarcely hear an order and repeated it as nonsense.

When these voice commands did not work, Davis again stepped out of the long file, grabbed his radioman and his runner, and sprinted toward the front. Where the trail bent left he ran into one of Lee's scouts. He held a finger to his mouth and with his other hand pointed to enemy mortar emplacements. Davis was tempted to order a platoon to take these emplacements out. But who knew what other Chinese units lurked nearby? A full-scale gunfight would mean the end of his mission to relieve Fox.

Davis sent his swift runner Private First Class Bob "Red" Watson, a Minnesotan, back with a nine-word warning for the bulk of the column: "No noise. Gooks ahead. No firing unless fired upon." He made Watson repeat the message back to him twice. Thereafter a procession of dark shadows whispered past the enemy emplacements.

Nearly simultaneously, two hundred yards up the line, Chew-Een Lee halted and turned back to Joe Owen. "Joe, better get back to Lieutenant Kurcaba," he said. "Tell him that without a Willie Peter starburst I can't go any farther unless they want me to lead everyone over a cliff."

Lee did not like many men, but he respected "Long" Joe Owen. When they had first met at Pendleton, Lee considered Owen just another wiseacre slacker. Owen's men had no discipline: they failed to stand at attention properly, they rarely saluted him, and several even had the audacity to call Owen by his first name. Lee, as a first lieutenant, outranked Owen. One day Owen had addressed him as merely "Lee," a common practice among junior officers in the Marines. Lee had shot back, "It's Lieutenant Lee to you, Second Lieutenant."

Lee thought that Owen's priorities were skewed. Lee himself hewed more to iron rule than to the Golden Rule, and according to Lee's Marine Corps sensibility the amiable Owen cared too much about the physical comfort of his men and too little about the bigger picture of war. In war, soldiers died. These deaths were honorable and were to be expected — but Lee felt that Owen did not respect this truth. Lee had also been disgusted in Hamhung, when Owen nonchalantly allowed his right-hand man in the mortar unit to commandeer a captured North Korean steam locomotive for a joyride. Owen had actually cheered the man on as he chuffed around the sooty industrial port town. Lee would have thrown him into the brig.

But Lee's opinion of Owen had changed in the hospital after the battle for Sudong Gorge. Lee had been wounded early in the fighting, and as more casualties from the Seventh Regiment poured into the temporary medical center, he had pulled up a chair and interrogated each Marine about the ongoing firefight. He heard the same story over and again: after his old Second Platoon had encountered its first Soviet tank of the war, the men had broken and fled in panic. Most disgracefully, to Lee, the retreat had been led by the officer, a veteran of World War II, who replaced him as platoon commander. But then the stories became interesting. As the Americans had taken flight, Lee was told over and again, Owen appeared in the middle of the road and stopped them.

"Stand and fight like Marines!" Owen had roared, physically lifting some men off their feet and throwing them back toward the enemy lines. Owen then led the counterattack that disabled the tank. From that moment on Chew-Een Lee had felt differently toward Joe Owen. There was probably not another Marine in the outfit to whom Lee could admit that he was human, that he needed assistance, that he was lost.

Now, no sooner had Owen turned back down the trail to find Lieutenant Kurcaba than he collided with a smaller man rushing up the path. It took him a moment to realize that he had knocked over Lieutenant Colonel Davis. The CO was exhausted, and even with Owen's aid he had to struggle to regain his footing. Nearby was a small depression, an abandoned Chinese dugout, and Davis dropped into it. Owen went back to get Lee, and then the two lieutenants squeezed in on either side of Davis.

They pulled their parkas over the hole, lit flashlights, and checked their compasses and maps. Through a process of comparison and synchronization, with occasional peeks at the stars appearing between snow clouds, they managed to reorient the column. But their minds were so benumbed that by the time they got up, they had forgotten which direction they'd decided on. They dropped down again, and this time Davis kept his finger pointed toward a second ridgeline several hundred yards to the northeast. They doused their lights. Incredibly, as they stood for the second time a word from Owen again made Davis forget exactly *why* he was

467

pointing in that direction. The three Marines had to confer one more time.

Davis returned to the center of the column
as Lee and his scouts, squinting in the
churning snowflakes, broke trail up the
slope toward the ridge. Even the hardy Lee
was so weak he was certain that an enemy
soldier could topple him with a gentle stab
of a finger. He felt like an old man, as if his
legs were stone, as if time had no meaning.
Still, he pressed on. He had not gone far
when he again stopped and sent a scout
back to find Davis. When Davis arrived, Lee
was standing with a semicircle of Marines,
staring down at a lump in the snow.

Before Davis could say a word a brawny
sergeant punched his fist through the crust
and lifted an ice-covered figure by the neck
of his quilted uniform. "Gook's still alive,
Captain," he said. The soldier was wearing
tennis shoes but no socks.

Davis peered at the man's eyes. They were
indeed moving, albeit very slowly. Davis
looked to either side of the trail. The white
terrain showed half a dozen similar bulges.
The big sergeant moved from one mound
to another, pulling a frozen Chinese body
from each one. All but the first man were
dead.

Davis thought of Fox Hill. Would he find

468

the same scene there, but with dead Marines buried in snowy graves? He passed up and down the line, reminding his men that the fate of Fox Company depended on them. Then he ran back to the point and urged Lee to move faster.

Following Lee, the relief column crested the next ridge and came on a small mountain meadow — level ground that stretched several hundred yards. It was pocked with huge boulders. Davis held the men back as Lee's point team picked its way through the rocks. The men on the team were halfway across the snowfield when the eastern and western slopes above them erupted in muzzle flashes. The Americans were shocked out of their frozen lethargy. At the first rifle report, Lee formed the Second Platoon into a skirmish line and charged. Davis and his main body followed.

Davis estimated that he was under siege from at least two enemy platoons, and he ordered his heavy machine gunners and mortar unit deployed between two attack columns. As the riflemen passed the mortar crews, they reached into their mummy bags and threw off 81-mm shells. Owen's tubes hit the Chinese hard. The attack columns following Lee — with Davis in the fore, firing his carbine — finished the job.

Lee's initial assault was so rapid that many Chinese were caught in their sleeping bags. Some fought back by throwing rocks. Lee shot two of them with his carbine, but neither went down. Much of the fighting was hand-to-hand, and several of Owen's ammunition carriers used entrenching tools to club enemy soldiers to death.

After the fight Davis called a ten-minute rest and re-formed his platoons. Lieutenant Kurcaba's men were so numbed from the wind and cold that he made them jog in place. Davis, meanwhile, met with his officers. Fox Hill was no more than two miles over the next ridgeline — a ridgeline occupied by at least one Chinese battalion and probably two. The Marines needed a plan of attack.

Davis was worried. His subordinates could barely stand, and their numbed minds were drifting. When he spoke, he made his officers repeat the words back to him three times to ensure they understood. But he himself was no better off — his saliva began to harden every time he opened his mouth, and he had a hard time forming words. For the first time in his life he wished he had been born and bred in a colder environment. Perhaps, he thought, if he had grown up sledding, skiing, and skating in Minnesota like Watson, he would have adapted better to this debilitating cold. There weren't many ski runs or frozen ponds in Georgia. He had everyone take a knee as he pondered assignments for the assault.

At 10 p.m. the Marines of Fox Company heard gunfire and mortar rounds echo off the heights behind the rocky ridge. Weary men looked at each other and shrugged. This was somebody else's problem.

They had no idea that the shots emanated from the guns of Lieutenant Colonel Ray Davis's First Rifle Battalion, which was trying to open the back door to Fox Hill.

DAY SIX

6

By 3 a.m., following another small gunfight, Lieutenant Colonel Ray Davis's Ridgerunners had been slogging overland for more than six hours, and had gone without sleep for nearly thirty. They were cold, hungry, and spent — nearly oblivious of the sporadic sniping from the surrounding peaks. How Company, the rear guard, had been given the responsibility of carrying the wounded from the meadow engagement, and its men had reached the limits of their endurance. They lagged several hundred yards behind the main force.

Davis called a halt. He established a temporary perimeter, to allow How to catch up. Every fourth man was instructed to stand alert while the rest crawled into mummy bags — which, by Davis's order, were to remain unzipped. The men could rest but not sleep. The NCOs and fire team

472

leaders circulated among the Marines who were lying down, urging them to stay awake. To Lieutenant Joe Owen, the men curled up in the snow looked like Eskimo sled dogs. Fourteen hundred yards to the southeast, less than a mile over the final rocky ridge, rose Fox Hill.

No sooner had the men of Baker, Able, and Charlie dropped where they had stopped than How radioed Davis for help. Its own rear guard had collided in the dark with two companies of Chinese, and it was taking heavy casualties. Davis sent two platoons — one each from Baker and Charlie — to bail out How, but by the time they arrived How's commanding officer had maneuvered his few men to the high ground above the interlopers and scattered them.

The Marines of Baker and Charlie escorted How back to the makeshift bivouac. Lieutenant Chew-Een Lee circled the encampment, yelling toward the hills in pidgin Chinese, urging all enemy combatants to surrender.

About an hour before daybreak Davis was patrolling the perimeter when he noticed a young Marine kneeling on an elevated knoll, silhouetted against the skyline. *Jesus Christ.* "Hey, Marine," he hollered. "Get down. Don't you . . ."

A sniper's bullet dented Davis's helmet, knocking him flat on his back into the snow. Corpsmen rushed over. He waved them off and summoned his platoon leaders. It was time to implement the plan of attack they had discussed earlier, in the mountain meadow.

As a gray dawn arrived Lieutenant Kurcaba led what was left of Baker Company, a few more than one hundred Marines, up the back slope of the rocky ridge of Toktongsan. Davis had ordered him to make contact with Fox Company on the other side. On their approach Kurcaba's men ran into the remnants of the same Chinese battalions that had pinned Fox down for five days, and the resistance was heavy. Chew-Een Lee — an inviting target in his bright marker panels — took another bullet, again in his wounded right arm, this time closer to the shoulder. Joe Owen rushed to his side and emptied two clips from his own M1. Lee, on his knees, began screaming in Chinese. So many enemy riflemen jumped from their hiding places to get a better bead on Lee that Owen guessed he was taunting them. Some even charged toward Lee. As fast as they came, the rest of Baker Company took them out; still, they kept coming.

When Baker faltered, Davis led Able and

Charlie into the breach. The battalion commander felt as if he were running in slow motion. Cold and exhaustion had taken a worse toll than the sniper's slug. As the firefight grew more intense, his brain started to form orders that he simply could not get out of his mouth. In the middle of a sentence he would lose his train of thought. He hollered to his lieutenants, asking if the commands he was issuing made any sense. They were not sure, either, but they continued to fight.

Now — as Kurcaba had predicted to Owen — their Marine training seemed to kick in. Simply out of habit, the men in the four rifle companies did indeed put one foot in front of the other, and gradually they cleared a path up to the rocky ridge.

At 7 a.m., while the fight on Toktong-san raged about him, Davis's radio operator shouted to his battalion commander, "Sir, I've got Fox on the radio!"

A pallid sun had just risen over the southeast corner of Fox Hill when John Bledsoe woke up. His hole mate Phil Bavaro was pounding his fists on Bledsoe's back and shoulders. Bledsoe was blanketed in six inches of fresh snow. Bavaro was too spent to show anger. He calmly informed Bledsoe that after his feet had gone totally numb he had decided to let his friend sleep through the night. He had taken the entire twelve-hour watch. But Bavaro was already hatching schemes to make Bledsoe pay back the favor.

Bledsoe was dumbfounded. How do you thank a man for such an act? His guilt increased as he watched Bavaro rip off his shoepacs and wool shoe pads. Bavaro's sweaty wool socks had frozen to his feet. He gingerly removed them and shook out the ice crystals. Candle-white splotches of frostbitten flesh ran from his toes to his ankles. He stuffed his shoe pads and socks under his armpits, and jammed his bare feet into his sleeping bag. He remembered the goddamn Reds who had stolen his pack with his spare socks from the hut on the first night. Even when he was wrapped in the mummy bag, his feet began to feel as if they had been thrust into a campfire. He inspected them again. Now they were blue and beginning to swell. He knew enough about frostbite — trench foot some Marines mistakenly called it, dredging up institutional memories of the flooded, muddy trench warfare of World War I — to realize that as long as his feet were in pain he still had a chance, that the tissue was not yet completely dead.

He cursed softly as he put his feet into his damp socks, shoe pads, and shoepacs. Even to stand up now was torture, but Bavaro had heard that spare socks might have been dropped by one of the cargo planes. Steeling himself, he began the long limp up the hill toward the aid station.

Before reaching the med tents he came upon the stack of American corpses. He saw a pair of dry shoepacs sticking out from beneath a poncho. He banished the thought of taking them — it was too morbid, too disrespectful. At the aid station a corpsman told him that the airdropped socks were only for the wounded, and at any rate they had all been distributed. Bavaro, slump-shouldered and miserable, trudged back down the hill.

Down near the spring the bazooka man Harry Burke crouched low, but there was no sniping from the woods near the South Hill this morning. He filled his canteen and edged over to the back of the large hut. He found the young Chinese soldier he had seen the day before, still leaning against the shack. The boy was frozen to death. A cursory check of the body revealed no new gunshot wounds.

■ ■ ■ ■

At 8 a.m., Captain Barber, having spoken to Lieutenant Colonel Davis and anticipating the arrival of the relief column, continued to oversee the general cleanup in preparation for the evacuation of the hill. At one point, however, he took a moment to stand by himself and gaze over the slopes, which were clean with new-fallen snow. His company had climbed this hunk of granite with 246 Marines and Navy corpsmen. Slightly more than eighty "effectives" remained, most of them wounded and frostbitten. Only one of his officers, Lieutenant Dunne of the First Platoon, remained unscathed.

Barber thought of an old saying that applied to his outfit: uncommon valor had become a common virtue. For a moment, both pride and sadness overwhelmed him. He took a final look at the hill and got to work.

He ordered empty C-ration tins, excrement, and sundry trash buried and all surplus equipment belonging to the wounded stacked near the med tents. A detail was formed to lug captured gear to the level terrain just off the road near the huts. There it would be set afire. Another squad was directed to be ready to strike the med tents and warming stoves on his signal. Finally, eight Marines were sent to move the stack of American corpses farther down the hill so that these could be more easily loaded onto the trucks that would arrive with Litzenberg's main column. This was a job no one wanted.

Barber also asked Sergeant Audas to take a squad to the hilltop for one final enemy body count. Audas returned with his best estimate: more than one thousand Chinese bodies lay on the ground from the saddle to the eastern crest and down the east slope. This number did not include the dead of the nearly four Chinese companies across the MSR and farther on toward the South Hill. How many of the enemy had been killed during the recon patrol's firefight at the rocky knoll, or by the machine gunners on the rocky ridge? How many more had been retrieved by their comrades, particularly during the confusion of the first night's battle, and lay in caves or shallow graves on the West Hill or the higher ridges of Toktong-san? Neither Barber nor Audas could hazard a guess.

What was certain was that Barber's company, outnumbered by at least ten to one, not only had survived five days and nights of frozen firefights but had dispatched more than three-quarters of the enemy it had faced.

The noisy bustle around the aid station woke Warren McClure at 9:10 a.m. He stumbled out of the med tent and into one of the last flurries of what had been a heavy snowstorm. Someone had just started a fire, and McClure poured himself a cup of coffee and scrounged another can of peaches. He went back in and again shared the fruit with the paralyzed Marine.

Then he made another effort to retrieve his kit from the west slope. He had made it halfway across the hill, about fifty yards, when he realized that although he might indeed reach his old hole, he would never get back. He returned to the aid station and again plopped down next to Amos Fixico. Cigarette smoke curled around the bloody bandage encasing Fixico's head. But his buddy, as well as all the other Marines basking in the morning sunlight, seemed in high spirits. They knew by now that relief was just over the rocky ridge.

McClure caught his breath and returned to the med tent. He found a rag to wipe the brow of the paralyzed Marine and fell asleep again.

At 10 a.m., Lieutenant Colonel Davis again made radio contact with Captain Barber. His column, Davis said, had fought its way nearly to the crest of the far side of the rocky ridge. He wanted to come in. The two officers spoke in a vague, unofficial code, but Barber recognized the unspoken message: *Hold your fire!*

Barber warned Davis about the Chinese still holed up in the caves and crevasses around the rocky knoll and — somewhat mischievously — volunteered to send a patrol out to escort the Ridgerunners across the saddle. Davis was not even sure if he would find any Marines of Fox Company able to walk, much less fight, when he reached Fox Hill. And here was their commander offering to take Davis's men in hand. Davis recognized the gentle barb as a Marine officer's dark humor leavened by esprit de corps — and respectfully declined the offer. He did, however, say that he carried no radios with a frequency to call in air support. He asked if Fox Company might contact the Corsairs to soften up the route. Barber said yes and warned Davis to get his point platoon back off the ridgeline and to keep the men's heads down.

The squad of Corsairs appeared at 10:20 a.m. Once again they did their best to incinerate the rocky knoll and the rocky ridge. As they flew off, Barber ordered all of Fox Company's 81-mm mortar units to begin a second barrage against the same positions. Then, as a feint, he sent a squad across the saddle as a patrol to harass any surviving Chinese troops.

At 10:30 a.m., Walt Klein shook the snow from his helmet and inched out of his hole on the eastern crest of Fox Hill. He spotted the hazy outlines of several dozen men etched against the skyline, marching down the rocky ridge about four hundred yards north of the rocky knoll. He hollered for the platoon sergeant, Audas.

"Chinamen walking that skyline."

Audas lifted his binoculars. "Those are Marines," he said.

Klein, Audas, and Frank Valtierra leaped from their holes and waved their arms over their head.

"Now, ain't that the greatest sight you ever saw," Klein said.

The climb down the ridge was slow going, and Lieutenant Kurcaba's point company took forty minutes to pick their way to the rocky knoll, where they dropped out of sight behind the huge outcropping. The

Marines of Fox Company heard gunfire, and suddenly scores of Chinese soldiers streamed from behind the big rock mound and down into the western valley. They made for the ravine and the woods skirting the West Hill. Some Fox Marines took potshots at the fleeing figures, but most were more interested in seeing who would emerge from behind the big rock.

At 11:25 a.m., the bedraggled Baker Company of the First Battalion, Seventh Marines, climbed down from the rocky knoll and began crossing the saddle. Sergeant Audas led a detail out to guide them through the trip wires attached to flares and hand grenades.

When Kurcaba and his exhausted men reached the crest of Fox Hill, their first request was for food. Guffaws exploded across the hilltop. Finally, a couple of boxes of C-rations were produced and handed out to the new arrivals. The Marines of Baker Company wolfed down the frozen chow without bothering to heat it.

Lieutenant Joe Owen dropped to his knees. His mind could not immediately comprehend the scene on the saddle. Hundreds, maybe thousands, of Chinese corpses littered the approach to Fox Hill. Many of the

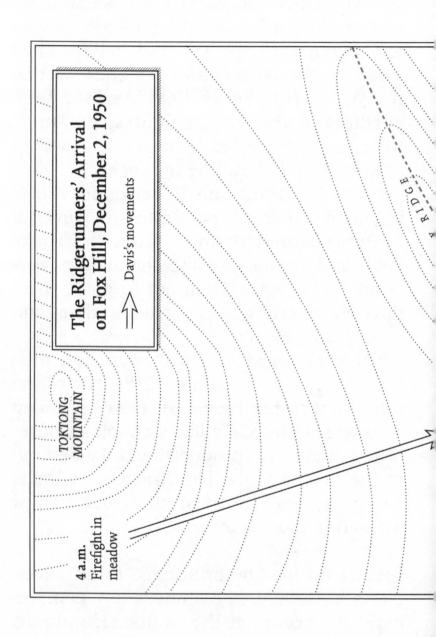

**The Ridgerunners' Arrival
on Fox Hill, December 2, 1950**

⇒ Davis's movements

TOKTONG
MOUNTAIN

4 a.m.
Firefight in
meadow

RIDGE

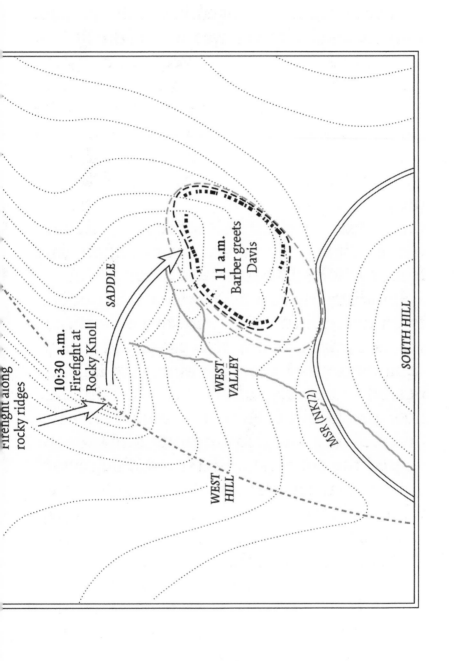

Firefight along
rocky ridges

10:30 a.m.
Firefight at
Rocky Knoll

SADDLE

11 a.m.
Barber greets
Davis

WEST
VALLEY

WEST
HILL

MSR (NK7)

SOUTH HILL

bodies seemed to be merely asleep, half buried under what looked like drifting white wool blankets. There was a straight line of snow-filled craters, hollowed out by Richard Kline's 81-mm mortars, along the land bridge, looking like stones just below the surface of a stream.

Owen looked around him. Some Ridgerunners stared in wonder. Others bowed their heads, as if praying. On the far side of the saddle brightly colored strips of parachute silk and air panels began popping up from foxholes like flags at a parade.

Standing beside Owen was a radio operator, Private First Class Howard Mason. He was stunned. From the ridges, the little squares he had seen pocking Fox Hill appeared to be rice paddies. He had wondered how the hell the Koreans could plant rice on the side of a mountain. Now, as he neared the crest, he understood. The rectangular constructions were American foxholes, with Chinese dead piled about them like sandbags.

Mason, however, did not have much time to be astounded. He was on a personal mission. Like Dick Gilling, Mason had been in a reservist unit with one of the Marines of Fox Company, Bob Ezell, with whom he'd attended high school. As he crossed the hill and took in the countless empty foxholes he grew anxious. He asked the first couple of Marines he encountered about Ezell. They must have been mortarmen, or enlisted men from the heavy machine gun units, because they had never heard of "Zeke" Ezell.

Joe Owen rose from his knees and began walking the one hundred yards toward the crest of Fox Hill. At first — possibly out of respect — he tried to avoid stepping on the enemy corpses. That proved impossible. He strode the last fifty yards across their backs, his feet hardly ever touching the ground.

Nearly as soon as they'd arrived, Baker Company was gone. On Lieutenant Colonel Davis's instructions, Lieutenant Kurcaba led them down the hill and across the MSR to set up overwatch positions on the high ground of the South Hill. The Chinese had abandoned their positions there during the night. With them went Howard Mason, who never did find Ezell.

It was close to 1 p.m. — with Able Company forming a rear guard high above on the ridges of Toktong-san — when Davis led the rest of his relief force through the American perimeter and onto Fox Hill. He walked directly behind the foxhole Fidel Gomez had held by himself for four nights.

Forty-eight hours earlier a potato masher had landed in Gomez's hole, and it had exploded near his face when he tossed it back. Coagulated blood from the shrapnel still encased the left side of his head — Lieutenant Peterson had congratulated him on being hit in the thickest part of his body — and he looked like a chewed sausage. Now Gomez recognized a Marine trailing Davis, a Greek-American kid with whom he had played high school football in San Antonio.

He yelled to the Greek, "What the hell took you so long?"

At first the Marine did not recognize the figure with the gruesome face hollering at him as Fidel Gomez. But then he yelled back. "We stopped at a tavern, over the other side of the ridge. If I'd known you were here I woulda brought you a beer."

All over the hill Marines from the various companies greeted each other as old friends. Men wearing blood-soaked compresses and slings, limping on crutches made of tree limbs, joshed about who, exactly, was relieving whom. Others commiserated over the loss of comrades. Most poignant was the arrival of the few survivors of "Hard Luck Charlie." The Marines from Fox and Charlie had taken the brunt of the Chinese attack south of the Chosin in two battles on the first night, which now seemed years ago. Men from these companies embraced despite the grit and stink of combat, with the identical remark: *You look like shit.*

Captain Barber was carried out of the CP tent on his stretcher. But with the help of his tree branch, he insisted on standing up to clasp hands with Lieutenant Colonel Davis. According to one account, the two exhausted officers "were too overcome with emotion to speak."

Finally, Davis asked where he could settle his twenty-two wounded men. Barber pointed out the aid station and Davis's medical officer, Lieutenant Arioli, introduced himself to Barber before hurrying off to the med tents.

At one point Barber leveled his gaze at the wounded Lieutenant Chew-Een Lee.

He must think I look like the guy who shot him, Lee thought.

In his little "fort" on the far right corner of the hilltop Dick Bonelli was praying. He had never been very religious, despite what the nuns had taught him, but he believed in God now. Not long after the campaign at Uijongbu he had received a letter from one of his mother's friends in the Bronx, an elderly Czech immigrant who lived in the same apartment building. When he'd ripped open the envelope he'd found a religious medal depicting the Infant of Prague. Prague? Bonelli was an Italian by descent. But what the hell? He'd worn the medal around his neck ever since, and he knew that it had brought him good luck. He'd also become accustomed to saying a short prayer to the Infant a couple of times a day, especially before and after gunfights. He was hunched over his light machine gun doing just this when a scarecrow of a Marine climbed over a large boulder behind him and startled him.

"Who the hell are you?" he said.

"Baker Company. Here to rescue you."

"Rescue? Do I look like I need rescuing? Who else is with you?"

"Abel, Charlie, and How."

At this Bonelli jumped from his hole. One of his best friends from the Bronx, a kid he had enlisted with named Randall Farmer, was with How Company.

"Where's How?" he said.

The scarecrow Marine jerked his chin toward an area down the draw near the command post. Bonelli looked past him and saw a line of green parkas shimmying down the slope. He had stashed two tins of

C-rations for a special occasion and he reached into his pack, grabbed one, and tossed it to the Marine. He stuffed the other into his parka. It was for Randall Farmer.

Bonelli started down the hill and the Ridgerunner hunched beside the light machine gun and ripped into the frozen food. A few paces out, three bullets — *chit-chit-chit* — tore into the snow at Bonelli's feet. He hit the ground and lay still for at least ten minutes, trying to pick out the sniper's position. He could not find it.

Eventually he raised himself to his knees and cautiously climbed to his feet. Still nothing. He took a step. A bullet tore into his chest, knocking him ass over teakettle.

Before Captain Barber led Lieutenant Colonel Davis to his CP tent to plot an exit strategy, he ordered all of Fox Company's remaining C-rations turned over to the starving First Battalion. The rearguard Marines of Able Company were the last to stagger into the Fox perimeter.

After a quick rest and some cold chow, Davis directed Able to move off the hill and across the road to join Baker Company digging in on the South Hill. Davis also ordered Charlie and most of How to move out before dark. He sent them three hundred yards down the MSR to secure the heights on the East Hill — but not before taking a small detail from How. These men were to remain on the hill to help Barber's men expedite the cleanup. As the bulk of the Ridgerunners moved off into the dark, what had been a festive afternoon for Fox Company became lonely again.

At the aid station Dr. Arioli busied himself securing the First Battalion's twenty-two wounded Marines. Two of them, he discovered, had died during the march; they were added to the stack of Fox Company's dead. Arioli also tended to the wounded of Fox Company, some of whom had only Scotch tape covering bullet wounds. Arioli was a skilled surgeon — a bone specialist — as well as a gifted general practitioner. He spent an exhausting night striding between the two med tents by candlelight, diagnosing injuries, changing bandages, administering morphine, pitching in wherever he could with what little medical supplies he carried.

Arioli lingered over Private First Class Dick Bernard, who had been shot in both legs manning the two tall rocks with Bob Ezell four days earlier. Bernard desperately needed to be in a hospital. Even morphine wasn't helping. Arioli decided that if, by some miracle, a helicopter evac showed up,

Bernard would be the first man on it. But realistically he knew this wasn't going to happen.

As Arioli went between the litters he passed Warren McClure's stretcher. McClure had no idea what the presence of this new doctor meant, and he didn't give it much thought. He was now intent on a single mission: retrieving his gear. He got up and tried again. It was another futile attempt. But this time, when he settled in at the campfire outside the med tents, he noticed more strange faces — American faces — passing by. He turned to Amos Fixico.

"Our relief," Fixico said. "We're getting off the hill."

How Fixico knew this with bandages covering both eyes was a mystery to McClure. But there was nonetheless a little extra lift to McClure's step as he wobbled back to the med tent. Inside he passed Hector Cafferata. Ken Benson was squatting beside him.

"Don't let them leave me behind, Bense. Don't let them leave me behind."

"Nobody's leaving you behind, Hector. You know I wouldn't go without you."

As the two spoke, Dick Gilling entered the med tent. When he spotted Benson and

Cafferata his eyes lit up. But as the three embraced and clapped one another's backs, Gilling noticed the extent of Hector's wounds.

"Remember our deal, Dickie?" Cafferata said.

"Don't worry about that, Hec. You're getting out and going home." It dawned on Gilling that if he was the one stuck in Korea, Cafferata would have to remember his end of the bargain. Now, exhaustion finally got the better of Gilling. "Say, guys," he said, "I've got to bed down somewhere. Know a good hole?"

A sly smile creased Hector Cafferata's haggard face. "We've got just the one for you," he said. "Kenny, why don't you show him."

On the west slope Freddy Gonzales approached Bob Kirchner's foxhole. He had seen his cousin Roger's name on the list of KIA posted at the aid station. He had also spoken to the wounded Walt Hiskett, who had watched Roger die. But he had been unable to locate Roger's body. He wanted to return Roger's dog tags to his family.

"Roger?" he said to Kirchner.

"There." Kirchner hooked a thumb over his shoulder, pointing toward the stack of bodies that ringed his hole. Roger Gonzales's body was near the bottom. There were at least two hundred bullet holes in it.

Kirchner braced for — he didn't know what. A fistfight? A shootout? Freddy Gonzales gazed at his cousin for a moment, and then looked back to Kirchner. "I would have done the same, I guess."

Together they extracted Roger's body and carried it over to the pile of dead Americans. When they had lowered it onto the stack, Freddy Gonzales gazed down at Kirchner's legs. His trousers had been shredded by shrapnel and streaks of frozen blood ran down each shin.

"What happened?" he said.

Kirchner was astonished. "Tell you the truth," he said, "I never even noticed it before now."

By 7 p.m., small and large cooking fires ringed Fox Hill. The flames attracted some long-distance sniping from Chinese riflemen, but all of it was ineffective.

This sniping did, however, provide Davis with a direction for his attack in the morning. He picked up his field phone and ordered the COs of his four companies to hit these pockets to the south and east at daybreak.

■ ■ ■ ■

Dick Bonelli awoke in a med tent. His entire left side burned. Two figures were standing over him: a corpsman he did not recognize and his buddy Randall Farmer. He did not like the look on their faces.

The corpsman said, "Sorry, Marine, morphine's all gone." Farmer remained silent but lit a cigarette and stuck it between Bonelli's lips. Then he removed Bonelli's gloves and began rubbing his hands.

"Tell my mother I love her and I was thinking of her," Bonelli said. It hurt to speak.

DAY SEVEN

DECEMBER 3, 1950

7

Except for the small cleanup detail from How Company, the last elements of Ray Davis's Ridgerunners cleared off Fox Hill by 1 a.m. They left their dead and wounded with Barber's corpsmen.

Ninety minutes later the distinctive *clank* of a tank grinding to a halt was carried across the hill by the wind funneling through the Toktong Pass. The heavy M-26 Pershing tank, leading the breakout from the Chosin, had paused in the hamlet of Sinhung-ni, three-quarters of a mile up the MSR from Fox Hill. Litzenberg and Murray were in a pickle. They'd successfully fought their way out of Yudam-ni and could not allow themselves to be encircled again. But their momentum was halting. The breakout column — trucks, Jeeps, tractors towing artillery, ambulances, and humping Marines — was three miles long and unwieldy. There were too many stragglers. They called a halt to tighten it up.

Farther down the MSR, at 6:30 a.m. Lieutenant Colonel Davis's four outlying companies sent out reinforced details to sweep the surrounding hills of any Chinese blocking the road south. Fifteen minutes later the main column of Americans at Sinhung-ni moved out. Hot on its trail were at least twelve enemy divisions — more than 100,000 Chinese troops.

Davis's patrols flushed the last remaining battalion of the CCF's Fifty-ninth Division. The enemy retreated northwest, pulling heavy machine guns on two-wheeled carts — directly into Litzenberg's and Murray's main column coming down the road. The Chinese were sandwiched in the southern valley almost directly below Fox Hill, and the haggard Marines of Fox Company were content to sit back and watch the ensuing bloodbath.

When the Chinese realized their predicament, they halted and turned confusedly in all directions. But they were trapped. Finally their officers formed them up to stand and fight. Captain Barber decided that fighting would not be necessary — at least for the Marines — and ordered Lieutenant Campbell to call in an artillery barrage from

Hagaru-ri. The Chinese were cut down by the howitzers.

When the artillery bombardment ceased, the Corsairs appeared overhead. Any enemy soldiers still standing were annihilated. Between six days of fighting on Fox Hill and this final engagement, the CCF's Fifty-ninth Division had been wiped out. It would not effectively re-form for the remainder of the Korean War.

Warren McClure stood beside Ernest Gonzalez and watched the bombardment from a high, rocky fold near the med tents. The two Marines, like the rest of the company, had been ordered to gear up for what would prove to be a daylong evacuation. When the slaughter was over neither said a word. After so much deprivation, neither felt a need to gloat. *Vae victis* — woe to the conquered. It was 8 a.m.

Fox Company's Headquarters Unit would be the first to leave, folding into the forward companies of Davis's First Battalion as it led the breakout column south to Hagaru-ri. As the Marines of the Headquarters Unit began to assemble on the MSR, McClure briefly considered trying to get back to his old foxhole for his kit. But he just could not find the strength to go up that slope.

Ernest Gonzalez, who had come down

from his position on the hilltop, already had his rucksack slung over his shoulders — he had abandoned all his souvenirs except the bayonet and the camera. He couldn't find his foxhole buddy Freddy Gonzales: he had lost Freddy in the excitement when the Ridgerunners entered camp. As Ernest was checking the med tents — he knew Freddy's feet had been frostbitten badly, but he did not know that Freddy's cousin Roger had died — he was handed a field phone by Sergeant Audas and was told he was the Third Platoon's new communications specialist. Audas reminded him to remain within eyesight of Captain Barber for the entire evacuation of the hill. "Or else," the sergeant said.

Barber, his stretcher propped up against a rock between the med tents, was only a few yards away, talking with Lieutenant Colonel Davis and several other officers and corpsmen. McClure and Gonzalez saw the new doc, Lieutenant Arioli, appear from under one of the tent flaps and walk toward the little group. Just as Arioli opened his mouth to say something, he was shot through the head by a sniper. He fell, dead, at their feet.

For the first time on the hill, Bill Barber felt like weeping. He turned his head for a moment and pretended to blow his nose.

Then he stiffened, swiveled, and directed a corpsman to add Dr. Peter Arioli's body to the frozen heap of American dead. The sniper was never located.

McClure and Gonzalez watched Arioli's body being carried off. They were struck by foreboding. No one wanted to be the last Marine to die on Fox Hill.

At 12:30 p.m., a helicopter from Hagaru-ri, piloted by a single Marine officer, landed on the hilltop and began unloading medical supplies. The chopper, peppered by small-arms fire from the enemy's last enclave on the West Hill, rose away the moment it had emptied its hold. It hovered for a moment, then spasmed and sputtered. To some Marines it appeared as if the pilot were doing aerobatics. They started to laugh: *Show-off.*

Then the helicopter spun out of control, flipped upside down, and crashed on the east slope, narrowly missing one of the First Platoon's light machine-gun emplacements. No one on the machine-gun crew was injured, but the chopper pilot, Lieutenant Robert Longstaff, was crushed to death on impact. Walt Klein and the mortarman Richard Kline helped carry his body back into the perimeter. They laid him next to

Dr. Arioli.

As the rejuvenated Marines of Fox Company hustled to secure the hill Private First Class McClure's quest for his gear had become almost tragicomic. At 2:40 p.m., fortified once again by a strong cup of joe, he began his trek up and across the slope. Midway there he saw the barrel of a Pershing tank emerging from behind the West Hill as it rounded the bend on the MSR. The tank was followed by a motley column of American vehicles filled with the wounded and dead.

McClure turned and stumbled down the hill as fast as his whistling lung would allow. Midway to the road he paused to catch his breath, not realizing he was standing next to the stack of American dead. One of the green ponchos laid over the bodies had blown away, and he saw a frozen arm sticking straight up out of the pile. The dead American's hand was open, as if waving for help. McClure shuddered and moved on.

After another fifty yards he had reached the road — or at least the ten-foot sheer cut bank. He took a chance and jumped. He landed with a thud and rolled; it felt as if a glass bottle had broken inside his chest. He crossed the MSR behind the tank and in front of a train of slow-moving bulldozers, trucks, and Jeeps. He dropped to his knees and made a feeble hitchhiking gesture with his good left hand. A Jeep carrying four Marines pulled to the side. A sergeant in the front passenger seat helped McClure climb in and wedged him between two wounded NCOs in the backseat.

The position was painful; McClure didn't care. He was off the hill. He wanted to turn to take one last look. Instead, he passed out.

Wayne Pickett had never been to Yudam-ni, but even in the pale moonlight he recognized the black ice of the "Frozen Chosin." Pickett was part of a small band of American prisoners who picked their way through the scattered detritus of battle, including the bodies of hundreds of Chinese who had frozen where they had fallen. It had taken three days for Pickett's group of POWs to walk to this site from the corral where he and Troy Williford had been held. He had no idea whether Daniel Yesko, the wounded Marine who had been carted away in the North Korean ambulance, was still alive.

The Americans in Pickett's group, perhaps three dozen by now, were marched to a hut near the shore of the reservoir and herded into a lean-to behind it. They were handed a ball of rice — the same food their captors ate, they noticed — and were only loosely guarded. The Chinese, intent on starting a warming fire, did not fear any escape into this frozen wilderness.

That morning a Corsair had machine-gunned their ragged little group as it descended from a ridge onto a spur path of the MSR, and Pickett had banged his knee hard on a rock when he dived for cover. His knee soon swelled to the size of a pumpkin, and as he lagged farther and farther behind the column of captives, his fear of being shot increased. Instead — to his surprise — his Chinese guards seemed to understand his predicament, and two of them slowed down and dawdled with him until he arrived at Yudam-ni three hours behind the rest. He was glad they were not North Koreans.

Inside the lean-to, a Chinese political commissar demanded that the Americans sign a prepared statement, written in English, attesting that they were being treated in accordance with the Geneva Conventions. Pickett hesitated until he saw two captured Marine officers put their names to the paper. He signed when his turn came.

Among the POWs were a few old China hands who spoke a little of the language, and news spread among the Americans that their final destination was a camp far to the northwest, near the border with China. The Marines had also come to understand that most of their guards were conscripts into the CCF who had fought against Mao during the Chinese civil war and were deemed too untrustworthy for the front lines. These soldiers appeared to hold no particular animus toward the United States and surreptitiously passed along snatches of intelligence when they could.

They told their prisoners that the other Americans were in disarray, running for the safety of Hagaru-ri. They did not seem to take any great joy in sharing this information — it was just another turn in the war. When Wayne Pickett asked after the fate of Fox Company on Toktong Pass, no one could answer him.

Sergeant Audas made the Chinese prisoners carry the Fox wounded down the hill. The Americans, swaddled in the blue, yellow, and red silk of the supply-drop parachutes, resembled bulky, oddly wrapped Christmas presents. A Marine from the Fifth Regiment slogged past Howard Koone's stretcher and recognized him from back home in Michigan. He stopped to light a cigarette for Koone and handed him a stick of gum.

Bob Ezell was laid on the road next to the semiconscious Lieutenant Lawrence Schmitt, the officer whose leg had been broken by sniper fire as he recovered supplies from the first airdrop. Ten days earlier, late on Thanksgiving night, Schmitt had written a letter to his wife: "We sang the 'Star-Spangled Banner,' 'America,' and 'My Country 'Tis of Thee.' The Chaplain said a prayer, and the Colonel gave a talk. Me, I have a lot to be thankful for: my wonderful wife and boy, our house, our health, and our faith. May the Good Lord continue to be generous to us. All my love, Larry."

Now Schmitt lay on a litter at the side of the road, his skin gray and his eyes yellow. A Marine from Yudam-ni passed by and saw Schmitt's Fox Company insignia. The man doubled back. "I hear you guys took out thirty-five hundred gooks," he said. "Great job. Saved our asses keeping the pass open."

Schmitt did not answer. The Marine looked at Ezell, who also said nothing.

Ezell watched as Eleazar Belmarez's stretcher was strapped to the hood of a Jeep and his wounded legs wrapped in dirty blankets. Next, Edward Gonzales — the Marine who was buried alive in the mysterious explosion during Fox's third day on the hill — was placed in a six-by-six. Gonzales had not yet regained consciousness (and wouldn't come to until the next day). Just as Ezell began to wonder when his turn would come, his litter was abruptly lifted from the road and tied onto the front passenger seat of a Jeep. He still could not move his legs. He asked for a weapon. Someone handed him a carbine. *Damn carbine,* he thought. *Aim for the head.*

Wounded men were still being loaded into every possible open space on every possible vehicle — some were even strapped to the barrels of howitzers. The bodies from Fox Hill, stiff as icicles, were piled in the lee of the larger hut. Toward the center of the Yudam-ni column were three heavy trucks packed with equipment. Captain Barber hailed them and ordered the dead piled on top of the gear. But there was not enough room. Eight bodies remained.

Barber, with Private First Class Bob Kirchner and Sergeant Kenneth Kipp supporting him under each arm, directed the eight corpses to be carried to a shallow gulley on the north side of the MSR, between the huts and the spring. He assembled what the official Marine Manual calls a "hasty burial detail." Spades and shovels chipped into the frozen ground. Someone found a chaplain from the Fifth Regiment and escorted him to the site. He opened his Bible and read a few words as a bonfire incinerating all of Fox Company's excess equipment and captured ordnance blazed not far away. In the shadows cast by the flames, several Marines of Fox Company vowed to return for their friends' bodies.

Phil Bavaro, the company cook, turned from the shallow graves and searched for a lift. Fox Company had been designated the main column's rear guard, and most of the vehicles were already well down the road. What Jeeps and trucks remained were crammed to overflowing with men wounded far worse than Bavaro. His feet swollen and painful, Bavaro grabbed hold of the tailgate of a truck inching down the MSR and resigned himself to the seven-mile hike to Hagaru-ri; he was afraid that he would fall asleep on his feet if he didn't hold on. Walt Hiskett, his arm in a sling, fell in next to Bavaro. Hiskett was guiding the blinded Amos Fixico.

It was 3:35 p.m. when Captain Barber, having ensured that every living man on his company roster left Fox Hill, was lifted into the passenger seat of a Jeep. Three dead Marines were strapped across its bumpers and hood. From the passenger seat, Barber turned over command of Fox Company to the most senior lieutenant on the scene, Lieutenant Ralph Abell of the Ridgerunners.

There was some emotion involved in this handover: Abell had commanded Fox Company's First Platoon before being transferred to Lieutenant Colonel Davis's staff, and now he was being given command of a battered company less than the size of that platoon. Of the seven officers who had formed Fox Company at Camp Pendleton in July, only he and Lieutenant Dunne still stood.

Barber's Jeep rolled down the road, and Ralph Abell noted that the captain did not look back.

Snow began falling again as the column of Marines moved south during the afternoon, through dusk and into the night. Occasional ten-minute breaks were passed up the line to allow stragglers to catch up. During one break a warming fire was lit, and word was passed to be on the lookout for lone Chinese soldiers attempting to infiltrate the American lines. This spooked some Marines. One approached his gunnery sergeant and said that "an armed gook" had indeed sneaked into the column.

"That's Lieutenant Lee," the gunny said. "Try not to shoot him."

Despite the rests, men still fell behind, slipping and falling on the icy road. Although the Marines did not come under attack, they could hear sniper fire ahead, at the front of the column, and they nervously eyed the hills overhanging either side of the MSR. Twice they saw long files of Chinese on the ridges, but neither side fired. The Americans' tension spiked when they passed a Pershing tank burning in a ditch on the side of the road, but nothing came of that, either. When Walt Hiskett described the scene for Amos Fixico, Fixico asked him not to say anything more until they reached Hagaru-ri.

Rollin Hutchinson — who had decided that the first thing he would do when he reached Hagaru-ri was find out if the Yankees had indeed swept the Phillies in the World Series — recognized a Marine from Chosin who was lagging behind. The man was a buddy from his reserve outfit in Toledo, Ohio. Hutchinson fell in next to him, urging him on. Soon they were both encouraging Ernest Gonzalez to keep up. Gonzalez's backpack and sleeping bag, as well as the company radio, were weighing him down. But he refused to jettison any gear, even when he slipped and fell into an icy drainage ditch. As he struggled to climb out, Hutchinson and the other Ohioan helped Gonzalez balance the equipment on his back, at least allowing him to walk in a little more comfort.

Lieutenant Bob McCarthy dozed fitfully in the cab of a six-by-six packed with the dead and wounded. About halfway to Hagaru-ri, amid much stopping and starting, gaps began to appear in the convoy. At a point in the road where there was a steep drop-off to both sides, McCarthy's young driver lost sight of the truck ahead and became too frightened to move.

Despite his leg wound, McCarthy climbed from the vehicle and hobbled several feet in front of the truck so the driver could see him. They finally caught up to the vehicle ahead, and thereafter McCarthy did not allow the forward six-by-six to leave his sight.

Several officers noticed that the Marines who were walking were having a hard go of it. During another short break Lieutenant Abell spread word that in Hagaru-ri the division cooks were already busy preparing hot coffee, flapjacks with real butter, and hot maple syrup for every man coming down the MSR. Abell said he had picked up this intel on his radio. In fact, Abell had heard no such thing; he didn't even have a radio. Anything to keep the men moving.

Somewhere on the road Lieutenant Elmo Peterson passed a corpsmen's Jeep that had tipped on its side. Someone had extracted its four injured passengers — two Navy corpsmen and two wounded Marines — and laid them on stretchers in the snow. Peterson bent over and spoke to the one conscious medic.

"We can't walk," the man said.

Peterson looked around. His own vision was blurred and his legs were quivering. There were no other vehicles in sight. His men were too spent to heft four loaded stretchers. He reached into a pocket of his field jacket and pulled out the pint of whiskey he had been carrying for seven days. There were only a few drops left. He handed the bottle to the corpsman and wished him luck. It was all he could do.

Dick Gilling awoke to silence. He was alone on Fox Hill. His exhaustion had finally overwhelmed him, and when Kenny Benson had led him to this slit trench the previous night, he'd dropped like a stone. He thought he'd awakened several times during the night to a horrific odor, but his mind was still awhirl from the ridgerunning. He decided that the odor was a part of bad dreams.

He saw now that it was not bad dreams. He stood up and brushed frozen excrement from his sleeping bag. His so-called pals had led him to a latrine. *Fucking Cafferata and Benson. I'll kill 'em.*

But Gilling had more immediate problems. A snowy fog was rolling up over the hill, obscuring any landmarks, including the ridges of Toktong-san. He had no idea in which direction the MSR lay. From somewhere far away he heard the basso reports of 105s. American? Chinese? He squinted, concentrated, trying to recall the difference in sounds. *Ours,* he finally decided.

He began walking overland toward the low rumbles. He had no idea that he was breaking a fresh trail, away from the road.

Phil Bavaro was daydreaming about the last time he had eaten — and about the hotcakes with real butter awaiting him — when he realized that at some point he had let go his grip on the tailgate of the truck. His feet hurt so much that he took baby steps, trying first to walk on his heels, then on his toes. Nothing eased the pain, and the column was rapidly leaving him behind.

Well after dark, as he passed the smoldering Pershing tank, it dawned on him that there were no Americans within sight. He was alone. He was listening to the distant echoes of the Corsairs of the First Marine Air Wing group bomb, strafe, and rocket the pursuing Chinese when he heard voices not far behind him. He racked the slide of his M1. A squad of Marines trotted into view. One of them said that they were the column's rear guard.

"Hey, buddy, you'd better shag ass," said another. "Nobody behind us but China-men." They vanished into the dark ahead of him.

It was hopeless. Bavaro could go no farther. He saw a large rock at the side of the road and sat down. He massaged his feet through his shoepacs. *All that bullshit just to die here.* More voices reached him from behind. He felt the sonic whine of a bullet pass near his head an instant before he heard the crack of a shot.

If Phil Bavaro had taken one lesson from boot camp to heart, it was that even when all seems lost a Marine always has one last burst of energy somewhere deep within him. He stood and began limping, then walking, then trotting, and finally running so hard he caught the rear guard. "Nobody behind me but Chinamen!" he shouted as he moved on.

DAY EIGHT
DECEMBER 4, 1950

8

At 1:30 a.m. on December 4, six hours after Lieutenant Colonel Ray Davis had escorted the point of the breakout column into Hagaru-ri, the sixty or so Marines and Navy corpsmen of Fox Company — along with Mr. Chung, the interpreter — arrived at the roadblock demarcating the perimeter of the American lines.

Above them, what was left of the First Battalion's Baker Company staked out the heights. In the distance, beyond a small bridge, they could see pillars of smoke, evidence of the smoldering fires from the previous days' firefights around the village. Lieutenant Abell approached the guard station, and the platoon leaders Lieutenant Dunne and Lieutenant Peterson called the company to attention. Dunne and Peterson formed the company into ranks according to their units. Abell saluted and announced that Fox Company did not know the password but wished to enter Hagaru-ri.

It was at this moment that Elmo Peterson finally faltered. Gray Davis happened to be looking at Peterson when the lieutenant tottered and fell to his knees. He remained kneeling for a few seconds, fighting off unconsciousness. But for the first time in a week Peterson's will failed him. He fell face-first into a snowbank. Davis and another Marine rushed to him and lifted him off the ground, one under each arm. They were not sure if he was dead. They carried him toward the roadblock. But after only a few steps Peterson regained consciousness and straightened up. He motioned the two men away and shook the loose snow from his uniform. Peterson rejoined the ranks next to Walt Hiskett, who was still bracing Amos Fixico.

The road barriers were raised and the column was allowed to pass. The ragged remains of Fox Company, Second Battalion, Seventh Regiment parade-marched into Hagaru-ri four men abreast, to a drill sergeant's cadence count. Someone began humming, softly at first, the Marine Corps Hymn. One by one, though their throats were dry and raw, the entire company picked up the tune. Soon each man was singing.

> From the halls of Montezuma to the shores
>   of Tripoli,
> we will fight our country's battles, on the
>   land as on the sea.
>
> First to fight for right and freedom, and to
>   keep our honor clean,
> we are proud to claim the title of United
>   States Marines.

As Fox Company crossed the checkpoint, a Navy corpsman stationed at the gate shook his head. He turned to a guard. "Will you look at those magnificent bastards," he said.

EPILOGUE

The first vehicles taking the most seriously wounded Marines from the Chosin Reservoir and Fox Hill into Hagaru-ri had already arrived hours before Fox Company's dramatic entrance into the village. A converted schoolhouse served as the UN forces' field hospital, where British Royal Marines removed injured men from vehicles and passed out hot coffee and cigarettes.

Warren McClure was helped down from his Jeep and left standing alone in the street among rows of stretchers. To his left was the field hospital. To his right was a mess tent. The Marines around him seemed dazed, wandering aimlessly, staring blankly. McClure was also cold and confused, having eaten nothing but three half-tins of peaches in six days. The smell of hot pancakes drew him like a magnet. He followed his nose and stumbled through the flaps of the mess tent.

A cook immediately assessed his sorry condition and attempted to steer him back across the street to the hospital. But Mc-Clure argued so stubbornly that the cook finally relented. He sat McClure in a corner at a picnic table and placed a gallon tin of peaches and a tablespoon before him. "Eat all you want," the cook said. "We're only going to end up burning everything left over before the Chinese get here."

Across the street Colonel Homer Litzenberg's Jeep pulled up to the field hospital. Lieutenant Colonel Lockwood approached Litzenberg to welcome him to Hagaru-ri. Litzenberg climbed stiffly from his Jeep without acknowledging Lockwood. All over the frozen ground were wounded men awaiting triage and identification. Among them was Captain Benjamin Read, How Company's commanding officer, who had paid for his refusal to move his guns back inside the safety of the Hagaru-ri perimeter with a sniper bullet through the knee.

Litzenberg exploded. He sought out the head corpsman and ordered him to eliminate the red tape and move the wounded inside on the double. It was "Litzen" at his most "Blitzen."

Inside the makeshift medical center, overwhelmed doctors and corpsmen rushed from station to station. Dick Bonelli opened his eyes and saw a roof over his head. He had no idea where he was. A crude mural above him depicted American planes machine-gunning Korean women and children. He looked around. Photographs and portraits of Kim, Mao, and Stalin hung from every wall. Bonelli had no way of knowing that the First Marine Division's commanding officer, General Smith, had ordered that none of the propaganda be removed from any North Korean structure. Not that Bonelli would have cared. His chest felt as if it were exploding, and he reached out to a corpsman who passed by wearing a bloody apron.

"Easy there, pal," the corpsman said. "You've got a shitload of broken ribs. Bullet bounced around inside you pretty good." Bonelli called out for a weapon, any weapon. The corpsman drew his forty-five-caliber pistol and let Bonelli feel the stock. Handling the weapon put Bonelli at ease. He slipped into unconsciousness again. The next time he awoke was in Osaka, Japan, where he was being given the last rites by a priest.

Not far away, beneath a bullet-pocked photograph of Joseph Stalin, corpsmen cut away Bob Ezell's dungarees and shoepacs.

521

The grenade had left his legs looking like ground meat, but only one wound — a deep gash in his right thigh — appeared life-threatening. Luckily for Ezell, the blood had frozen and coagulated almost immediately. His feet were another story. Both were black with frostbite and covered with ugly red blisters.

Another corpsman was looking warily at Eleazar Belmarez, who was in a cot next to Ezell. The medic suspected that Belmarez's shot-up legs were in worse shape than Ezell's, but Belmarez was delirious and refused to relinquish either his M1 or the several live hand grenades attached to his field jacket beneath the two bandoliers of ammunition crisscrossing his chest. Finally one corpsman gingerly examined Belmarez's wounds while a second hung back. After a brief consultation they concluded that he was in no danger of dying and decided to leave him for the Division docs to deal with.

Walt Hiskett led Amos Fixico into the field hospital and remained at his side while a medic unwrapped the filthy bandages that had covered his head. His left eye was swollen shut and his right eye was a small slit beneath the shrapnel wounds. "Walt, I can see a little out of this one," he said. Hiskett had his own shoulder wound treated and joined Fixico near a coffee urn in the corner of the building. He poured two cups.

A British commando took one look at Howard Koone, trussed up in a red parachute, and asked a buddy to lend a hand. "Here, Harry, they've got this fucking Yank all tied up like a Christmas present." After they cut Koone loose he was carried inside, his snapped ankle was reset, and someone handed him a few Tootsie Rolls. He passed them out to the men around him. He hated Tootsie Rolls. He drifted off to sleep and woke up on a cargo plane bound for Japan. His parka was gone. In its place someone had wrapped him in a clean wool blanket.

Dick Gilling walked the seven miles overland from Fox Hill and stumbled into an outlying artillery command post staffed by Marines from How Company. He had never found the MSR, and when he entered the compound he looked like a snowman. A corpsman attempted to remove his boots but Gilling stopped him. "Don't. My feet are frozen solid." The medic complied and instead pumped Gilling full of penicillin before transporting him to Hagaru-ri.

On it went. Lieutenant Bob McCarthy's leg wound was freshly dressed and he was wheeled to a corner of the makeshift hospital. He pulled a small leather notebook from his field jacket and began writing down his recommendations for battlefield citations. The first two names he jotted were Captain William Barber and Private Hector Cafferata. McCarthy planned to nominate both for the Congressional Medal of Honor. He smiled to himself as he wrote down Dick Bonelli's name. He'd never thought much of the wiseass New Yorker; now he planned to put him up for a Silver Star. McCarthy was airlifted to Fukuoka, Japan, the next day.

Aside from a small rear guard set up outside the perimeter, the ambulatory survivors of Fox Company were the last Marines to enter Hagaru-ri. They surged into the mess tent. To Ralph Abell's great surprise, hot coffee, pancakes with syrup, and buttered noodles with beef stew awaited them. It was their first hot meal in seventeen days. Abell was speechless as Marines clapped him on the back, congratulating him for his accurate prediction about precisely what chow they could expect if they made it to the village.

Outside the mess tent Gray Davis slouched in a snowbank, too tired to move. He had come down from Fox Hill the same way he went up, and this time he felt he had earned a little rest without some gunny threatening to direct a shoepac up his butt. Somewhere in the distance a radio was playing, and Davis heard Billy Eckstine's "Bewitched, Bothered, and Bewildered" for the first time. He thought it was beautiful, and it became his favorite song for the rest of his life.

Around 2 a.m., the company was led from the mess hall to warming tents. Phil Bavaro found a corner near a stove, peeled off his shoepacs, shoe pads, and socks, and baked his mangled feet as close to the fire as he dared. Like most of the rest of the company, he slept for the next twelve hours. Before nodding off, however, he filed away a cooking tip. He had watched a wounded Marine in the next cot slap a slice of the doughy, Marine-issue white bread onto the side of a field stove. When it fell off, it was toast on one side. *Wait'll I start serving toast next time we're in the shit.*

Someone helped Gray Davis out of the snowbank and into a warming tent. He collapsed onto a cot, but had trouble staying asleep — every fifteen minutes he would sit bolt upright. This happened all night. Finally the reason hit him: the tent was too warm for the kid from Florida. His body, he realized, had become too accustomed to the weather on Fox Hill. *Jesus, don't that beat all?*

The evacuation to Japan began at daybreak. Over the next four days more than four thousand wounded Marines and Army troops, a third of them victims of frostbite, were flown out by an international airlift staged from Hagaru-ri. Bob Ezell was put on a Greek C-47 and Dick Bonelli was strapped into a tiny Piper Cub. Elmo Peterson's cargo plane ran off the runway on takeoff and crashed into a small creek. No one was seriously injured, but Peterson had to wait another twenty-four hours before being flown out. He was evacuated on the same plane as Bill Barber and Hector Cafferata.

At just past 9 a.m., Warren McClure stumbled from the mess tent toward the field hospital. He recognized Eleazar Belmarez, unconscious, being carried on a stretcher into the hold of a cargo plane. McClure ached for his own turn. But in the med tent a corpsman mistook the three-inch-long, scabbed-over tear where the bullet had exited beneath McClure's shoulder blade for a "flesh wound" and directed him to return to his company. McClure flagged down a passing doctor, who put a stethoscope to his chest. Without a word the doctor motioned him toward the line of walking wounded awaiting evacuation. Around him stretchers were stacked four deep on both sides of the passageway that led to the airfield.

As McClure inched closer to the door he could hear a C-47 revving its engines on the muddy landing strip. He had almost reached the exit when a Marine two places in front of him dropped a live grenade and fell on it. The Marine's body absorbed most of the explosion, but McClure was knocked backward. *Accident? Suicide?* McClure, dazed and numb to the point of apathy, stepped over the corpse and walked out onto the tarmac. He boarded the C-47 in a trance, found a place to lie down in the hold, and woke up in Fukuoka.

By 11 a.m., Phil Bavaro had made an uncomfortable decision. Fox Company was down to about sixty effectives, and he knew they would soon be ordered to join the fight to break out of the encircled village of Hagaru-ri. He hated to leave the outfit in the lurch, but his feet were so inflamed that he told John Audas he had to see a corpsman. The doctor who examined him glanced at the shrapnel wound on his thumb and waved him away. Bavaro nearly collapsed.

"It's my feet," he said.

The physician cut off his shoepacs, took one look at Bavaro's misshapen and discolored feet, and tied an "EVAC" tag to a button on his parka. Bavaro waited for most of the afternoon on the long evacuation line, occasionally catching glimpses of Fox Company Marines who had been wounded weeks ago disembarking from planes. They were reinforcements.

It was dusk when his turn to board finally came. He limped out onto the tarmac but was halted just as he was about to climb the clamshell into the hold of a cargo plane. "We're full," a corpsman on the loading detail told him. "Next one's tomorrow morning."

Heartsick, Bavaro turned to gimp back to his tent when he heard the pilot yell from the cockpit, "Got room, send up one more." Bavaro scrambled toward the nose of the plane, the pain in his feet miraculously eased. He settled into the copilot's seat next to the gray-haired World War II veteran at the controls.

"Pretty rough up there?" the pilot said.

"Could have been worse."

"Well, put on your seat belt. And don't touch anything!"

The pilot gunned the engine, released the

brakes, and shot down the runway. Bavaro watched a mountain at the end of the runway looming larger and larger. *There's no way we clear it,* he thought. He said nothing. The pilot threw the cargo plane into a steep bank. Bavaro, peering straight down, could see the muzzle flashes from Chinese snipers issuing from the trees across the heights. *OK, we clear the mountain, but there's no way I don't get shot.*

When the cargo plane skipped over the mountaintop by a few yards, the pilot turned again to Bavaro, who was ashen. "See anybody you know down there?" he said.

A detail from the Marine Graves Registration Unit collected all the dead Americans who had been transported down from Fox Hill and both sides of the Chosin Reservoir. Their dog tags were sorted — one for the official files, one to be buried with the body — while bulldozers gouged several trenches in the frozen soil, six feet deep by six feet wide. The bodies were stripped and laid side by side in the holes, each man wearing only a dog tag around his neck. Their uniforms were burned.

The few Marines who attended the service thought the bodies didn't even resemble the friends and comrades they had known and fought with. It was if they were burying rows of white wax figures. The bulldozers covered them with dirt, and the sites were marked on maps for future recovery.

At roll call on December 5, sergeants Audas and Pitts inspected the approximately sixty Marines of Fox Company who could still fight. They announced that the Seventh Regiment's three battalions would lead the next day's breakout from Hagaru-ri to Koto-ri, and Fox had the point.

To the Marines, "the pogue Army generals" MacArthur and Almond had failed to get them all killed on Fox Hill, and now they were determined to get it right. There wasn't a damn thing any of them could do about it. Audas told the men that anything left behind would be incinerated; this meant that the food storehouses were fair game. Ernest Gonzalez ran over and scrounged a large carton of powdered chocolate. He immediately mixed a small portion of it with the melted snow in his canteen.

At 6 p.m., the ready, able, and effective Marines of Fox Company, still under the command of Lieutenant Abell, gathered after chow to find that the outfit had been supplemented by nearly one hundred replacements. Most were new boots flown in from Japan; others were Marine airmen from cargo planes and technicians and clerks cannibalized from regimental and battalion headquarters units.

One of the replacements was Bob Duffy, an enlisted man who had been a part of the Marine crew dropping supplies on Fox Hill. He had sought out several Marines from Fox when they had reached Hagaru-ri, and he did not wait to be conscripted into the company. When an officer announced that men were needed to fill out the ranks of several units, Duffy stepped up and volunteered for Fox. He would fight with the outfit through the rest of his tour in Korea.

Replacement officers, however, remained scarce. Lieutenant Dunne still led Fox's First Platoon, but the Second and Third platoons were commanded, respectively, by an artillery officer and a bewildered young reserve lieutenant who a day earlier had been the First Division's assistant historian. Everyone was told to be ready to move out at dawn.

One of the replacements, Private First Class Everett Jensen, was a veteran of Fox Company who had developed frostbite after Sudong and was transferred to the motor pool at Hagaru-ri. Jensen beamed when he saw Gray Davis, his buddy from the Second Platoon.

"Hey, Gray," he said, motioning over his shoulder in the general direction of Fox Hill, "what the hell happened up there?"

The two spoke for a while before the paucity of survivors dawned on Jensen.

"How's Iverson doing?"

"Dead."

"Farley?"

"Dead."

"Peoples?"

"Dead."

"Parker?"

"Dead."

With each response Jensen's voice became softer, until it was almost inaudible. Jensen tried half a dozen more names before both Marines became too choked up to speak. Jensen cried. Davis did not. After a moment they walked toward the bivouac tent in silence. Behind them the supply dumps were already beginning to burn.

There would be more, much more, bloody fighting to come before Fox Company and the First Marine Division reached the safety of the sea near Hungnam on December 11. But as one Marine wrote in his journal, "That is another story."

AFTERWORD

In a postwar interview with the military historian S. L. A. "Slam" Marshall, Major General Oliver P. Smith of the Marine Corps confessed, "The country around the Chosin Reservoir was never intended for military operations. Even Genghis Khan wouldn't tackle it."

Any Marine from Fox Company could have told the general this. But the outfit's travails did not end on the Toktong Pass overlooking the Chosin Reservoir. Shortly before noon on December 8, 1950, First Lieutenant John M. Dunne, the only officer to survive Fox Hill unscathed, was shot dead in an ambush on the road to Koto-ri.

In the same encounter, during a strange, foggy snowstorm, the bazooka man Corporal Harry Burke and the rifleman Corporal Rollin Hutchinson were wounded by grenades, and Private First Class Kenny Benson was hit by a bullet from a Thompson submachine gun. All three were returned to Hagaru-ri and airlifted to American military bases in Japan. Hutchinson and Benson were sent home to the United States; Burke returned to duty with Fox Company in May 1951. Ten days later shrapnel from a Chinese artillery round shredded his back. He was then also shipped home, with two Purple Hearts.

The day after Dunne's death, Fox was again ambushed on the road to Koto-ri. Sergeants Kenneth Kipp and Clyde Pitts were killed, and Sergeant John Audas was seriously wounded in the right leg, which eventually had to be amputated. As Pitts lay bleeding out in the snow, with two bullets in his chest, Private First Class Walt Klein held Pitts's head in his lap. "I always knew it would end like this," Pitts said in his deep Alabama drawl.

Lieutenant Abell was wounded in the arm the following day. When Fox finally reached the evacuation port of Hungnam on December 11, there were no officers left standing. The platoon sergeant Richard Danford commanded the company, which now consisted of fewer than three dozen men. Private First Class Walt Klein and Ernest Gonzalez were the only members of the Third Platoon remaining. Gonzalez was hospitalized in South Korea with severe frostbite on December 18. He was flown to Japan a week later, and from there he returned to southern California.

Private First Class Phil "Cookie" Bavaro spent months in hospitals in Fukuoka, Japan; Hawaii; California; and New York before being honorably discharged from the Marine Corps in August 1951. One of his small toes and large portions of both heels were amputated because of frostbite. On his first day in the Fukuoka army hospital he was weighed. He had lost thirty-five pounds on Fox Hill.

On his return to the United States, Bavaro learned that during the days of the breakout his parish in Newark, St. Charles Borromeo, had organized prayer vigils for his safe return. One of his family's neighbors, a Mr. Katz, had held similar religious services at his temple, and the black landlord where Bavaro garaged his car, a Baptist minister, had also organized prayer meetings for him. When Bavaro remembered the last bit of energy he had summoned to escape the pursuing Chinese on the MSR from Fox Hill, he was certain that these prayers had saved his life.

Corporal Eleazar Belmarez was evacuated from Japan to the naval hospital in Corpus

Christi, Texas, close to his home in San Antonio. His left leg was amputated six inches below the kneecap, and he also lost a section of his right foot as a result of frostbite.

Dick Bernard was returned to the United States and was hospitalized for six months. Because he had gone too long on Fox Hill without medical attention, both of his legs had to be amputated.

In 1981, Fidel Gomez was invited to a party at a lake outside San Antonio to meet the family of the man who had proposed to his daughter. As he was talking to a young man at the party the subject of Korea came up, and the man mentioned that his father also fought there. Gomez asked to meet him, and the next minute he was introduced to David Goodrich. Each had thought the other died on Fox Hill.

Lieutenant Elmo Peterson was awarded the Navy Cross for his actions on Fox Hill. He was back fighting in Korea as a platoon commander in Fox Company six months after his evacuation from Hagaru-ri. He led a platoon that included Walt Klein. Both went home permanently in November 1951.

After Private First Class Dick Bonelli was given the last rites, he remained on the critical list at the Army hospital in Osaka for three days. He endured several agonizing spinal taps before the thirty-caliber bullet was finally removed from his chest. It had narrowly missed both his spine and his heart. The surgeon who operated on him was of Chinese-American descent. When Bonelli awoke, the surgeon handed him the small, misshapen chunk of metal he had extracted.

"You take it out?" Bonelli said.

The surgeon nodded.

"How do ya like that? A Chinaman put it in and a Chinaman took it out."

When Bonelli returned to the United States, he found a woman who would tame him — up to a point. He and his wife, Mary, had eight children and twenty-four grandchildren.

Private First Class Bob Ezell never played baseball again. In addition to his leg wounds, he had developed frostbite on his left foot while he was in the med tent on Fox Hill, and all five toes on that foot were eventually amputated. When he returned to California he graduated from college and became a baseball coach in the Los Angeles city school district. Eight years later, in the 1960 World Series, the Pittsburgh Pirates defeated the New York Yankees in seven games. It was a bittersweet experience for

"Zeke" Ezell — his old friend and fellow high school graduate George Witt, who had also served in the Marine Corps, pitched in three of the games.

Sergeant John O. Henry made it through the breakout unscathed and on the road to the port of Hungnam actually oversaw the evacuation of his younger brother, George, another machine gunner who had developed a severe case of frostbite at the Chosin. John was awarded the Silver Star for his actions on Fox Hill, and then a Bronze Star with a V for valor for actions, later, at Koto-ri. He remained a Marine until his retirement in 1968. The Henry Machine Gun Range at Basic School in Quantico is named in his honor.

Private First Class Bob Kirchner made it off Fox Hill and out of Hagaru-ri without injury. He returned to Pittsburgh to his wife and baby daughter. He then visited Roger Gonzales's family in San Pedro, California, to ask their pardon for using Roger's body as cover. They told him they understood and forgave him.

Corporal Wayne Pickett of Duluth, Minnesota, was held as a prisoner of war by the Chinese in North Korea for 999 days. He endured starvation, torture, dysentery, and the burials of many of his fellow prisoners, who died from sickness or from lack of the will to survive.

Following the battle for Fox Hill and the subsequent breakout, Pickett was moved to the town of Chang Song in the far northwest of the country, to a facility that officially became known as North Korean Prison Camp Number 1. Escape from Chang Song was impossible, and the few who attempted it were soon caught and punished severely. Not until more than a year after his capture did the U.S. government notify Allan and Clara Pickett that their missing son was a prisoner of war. The Picketts quickly got word to Wayne's fiancée, Helyn Bergman.

As part of the cease-fire agreement with North Korea on August 23, 1953, Pickett and the other American prisoners were driven on flatbed trucks to the city of Panmunjom. There they crossed a small bridge to where UN ambulances awaited them. Pickett — sixty pounds lighter — was back in Duluth eleven days later.

Today, Wayne Pickett says he has no animus toward his Communist captors. He adds that he will never forget "the hills. Hills and mountains every direction you looked. I would imagine under different circumstances some people would even say that North Korea is really a beautiful country."

Walt Hiskett had the slug removed from his shoulder at a U.S. naval hospital in Guam. After his recovery he was promoted to sergeant, and he returned to the United States in August 1951. He was discharged two months later.

Hiskett kept his commitment to God. In Chicago, Hiskett passed the GED test and received his high school diploma. He earned a college degree attending night school while working at construction jobs, and then attended Chicago Lutheran Seminary. After his graduation he enlisted in the Navy; he served twenty-four years as a chaplain, retiring as the Head of Marine Chaplains in the Navy. He saw combat again in 1968 in Vietnam, with Fox Company, Second Battalion, Seventh Regiment.

First Lieutenant Chew-Een Lee took command of Baker Company when Lieutenant Joe Kurcaba was killed just south of Koto-ri on December 8. Lieutenant Joe Owen suffered multiple gunshot wounds in the same engagement and was evacuated to Japan by air transport from Koto-ri. Baker Company reached Hungnam by train with twenty-seven Marines still standing. In addition to his two Purple Hearts, Lee was awarded the Navy Cross for his actions at Sudong Gorge.

He recovered from his wounds and remained in the Corps until his retirement, with the rank of major, on December 31, 1968.

By far the most famous Ridgerunner to come out of the Chosin Reservoir campaign was Lieutenant Colonel Raymond Davis. Three days after arriving in Hagaru-ri he was named executive officer of Colonel Homer Litzenberg's Seventh Marine Regiment. Two years later, Davis was awarded the Congressional Medal of Honor for his role in the relief of Fox Hill by President Harry S. Truman in a ceremony in Washington, D.C. Davis went on to command the Third Marine Division in Vietnam. After his promotion to general, he became the assistant commandant of the U.S. Marine Corps.

In the autumn of 2002 Davis was among the small party of Korean War veterans — four vets, with family members — allowed to visit Yudam-ni, Toktong Pass, and Hagaru-ri on a trip arranged by the U.S. Defense Department, the first of its kind since the war. A year later Davis — one of the most decorated Marines of his generation — died of a heart attack.

Lieutenant Bob McCarthy remained a Marine after the Korean War, served at various posts in the Pacific, and retired in 1957 as a major. He subsequently enlisted in the U.S. Army and spent three years running an Army training facility at Fort Gordon, Georgia. Soon after his evacuation from Hagaru-ri, McCarthy nominated both Captain William Barber and Private Hector Cafferata for the Congressional Medal of Honor. Of that first night on Fox Hill, McCarthy recalled, "I figured Cafferata flat killed about a hundred, but I only wrote it up for thirty-six because I didn't think anybody would believe one hundred."

Following his evacuation, Cafferata spent the next eighteen months undergoing surgery in hospitals in Japan, Hawaii, California, Texas, and New York. A nerve in his right arm had been severed by the sniper's bullet. To this day, he cannot eat or write with his right hand, although he relearned to pull a trigger. Hunting and fishing remain his passion. In 1952, at home in New Jersey, he was informed by telegram that he had been awarded the nation's highest military citation and was to travel to Washington, D.C., for the presentation ceremonies. Never much for pomp, he replied that he would prefer to have the award mailed to him. He was subsequently contacted by an irate Marine officer, who told him, "You *will* get down here so that President Truman can personally give this Medal of Honor to you!" Cafferata obeyed, and the award was presented to him on November 24, 1952. What he remembers most about the ceremony is that the undersized Truman had to stand on Cafferata's freshly shined shoes to place the ribbon and medal over his head.

Captain William Barber was evacuated from Hagaru-ri to Yokosuka, Japan, on December 8, 1950. He spent three months in various hospitals while his infection was treated and the bullet lodged in his hip bone was finally removed. He returned to the United States in March 1951, and in August 1952 he was awarded the Congressional Medal of Honor by President Truman for his leadership in the defense of Fox Hill. "One bullet doesn't stop a man," he told reporters after the ceremony.

He went on to serve in Okinawa and Bangkok, and to become, like Davis, one of the few men in any branch of the U.S. military to have held commands in World War II, Korea, and Vietnam. In Vietnam he served as psychological operations officer for the III Marine Amphibious Force. For his service in Vietnam he added the Legion of Merit with Combat V to his war chest of commendations, medals, and awards.

He retired from the active-duty Marine Corps as a full colonel in 1970 and returned to the now renamed Morehead University to finish his studies and receive his degree — three decades after he had dropped out "to see the world." He became a civilian military analyst for the Northrop Corporation. William Barber died of bone marrow cancer in 2002 at the age of eighty-two. He was buried with full honors at Arlington Cemetery. Four years later his widow, Ione, died. Her ashes were interred in her husband's grave.

Throughout his life, Barber resisted attempts to compare Fox Company's six-day ordeal on Toktong Pass to an apparently obvious parallel — the Spartan general Leonidas's last stand against an overwhelming Persian invasion at the Greek pass of Thermopylae. *Mythology is what never was, but always is.* He was quick to point out that the effect of his company's actions at Fox Hill on world history was nowhere near the effect of Thermopylae. He also noted that during the Korean War several other surrounded, outnumbered Marine and Army units had held out against much greater odds. "And don't even get me started on Bastogne," he would say with a laugh.

Yet it is fair to say that no Marine unit —

or any other unit — fighting in Korea in 1950 held a more strategic piece of land against more crushing odds, and despite such severe isolation, as Fox Company on Fox Hill. Writing in the archives of the Marine Corps Association, the eminent military historian H. Lew Wallace put the battle for Fox Hill into perspective: "If the actions of Barber and his men did not alter the broad sweep of history, they did alter the margin between a potential rout and the controlled breakout that actually occurred, between moderate and unacceptable losses, indeed between life and death for 8,000 Marines."

One hundred thirty-one Medals of Honor were earned during the fighting in Korea. Davis, Cafferata, and Barber were three of only thirty-seven men who were not awarded the medals posthumously.

In 1981 the former Marine Corps commandant General Robert H. Barrow wrote in a letter to Barber, "I regard your performance as commander of Fox Company at Toktong Pass from 27 November to 2 December 1950 as the single most distinguished act of personal courage and extraordinary leadership I have witnessed or about which I have read."

At Bill Barber's funeral service, one side

of the church was filled with veterans of Fox Company who had traveled to California from across the United States. On the other side of the aisle, behind his family, friends and other military veterans, including several fellow recipients of the Congressional Medal of Honor, packed the pews. Moments before the ceremony began, Barber's only son, John Barber, stood, kissed his mother, and walked across the aisle to sit with Fox Company.

POSTSCRIPT 2008

After the Korean War the veterans of Fox Hill scattered to their homes around the country. Except for several informal, regional get-togethers, most of them remained apart for forty-one years.

Then, in 1991, Fox Company held its first official reunion. Fifteen years later, in November 2006 — more than five decades after one of the greatest stands against an enemy in U.S. military history — the Marines of Fox 2/7 gathered in Quantico, Virginia, on the weekend celebrating the dedication of the new National Museum of the Marine Corps.

Four sections of this magnificent structure are devoted to signature U.S. Marine Corps actions in twentieth-century American wars: Belleau Wood, Iwo Jima, Khe San, and Fox Hill. The Korean War gallery presents a tableau of Fox Hill — complete with air-conditioning to simulate (to a point) the freezing cold. Captain Bill Barber's bullet-pocked parka is worn by the figure depicting him — he had put it over a wounded Marine in Hagaru-ri, and it was discovered in an attic several years ago.

A few of the veterans from Fox Company grumbled about some of the details, but most seemed pleased by the attention and the sentiments. Following the ceremony, on the evening of Saturday, November 10, 2006 — the 231st birthday of the Corps — some of the former Marines commandeered a meeting room at their hotel, pulled bottles from their suitcases, and proceeded to catch up on each other's lives, and to swap tales about a time when ordinary men won an extraordinary battle on the other side of the world.

Later there was a dinner in a conference room at the same hotel. The keynote speaker was Major (Ret.) Chew-Een Lee, still ramrod straight in his uniform covered with medals, and still with a chip on his shoulder. Bill Barber's daughter and son, Sharon and John, attended. They were in town to bury the ashes of their mother, Ione, with their father at Arlington National Cemetery.

By the time Fox Company met again a year later, in Orlando, Florida, the survivors were waging a different kind of war —

against age and its depredations. Dick Bonelli, now seventy-six, had coordinated this reunion. He seemed to have enough energy for the entire company, but some of the men weren't up to making the trip. Elmo Peterson, slowed by a stroke and an eye disorder — macular degeneration — stayed at his home, near one of his daughters, in Tucson, Arizona. Bob McCarthy remained in North Carolina because of leg problems. The machine gunner John Henry had planned to attend but was having heart trouble and was grieving over the recent death of his wife of fifty years. Kenny Benson, who had journeyed from New Jersey to Quantico a year earlier, did not have the strength to make this journey in his wheelchair. Fidel Gomez had also attended the museum dedication, but this year his wife was too ill for him to get away. (She died two days later.)

But there was still a good turnout. Warren McClure, Edward Gonzales, Harry Burke, and Wayne Pickett attended with their wives, as did, among others, Clifford Steen, Eleazar Belmarez, Bob Duffy, Richard Danford, Bob Kirchner, Walt Klein, Richard Kline, Bob Ezell, and Bob Watson from the Ridgerunners.

As the weekend came to a close, a room

at the hotel in Orlando was set aside on Sunday morning for a memorial service to honor those who had fallen on Fox Hill. The service was conducted by the Reverend Walt Hiskett, who was also grieving; his wife, Marilyn, had died the previous March.

A few minutes before 11 a.m., the men and their wives, along with several adult children, filed in to sit in a semicircle around a table Hiskett had set up. As Hiskett spoke to the veterans and their families about a war, in David Halberstam's phrase, "orphaned by history," he stepped from the table and moved to a podium to deliver a homily.

He began by speaking about a stained-glass window in the old chapel next to Arlington Cemetery that is dedicated "in honor and memory of all deceased Marines." The scene on the window depicts Gideon and his three hundred vastly outnumbered soldiers as they prepared for battle. But Hiskett did not speak of death or glory — he spoke to the men about peace. "Gideon was tasked by God to organize an army to rout the Midionites and Amalekites in order to restore peace to the people of Israel," he said. "Not unlike the task given to the Marine Corps when the North Koreans swooped down across the

38th Parallel in June of 1950 — we were tasked to restore peace."

Every eye was on Hiskett as he spoke of his "brothers" on Fox Hill. "We are here today because when we were faced with overwhelming odds, we fought, and many died, not just for self-survival, but for our Corps and for one another. We commemorate the memory of our heroic dead. They were the life, the spirit, and soul of our Corps. We will not, nor can we ever, forget the lessons they taught us about honor and faithfulness."

Here Hiskett paused, trying to keep his composure. He was choking on the words. He raised his right hand and continued, his voice strengthening as he declared, "We are the Marine Corps, and *Semper Fidelis* is our motto. Always faithful. That was the spirit that keeps our Corps alive today. That was the spirit of the Marines we honor here today. We are here today because they made the sacrifice then. They will live on forever in our hearts and minds because we are a part of them and they are a part of us."

When Hiskett finished the service, the men of Fox Company, Second Battalion, Seventh Regiment, First Division, stood and closed ranks once more. Then it was time for these Marines and their families to go home.

ACKNOWLEDGMENTS

We have been humbled by the enormous generosity of the men of Fox Company and their families. When we initially sought them out and introduced ourselves and our book idea, there was some caution on their part: Who are these two guys? Can we trust them to tell the story? Can we trust them to tell it right? Over time, however, the surviving members of the Marines who fought on Fox Hill became most charitable with us — sharing their memories, private letters, journals, oral histories, and official reports — as well as allowing us into their lives. For that we thank them, most especially Warren McClure and Dick Bonelli.

In McClure's case we took advantage of his years of dedication, as the secretary of the Fox 2/7 Association, in collecting, coordinating, and preserving the hundreds if not thousands of details, individual narratives, and maps of the events on Fox Hill during that week in late November and early December of 1950. Given that Mc-Clure is a writer of wonderful verse, we feel that we have met a true modern-day warrior-poet. As for Bonelli — quite simply there would have been no book without his input, participation, friendship, and coordinating abilities. He has as much considerable energy today as he had in Korea fifty-eight years ago.

We are also grateful for the recollections of Eleazar Belmarez, Ken Benson, Hector Cafferata, Jack Coleman, Dick Connelly, Richard Danford, Victor M. Davis, Bob Duffy, Harry Burke, Bob Ezell, Dick Gilling, Fidel Gomez, Edward Gonzales, Arnie Hansen, John Henry, Walt Hiskett, Rollin Hutchinson, Barry Jones, Bob Kirchner, Walt Klein, Richard Kline, Chew-Een Lee, Howard Mason, Bob McCarthy, Joe Owen, Chuck Pearson, Elmo Peterson, Wayne Pickett, Harrison Pomers, David Seils, Jerry Triggs, and Bob Watson, as well as for the accounts of the battle set to paper by Phil Bavaro, Don Childs, Graydon Davis, Raymond Davis, Vic Dey, Billy French, Stan Golembieski, Ernest Gonzalez, Lemuel Goode, Lee Knowles, Howard Koone, Minard Paul Newton, Clifford Steen, and Allen Thompson.

In addition to those veterans of Fox Hill, we would also like to thank Woodrow Barber, Jerry Courtier, Jean Sheets, and Sharon Waldo for their contributions.

Even with the recollections and written testimonies of those who participated in the Battle for Fox Hill, we also took advantage of a wide range of research sources to add more details to the narrative. We thank the following for their courteous help: Danny Brandi of the Denver, Colorado, "Chosin Few" organization; William Dillon; Paul Hughes; the Korean War Educator (www.koreanwar-educator.org); the Korean War Project in Dallas, Texas; Lee Mead; staffers at the National Archives and Records Administration in College Park, Maryland; Dr. Charles P. Neimeyer, Robert Aquilina, and their colleagues at the Reference Branch at the Marine Corps History Division in Quantico, Virginia; the Marine Corps Heritage Foundation; and the National Museum of the Marine Corps, also in Quantico.

We have been fortunate to have assistance and encouragement from friends and others in the preparation of the manuscript. We are most grateful to James Brady, David Hughes, Colonel (Ret.) Joseph C. Long, Major General (Ret.) J. Michael Myatt of the Marines Memorial Association, David Winter, Valerie Pillsworth, Kelly Olsen, Bob Rosen and Jennifer Unter at RLR Associates, and Alison Thompson.

It has been written many times before yet it is still true: Without the expertise and support of the professionals who made *The Last Stand of Fox Company* a reality, we wouldn't have the privilege of thanking them for this book. And we are very happy to thank Morgan Entrekin, Jofie Ferrari-Adler, and Nat Sobel.

Finally, to our family members and loved ones — Brendan Clavin, Kathryn Clavin, Liam-Antoine DeBusschere-Drury, Denise McDonald, and Leslie Reingold — you have given us more than we deserve.

APPENDIX

According to United States Marine Corps records, the following men were assigned to Fox Company, Second Battalion, Seventh Marine Regiment, along with various attached Marines and United States Navy corpsmen, on the official November/December 1950 roster. Marine Corps historians attribute the seven-man discrepancy between this roster and the 246 Marines and Navy corpsmen who fought on Fox Hill to last-minute replacements and evacuations, as well as "the fog of war."

1. Adams, Douglas H., Private First Class
2. Aguilar, Jose R., Private First Class
3. Anderson, Robert, Private First Class
4. Arcuri, Nickolas M., Private
5. Ashdale, Thomas G., Corporal
6. Audas, John D., Staff Sergeant

7. Balcezak, Benjamin, Private First Class
8. Barber, William E., Captain
9. Batdorff, Robert L., Private First Class
10. Bean, Harry H., Sergeant
11. Belmarez, Eleazar R., Corporal
12. Bendy, Cecil J., Private First Class
13. Benson, Kenneth R., Private First Class
14. Bernard, Richard J., Private First Class
15. Blacklidge, Jack W., Corporal
16. Blunk, Albert W., Private First Class
17. Bolstad, Richard E., Private First Class
18. Bonelli, Richard A., Private First Class
19. Boudousquie, William, Private First Class
20. Brady, Joseph J., First Lieutenant
21. Bryan, John C., Private First Class
22. Brydon, William H., Corporal
23. Bunch, William H., Master Sergeant
24. Burkard, Raymond L., Corporal
25. Burke, Harry L., Corporal
26. Cafferata, Hector A., Private

27. Campbell, Donald, First Lieutenant
28. Cavanaugh, James P., Private First Class
29. Childs, Donald L., Private First Class
30. Chung, Mr., Korean Interpreter
31. Cilek, Gene, Private First Class
32. Clark, Thomas L., Corporal
33. Connelly, Richard W., Corporal
34. Conrad, Richard A., Private First Class
35. Cornelison, Roy J., Private First Class
36. Cunningham, Alfred, Corporal
37. Dana, Charles C., Master Sergeant
38. Danford, Richard E., Staff Sergeant
39. Danilowski, Henry J., Private First Class
40. Davis, Graydon W., Private First Class
41. Davis, Roger R., Private First Class
42. Daugherty, James H., Private First Class
43. Dunne, John M., First Lieutenant
44. Dytkiewicz, Alvin T., Corporal
45. Elknation, Rueben A., Private First Class
46. Elrod, Judd W., Sergeant

47. Erwin, Louis E., Private First Class
48. Evans, Walter, USN Corpsman
49. Ezell, Robert W., Private First Class
50. Farley, John D., Corporal
51. Fenton, Charles E., Private First Class
52. Fich, Richard A., Private First Class
53. Fitzgerald, Thomas, Private First Class
54. Fixico, Amos, Private First Class
55. French, Billy M., Private First Class
56. French, James, USN Corpsman
57. Friend, Harvey J., Corporal
58. Fry, William L., Private First Class
59. Gagner, Eugene E., Private First Class
60. Gaines, Robert L., Corporal
61. Gajda, Thadeus M., Private First Class
62. Gamble, Clifford, Private First Class
63. Garza, William F., Private First Class
64. Geer, Harmony, Private First Class
65. Gleason, William P., Private First Class

66. Godwin, Eugene R., Private First Class
67. Goldstein, Bernard, Private
68. Golembieski, Stanley, Corporal
69. Gomez, Fidel G., Private First Class
70. Gonzales, Alfredo (Fred) D., Private First Class
71. Gonzales, Roger, Private First Class
72. Gonzales, Edward, Private First Class
73. Gonzalez, Ernest T., Private First Class
74. Goodrich, David J., Private First Class
75. Gose, Roger D., Private
76. Griffith, Jack B., Corporal
77. Groenewald, William, Staff Sergeant
78. Gruenberg, Arthur H., Staff Sergeant
79. Gruenewald, Harold, Private First Class
80. Haggard, Barner W., Private First Class
81. Hall, David T., Private First Class
82. Halstead, Raymond P., Private First Class

83. Hammond, Phillip O., Private First Class
84. Hancock, Harold E., Private
85. Haney, Alvin R., Private First Class
86. Harvey, Edward E., Corporal
87. Harvey, William L., Private First Class
88. Hedinger, Larry M., Private First Class
89. Heinz, Erwin C., Corporal
90. Henry, John O., Staff Sergeant
91. Hess, Erwin W., Private First Class
92. Hiskett, Walter A., Corporal
93. Holt, James, Private First Class
94. Homan, Elmer P., Sergeant
95. Horn, Jack, Private First Class
96. Hostetler, James S., Private First Class
97. Hough, Bruce B., Private First Class
98. Hutchinson, Rollin, Corporal
99. Hymel, Benjamin A., Private First Class
100. Iverson, James E., Corporal
101. Jackson, Norman A., Private First Class
102. Jacob, Ernest E., Corporal
103. Jaskiewicz, Chester, Private First Class

104. Johnson, Maurice W., Private First Class
105. Johnson, Norman J., Corporal
106. Jones, Edward, USN Corpsman
107. Jones, Roy J., Corporal
108. Jones, Rosco, Private First Class
109. Kalinowski, Richard, Private First Class
110. Kanouse, James C., Private First Class
111. Kaser, George C., Private
112. Keirn, Meredith F., Sergeant
113. Keith, Clarence V., Private First Class
114. Kipp, Kenneth R., Sergeant
115. Kirchner, Robert, Private First Class
116. Klein, Walter, Private
117. Kline, Richard, Private First Class
118. Knowles, Lee E., Private First Class
119. Kohls, Robert, Staff Sergeant
120. Komorowski, Joseph, Sergeant
121. Koone, Howard, Corporal
122. Kuca, John F., Corporal
123. Ladner, Hobert P., Corporal
124. Lavecchia, Joseph F., Private First Class
125. Lawson, Robert E., Corporal

126. Lawton, John D., Private First Class
127. Leach, James C., Private First Class
128. Ling, Jack D., Sergeant
129. Longstaff, Robert A., First Lieutenant
130. Lowry, Private First Class
131. Mann, Robert R., Private First Class
132. Martin, Clifford O., Corporal
133. Mathews, Kenneth J., Private First Class
134. Maurath, Mervyn (Red), USN Corpsman
135. McAfee, Johnson, Sergeant
136. McCarthy, Robert C., First Lieutenant
137. McClelland, Herbert, Private First Class
138. McClure, Warren L., Private First Class
139. McLean, William, USN Corpsman
140. Mercadante, Louis J., Private
141. Mertz, Kenneth N., Corporal
142. Monagan, Homer, Private First Class
143. Montville, Daniel M., Corporal
144. Moore, Walter M., Private First Class

145. Morrissey, James, USN Corpsman
146. Myers, Raymond F., Private First Class
147. Nemire, Olen D., Private First Class
148. Newhoff, Elmer W., Private First Class
149. North, Charles R., Corporal
150. O'Leary, John, Private First Class
151. Pacter, Paul F., Private First Class
152. Page, Jack, Corporal
153. Parker, Charles W., Private First Class
154. Parker, Richard A., Private First Class
155. Parks, Lloyd M., Private First Class
156. Pearson, Charles M., Sergeant
157. Peck, Raymond F., Corporal
158. Peek, Oma L., Corporal
159. Penn, Homer K., Private First Class
160. Peoples, Claude, Private First Class
161. Peterson, Charles H., Corporal
162. Peterson, Elmo C., First Lieutenant
163. Phillips, Alfred P., Technical Sergeant
164. Pickett, Wayne A., Corporal

165. Pietkowski, Robert, Corporal
166. Pilcher, Donald R., Private First Class
167. Pitts, Clyde T., Sergeant
168. Pomers, Harrison, Private First Class
169. Ramey, James R., Private First Class
170. Reed, Billie W., Private First Class
171. Reitz, George W., Sergeant
172. Rittennour, Donald E., Private First Class
173. Robaczynski, John, Private First Class
174. Roberts, Gerald, Private First Class
175. Robicheau, Staff Sergeant
176. Rodien, David L., Private First Class
177. Rodrigues, Nicholas, Private First Class
178. Rodriguez, Manuel V., Private
179. Salyer, Walter E., Private First Class
180. Schmidt, Robert H., Private First Class
181. Schmitt, Lawrence, First Lieutenant
182. Scott, John L., Private First Class
183. Scully, Robert P., Sergeant

184. Seils, David, Private First Class
185. Senzig, John F., Private First Class
186. Shilney, Richard A., Sergeant
187. Slapinskas, Daniel, Sergeant
188. Smith, David, Sergeant
189. Smith, Gerald J., Private First Class
190. Snyder, Walter R., Private First Class
191. Stanley, Glen J., Sergeant
192. Steen, Clifford, USN Corpsman
193. Stein, Richard J., Private First Class
194. Stevens, Marvin L., Private First Class
195. Stiller, Daniel J., Private First Class
196. Stillwell, Charles R., Private First Class
197. Stonebreaker, John G., Corporal
198. Stritch, John T., Private First Class
199. Strommen, Ronald D., Private First Class
200. Sulem, Kenneth M., Private First Class
201. Svicarovich, George, Sergeant
202. Szabo, Antal J., Private First Class
203. Tallbull, Clarence, Private First Class

204. Temple, Johnny L., Private First Class
205. Teter, Lowell D., Private First Class
206. Thomas, Evan D., Private First Class
207. Thompson, Allen S., Private First Class
208. Thornton, Donald R., Corporal
209. Thrower, Louis V., Private First Class
210. Tilhof, Peter, Private First Class
211. Timbes, Ralph, Private First Class
212. Tranchita, Carmelo, Corporal
213. Triggs, Jerry D., Private First Class
214. Troxell, Paul T., Private First Class
215. Trujillo, Adam, Private First Class
216. Turnipseed, Roy B., Private First Class
217. Umpleby, James P., Private First Class
218. Urrutia, Joe C., Private First Class
219. Valek, Raymond L., Private First Class
220. Valtierra, Frank, Private First Class
221. Vanderveer, John S., Private First Class
222. Vaydice, John S., Private First Class
223. Vey, Arnold R., Private First Class

224. Waddell, Joseph L., Corporal
225. Waldoch, Daniel C., Private First Class
226. Watson, Wayne E., Staff Sergeant
227. Welsh, Robert T., Private First Class
228. Westin, John L., Corporal
229. Whitaker, Billy J., Private First Class
230. Whittaker, USN Corpsman
231. Wiedau, James L., Private First Class
232. Willard, James P., Private First Class
233. Williams, James E., Sergeant
234. Williford, Troy A., Private First Class
235. Wilson, Lee D., Private First Class
236. Wright, Clark B., First Lieutenant
237. Yeager, Kenneth E., Corporal
238. Yesko, Daniel D., Private First Class
239. Zacher, Kenneth L., Private First Class

SELECTED BIBLIOGRAPHY

All historical records are complicated, none more so than accounts of any war's individual battles and firefights. In addition to relying on official United States and Marine Corps historical records, contemporary media accounts, and the works referenced in this selected bibliography, we have reconstructed the events of the Battle of Fox Hill — particularly the quoted conversations among participants — from journals and personal letters written by Marines soon after the "Last Stand" took place and from reminiscences of the remaining members of Fox Company and the Ridgerunners that were obtained in personal interviews during the last two years. We acknowledge that fifty-year-old memories can play tricks, so whenever possible we have tried to confirm those conversations with each participant.

Books

Appleman, Roy E. *East of Chosin: Entrapment and Breakout in Korea, 1950.* College Station: Texas A&M University Press, 1987.

Brady, James. *The Coldest War: A Memoir of Korea.* New York: Orion Books, 1990.

Clark, Johnnie M. *Gunner's Glory: Untold Stories of Machine Gunners.* New York: Ballantine Books, 2004.

Cumings, Bruce. *North Korea: Another Country.* New York: New Press, 2004.

Daniel, Clifton, ed. *Chronicle of the 20th Century.* New York: Dorling Kindersley, 1995.

Davis, Raymond. *The Story of Ray Davis.* Fuquay, VA: Research Triangle Publishing, 1995.

DuPuy, R. Ernest and Trevor N. *The Encyclopedia of Military History: From 3500 B.C. to the Present* (second revised edition). New York: Harper & Row, 1986.

Geer, Andrew. *The New Breed: The Story of the U.S. Marines in Korea.* New York: Harper & Brothers, 1952.

Halberstam, David. *The Coldest Winter: America and the Korean War.* New York: Hyperion, 2007.

Hammel, Eric. *Chosin: Heroic Ordeal of the*

Korean War. Novato, CA: Presidio Press, 1981.

Hopkins, William B. *One Bugle No Drums: The Marines at Chosin Reservoir.* Chapel Hill, NC: Algonquin Books, 1986.

Jackson, Robert. *Air War Over Korea.* New York: Charles Scribner's Sons, 1973.

Knox, Donald. *The Korean War — An Oral History: Pusan to Chosin.* Orlando, FL: Harcourt, 1981.

Leckie, Robert. *March to Glory.* New York: Simon & Schuster, 1960.

Mahoney, Kevin. *Formidable Enemies: The North Korean and Chinese Soldier in the Korean War.* Novata, CA: Presidio Press, 2001.

Manchester, William. *American Caesar — Douglas MacArthur, 1880–1964.* Boston: Little, Brown, 1973.

Marshall, S.L.A. *Battle at Best.* New York: Pocket Books, 1964

———. *Pork Chop Hill.* Nashville, TN: The Battery Press, 1986.

Montross, Lynn, and Canzona, Capt. Nicholas A. (USMC). *U.S. Marine Operations in Korea 1950–1953; Volume III: The Chosin Reservoir Campaign.* Austin, TX: R. J. Speights, 1990.

Murphy, Edward F. *Korean War Heroes.*

Novato, CA: Presidio Press, 1992.

Odgers, George. *Across the Parallel: The Australian 77th Squadron with the United States Air Force in the Korean Air War.* Australia: William Heinemann, 1952.

O'Neill, Robert. *Australia in the Korean War.* Australian Government Publishing Service, 1981.

Owen, Joseph R. *Colder Than Hell.* Annapolis, MD: Naval Institute Press, 1996.

Roe, Patrick C. *The Dragon Strikes: China and the Korean War: June–December 1950.* Novato, CA: Presidio Press, 2000.

Russ, Martin. *Breakout: The Chosin Reservoir Campaign, Korea 1950.* New York: Penguin Books, 1999.

Schlesinger, Arthur M. *War and the American Presidency.* New York: W. W. Norton, 2004.

Smith, Larry. *Beyond Glory: Medal of Honor Heroes in Their Own Words.* New York: W. W. Norton, 2003.

Sun-tzu. *The Art of War.* London: Oxford University Press, 1963.

Warren, James A. *American Spartans — The U.S. Marines: A Combat History from Iwo to Iraq.* New York: Free Press, 2005.

Wilson, Jim. *Retreat, Hell: The Epic Story of*

the 1st Marines in Korea. New York: Pocket Books, 1988.

Magazine and Newspaper Articles

"Angels or Gooney Birds?" William O. Brennan, *Marine News Digest,* July–September, 2005.

"Finally, Back at Chosin!" W. G. Ford. *Leatherneck,* December, 2002.

"Gen. Raymond Davis, War Hero, Dies at 88." Richard Goldstein, *New York Times,* September 5, 2003.

" 'Marine's Marine' Laid to Rest." Bill Hendrick. *Atlanta Journal-Constitution,* September 9, 2003.

"Official Reports Describing the Fighting in Korea." *New York Times,* December 13, 1950.

"Ridgerunners of Toktong Pass." Lynn Montrose, *Marine Corps Gazette,* May, 1953.

"Sudong-ni: The Historic Clash as American Marines Meet Red Chinese Volunteers in the Korean War." *Combat Magazine* ISSN 1542–1546, volume 05, number 04, October, 2007.

"Toktong Ridgerunner." Bob Jordan. *Leatherneck,* December, 1985.

"Toktong Ridgerunners — 1st battalion, 7th Marines." Dick Camp. *Leatherneck,* December, 2000.

"Truman's Letter." *Marine Corps Times,* Dr. Charles P. Neimeyer, July 30, 2007

Video and Electronic Sources

"Battle for the Frozen Chosin." *War Stories with Oliver North.* Fox Network.

"Col. Bill Barber." Radio Interview with Hugh Hewitt, May 25, 2001.

"Korea: Medal of Honor." *U.S. News & World Report,* 1990.

"Korean War Stories." PBS Home Video, 2001.

Miscellaneous

"A Prayer Vigil on a Hill." Walter Hiskett. *The Fox Two Seven Association Newsletter,* April, 2007.

"Cold Injury." Jerrod E. Johnson, MD. *The Scuttlebutt Newsletter,* November, 1998.

"F-2–7 Battles South Korea, 1951." Jack Strong. *The Fox Two Seven Association Newsletter,* June, 2007.

Historical Reference Branch, U.S. Marine Corps, Quantico, Virginia.

Letter to General C. B. Cates, USMC, from General Oliver P. Smith, USMC, November 15, 1950.

"Night March to Fox Hill." Joesph R. Owen. *Marine Corps Association Newslet-*

ter, December, 1984.

"Personal Notes Covering Activities of Lt. Gen. E. M. Almond During Military Operations in Korea 31 August 1950–15 July 1951."

Special Action Reports of the 1st Marine Division, November and December, 1950.

"Turkey Shoot at Turkey Hill." Joseph R. Owen. *First Battalion Seventh Marines Newsletter,* 1970.